# Teaching Literature in a Second Language

Edinburgh Textbooks in Applied Linguistics
Series Editors: Alan Davies and Keith Mitchell

# Teaching Literature in a Second Language

Brian Parkinson and
Helen Reid Thomas

Edinburgh University Press

© Brian Parkinson and Helen Reid Thomas, 2000

Edinburgh University Press Ltd
22 George Square, Edinburgh

Typeset in Garamond
by Norman Tilley Graphics, Northampton,
and printed and bound in Great Britain
by MPG Books Ltd, Bodmin

A CIP record for this book is available from
the British Library

ISBN 0 7486 1259 9 (paperback)

The right of Brian Parkinson and Helen Reid Thomas
to be identified as authors of this work
has been asserted in accordance with
the Copyright, Designs and Patents Act 1988.

# Contents

# Series Editors' Preface

This new series of single-author volumes published by Edinburgh University Press takes a contemporary view of applied linguistics. The intention is to make provision for the wide range of interests in contemporary applied linguistics which are provided for at the Master's level.

The expansion of Master's postgraduate courses in recent years has had two effects:

1. What began almost half a century ago as a wholly cross-disciplinary subject has found a measure of coherence so that now most training courses in Applied Linguistics have similar core content.
2. At the same time the range of specialisms has grown, as in any developing discipline. Training courses (and professional needs) vary in the extent to which these specialisms are included and taught.

Some volumes in the series will address the first development noted above, while the others will explore the second. It is hoped that the series as a whole will provide students beginning postgraduate courses in Applied Linguistics, as well as language teachers and other professionals wishing to become acquainted with the subject, with a sufficient introduction for them to develop their own thinking in applied linguistics and to build further into specialist areas of their own choosing.

The view taken of applied linguistics in the Edinburgh Textbooks in Applied Linguistics Series is that of a theorising approach to practical experience in the language professions, notably, but not exclusively, those concerned with language learning and teaching. It is concerned with the problems, the processes, the mechanisms and the purposes of language in use.

Like any other applied discipline, applied linguistics draws on theories from related disciplines with which it explores the professional experience of its practitioners and which in turn are themselves illuminated by that experience. This two-way relationship between theory and practice is what we mean by a theorising discipline.

The volumes in the series are all premised on this view of Applied Linguistics as a theorising discipline which is developing its own coherence. At the same time, in order to present as complete a contemporary view of applied linguistics as possible other approaches will occasionally be expressed.

Each volume presents its author's own view of the state of the art in his or her topic. Volumes will be similar in length and in format, and, as is usual in a textbook series, each will contain exercise material for use in class or in private study.

Alan Davies
W. Keith Mitchell

# Preface

This book is intended to help those who teach literature in a foreign language, whether in situations where literature is emphasised and language has a supporting role, or where the reverse applies, or at any point between these two extremes.

It is, however, concerned with the teaching of literature rather than with literary criticism or analysis; ideas from literary theory are touched upon, some are dealt with in more depth, but it is their pedagogic implications which are emphasised. A communicative attitude to teaching, and a concern with the realities of classroom process, inform a systematic consideration of objectives, teacher and learner roles, affective and cognitive issues and problems, syllabus choices, moment-to-moment classroom decisions and associated areas of research. Although the book contains practical ideas, the emphasis is on principles rather than on specific recipes or model lessons, and the aim is to inform teacher choice rather than promote a particular method. Although most of the examples are taken from literature written in English, with a few from German and French, it is hoped that the principles explored will be relevant to the teaching of literature in other languages.

# Acknowledgements

1. Arthur Waley, *Chinese Poems*, George Allen & Unwin, London, 1946 and The Arthur Waley Estate.
2. Philip Larkin, 'Mr Bleaney' in *The Whitsun Weddings*, Faber & Faber.
3. *Guidelines 5.1: Classroom Tests*, RELC, 1983.
4. B. Gardner, *The Terrible Rain*, OUP, 1983, by permission of Oxford University Press.
5. Alexander Scott, 'Continent O Venus' in *Latest in Eligies*, Caledonian Press, 1949. Every effort has been made to trace copyright holders but if any have inadvertently been overlooked, the editor and publishers will be pleased to make the necessary arrangements at the first opportunity.

# Chapter 1

# Introduction

## 1.1 GENERAL INTRODUCTION

This book has been written by two people who were for some years colleagues in the Institute for Applied Language Studies at the University of Edinburgh, where together they developed a course on the language of literature. As you read, it will become apparent to you that the authors occupy rather different positions on the language–literature continuum. We were slightly anxiously aware of this when we began to write, but it became increasingly clear as we continued that this, rather than being a limitation or an obstacle, was in fact one of the strengths of our collaboration. Like any co-authors, we have expressed different views on a number of occasions, but these have not been irreconcilable disagreements. Our practice simply reflects a difference of emphasis and approach to the relationship between the two poles of language teaching and literature teaching, between what Maley (1989) calls the use and the study of literature.

If we picture language and literature teaching as a continuum, we could say that Brian Parkinson occupies a position towards the language teaching end, and is most concerned with teaching situations where literature in the classroom has a primarily instrumental function, what is sometimes referred to as the 'literature as topic' or 'literature as resource' approach. Helen Reid Thomas' approach is situated closer to the 'literature as object of study' end of the continuum, where literature appears as an academic subject on the timetable, but with a focus on the language that is used in that literature. This partly reflects our respective backgrounds: Brian Parkinson's interest in English language teaching has its roots in a broader experience of modern language teaching, particularly German and French; Helen Reid Thomas' work has been more specifically concerned with ways of reading and teaching literature, recently to British undergraduates but also in India, Malaysia and Bulgaria, where literature in English is taught for a variety of reasons and in a variety of ways, but all in a context where English is a foreign language.

The distinction between 'literature as object of study', which for brevity we will sometimes call 'Type A', and 'literature as topic/resource' (in 'language improvement' classes), which is our 'Type B', is more important in some chapters and sections of this book than others. Broadly speaking, sections 1.3.1, 1.5 to 1.8.1, 8.3.4, 9.3, 9.4, and almost all of Chapter 2, seem to us more relevant to Type B teaching, while sections 1.4, 1.9 to 1.11, 7.3, 7.4, 8.3.3, 9.1, 9.2, as well as Chapters 4–6, seem more relevant to Type A, and the rest of the book equally relevant to both types. The distinction is perhaps most important when we are writing about reader response and about general objectives, both in the present chapter, and about assessment in Chapter 8.

The boundaries between the two types, however, should not be drawn too sharply. Many real-life teaching situations have features of both 'types', together with a measure of ambiguity and room for negotiation, and even when the 'types' are distinguishable, identical or analogous theoretical reasoning or practical procedures can sometimes be usable in both. For this reason we have deliberately not labelled chapters and sections as 'A' or 'B', or used these terms in the text, except very sparingly in places where we find the distinction especially important.

Exchange of ideas between the two types has become particularly extensive in recent decades. Borrowing by language improvement (Type B) teachers, especially EFL teachers, is well known and perhaps unsurprising: such teachers are often proud of their eclecticism, and the logic of modern approaches favours preparing for, simulating and borrowing from other types of classroom (for example, 'English for Academic Purposes') as well as the outside world. Less well known, but now quite common – and certainly advocated in the present book – is borrowing in the other direction. In all the Type A situations mentioned above (Britain, India, Malaysia and Bulgaria), strategies that have been developed in the 'communicative' foreign language classroom can be very relevant. In terms of classroom management, pair and groupwork can be used within the more traditional tutorial or seminar context; where teachers and students are required to concentrate on prescribed texts, this apparent limitation can be transformed by 'playing' with the texts, cutting them up, rearranging them, altering point of view and so on. A further advantage of this kind of approach is that learner independence is encouraged in that there is a shift away from the kind of teacher-dependent organisation which is so much a feature of the traditional literature classroom towards the active engagement of the learner in particular tasks.

Another unifying thread in this book is the concern of both authors with the metalanguage (that is, 'language about language') involved in the study of literature and with the language that emerges from classroom practice. There are sections specifically devoted to a discussion of classroom process and the language required for this. Likewise, particularly in the chapters that deal with the various literary genres of poetry, prose fiction and drama, you will find, as well as a small number of technical terms, language that may not be particularly technical but which enables us to talk and write with precision about literature.

Our main aim has not been that of bibliographic review. We have referred extensively to what others have written, but have selected and tailored such references to fit our objectives as stated in the preface. If you seek a guide to further reading, the literature review article Gilroy and Parkinson (1996) may be used to supplement this book in certain areas, especially within Type B.

## 1.2  THE PLACE OF LANGUAGE IN THE LEARNING AND TEACHING OF LITERATURE

Language is involved in the teaching of literature in two main ways:

1. The language of the texts themselves. This includes any special features which make them difficult for non-native language users – either difficult to understand at all, or difficult to 'appreciate' and respond to as widely and fully as might a native user of suitable background and experience.
2. 'The language of the classroom'. This refers to all the language used by teachers and learners in writing and talking about the texts and related matters. It includes language used outside the classroom but related to it: in the teachers' case mainly in the form of worksheets, in the learners' case mainly in the form of written homework, but in all cases also other, rarer types, such as self-recorded audio and video material.

These two subsets overlap with each other and with other relevant subsets, such as the language a given group of learners already knows at the start of the course, and what they need or want or hope to know, or others hope they will know, at the end.

Language is, of course, never more than part of the story, and its study can never be completely separated from the study of non-linguistic areas. In the case of texts, these include history, politics, philosophy, sociology, psychology, cultural traditions and other arts (and also, for 'performed' texts including theatre, film and so on, concrete aspects of staging and of performance generally). In the case of classrooms, areas to be considered alongside language include most of the above, especially sociology, psychology and politics, plus more narrowly educational and pedagogic theories. In a book about applied linguistics, albeit in a wide sense, such areas can only be mentioned in passing, but they are always present in the background. We have striven to remember, as should our readers, that much of what we regard as normal is socially contingent, might not apply everywhere today, and may be rare or unknown in a few decades' time as a result of technological, political or cultural changes.

## 1.3  FINDING ONE'S OWN TEXT: A BASIC POSITION

The following poem, in Reber (1986), provides a way into our general view of literature, and of reading, learning and teaching literature.

```
selbst in den fremdesten texten den eigenen text entdecken
selbst fremdesten texten den eigenen text entdecken
fremdesten texten den eigenen text entdecken
den eigenen eigenen text entdecken
eigenen text entdecken
eigenen text entdecken
entdecken
entdecken
```

Claus Bremer

The German sentence may be translated as something like: 'Even in the strangest [most alien, most "somebody else's"] texts, to discover one's own text'. The exact meaning of the typography must, for obvious reasons, be left to the reader to decide!

The idea of 'reader response' is crucial to most – dare we say all? – modern ideas in this field. It provides a striking example of the principle of convergence, when strands of thought and practical experience in widely different fields lead to the same or similar results at roughly the same time. In this case the fields are literary theory, general educational ideas and 'communicative' approaches to foreign language teaching. The common conclusion (though agreement can be exaggerated and terms borrowed inappropriately – see Hirvela 1996) seems to have two elements:

1. That response is (or can be or should be) individual, with no belief or reduced belief in 'right' and 'wrong' answers;
2. That response is creative, not just understanding the text, not even just 'appreciating' it, but doing something active with it, creating another text, perhaps even creating the original text.

### 1.3.1 Pedagogic justification of the basic position

The process of learning, and more generally those of reading and listening, and more generally still all perception through the senses, are increasingly understood to be active processes. We do not simply take in and store information, but seek it out and pass it through all kinds of mental filters. Less obviously, we constantly predict what we are going to see, hear, read and so on, and match reality with expectation, rather than let our minds be blank sheets on which anything can be written. If we see or hear something totally unexpected, we often cannot even begin to understand it for a few moments, until we have devised a schema into which it will fit. A few moments' introspection should confirm this from your own experience – 'mystery photographs' which you could not begin to interpret until you were given a title, or incidents when someone began to speak in an unexpected language, or on an unexpected topic, and the first few words or even sentences were totally lost. For reading, the argument is less obvious, as we can normally start again when we are confused – or throw the book away – but psycholinguistic experiments (see for example Bransford and Johnson 1972) have shown that readers do not feel comfortable with a text, perhaps do not even understand it, until they have a framework into which it can be fitted. If the same text is given to different groups with and without a title, or with two different titles, this can radically affect how much is understood, and what is understood. The problems are, of course, typically greater in a foreign language, and with a text which is culturally remote from the reader.

These problems, or rather some aspects of them, have long been implicitly or explicitly recognised by teachers of literature in a foreign language and materials writers. The traditional response has been preparation of content and 'pre-teaching' of language. The former term is fairly self-explanatory: information is given about such topics as the novel (for instance) from which an extract is drawn, other texts by the same writer, the writer's life, the historical and cultural background, and perhaps even guidance on how the reader is supposed to judge the text: 'This is one of the greatest writers/poems of the twelfth century'. Pre-teaching means teaching selected language from the text – mostly vocabulary, sometimes a few grammatical or other features – before the learners are exposed to the text itself.

In modern approaches, there is still a place for preparation of content, though perhaps a reduced one: it is more 'communicative' to let learners find out what they can, or make guesses and confirm them later. The pre-teaching of language, though, is under serious theoretical assault, and widely condemned or discouraged by teacher-trainers, advisers and writers (though still common in actual classrooms!). The main reason is that giving too much information in advance makes the task inauthentic and inhibits the development of the skill of reading, which includes the developing of ways to cope with unknown language, whether by consulting reference books, making guesses and provisional hypotheses, or deciding that unknown elements are not important. All of these strategies, especially the last two, force the reader to be active, to create a provisional text of his or her own, which is constantly matched with the text on the page, but never is, and does not aspire to be, identical with it.

We shall see later more of what it can mean for the learner to become active, but it is worth saying at this stage that support for the notion of active learning does not imply a blanket approval for all 'modern' approaches in all situations. Pairwork, discovery learning, learners writing their own poems – all these can sometimes be the very opposite of truly learner centred, and at conferences for teachers one now regularly sees presenters who have adopted these surface tricks but with no con-comitant change in underlying philosophy. Conversely, teacher lecturing and other traditional teaching techniques are not necessarily antipathetic to learner centred-ness, especially where they fit learner expectations, though they should be part of a wider pedagogy which includes learning how to learn in different ways. The teacher can be a guide for a large part of the journey, but the last step always has to be taken by the learner.

We have emphasised reading and preparation for reading, but speaking and listening are equally or more important in most 'communicative' classrooms. Even unsophisticated teachers use literary texts as stimuli for discussion in the foreign language, sometimes with rather limited concern for the details of the text:

> Now that we've read *Die Verwandlung* [Kafka's *Metamorphosis*], tell your partner how you feel about insects.

Although literary and linguistic sophisticates mock such approaches, they may be better for language learning than the other (or one other?) extreme, a 'close reading' designed to guide the class towards an expert analysis pre-planned by the teacher. (One version of the latter, found in German teacher-training courses, is the *Tafelbild*, an elegant analysis of a text fitted into a diagram using all the spaces on the large, multi-surfaced German school blackboard: the teacher is supposed to compile this using ideas supplied by the pupils, but also to have a sketch in his/her pre-lesson teaching plan showing how the *Tafelbild* will look at the end.) Modern opinion favours a compromise, in which learners are guided to look at the text in far more detail than in the Kafka example, but there is still room for genuinely unpredictable and personal response. This can include responses which have little to do with the text, and more with the learners' own lives, provided that they are offered and recognised as such. The principles of autonomy, responsibility for one's own learning and learner empowerment should also mean that there is room for learners to make, or participate in, other kinds of decision – to stop reading a boring text, to choose non-traditional text types (including films for example), to read with or without questions or exercises to follow, to concentrate on language or content or both, to come to class or to read at home, to write as well as read.

The last point returns us to the other element in Bremer's poem, and to the 'reader response' idea. If all reading involves creating one's own text in one's head, perhaps learners should go further and create their own text in writing – or possibly in sound, for unscripted (but perhaps recorded) oral performance? This again is a simple 'tip for teachers' which can be done, and often is, with no conscious theoretical basis, but there is also an impressive intellectual foundation for such procedures, mainly from Widdowson, as well as support from textbooks of varying quality.

Widdowson's approach is most fully developed in Widdowson (1992), though much of it is also present in his earlier works, notably Widdowson (1975). It starts with interpretation of a text, which he sees a very individual activity: he favours 'precision of reference … in support of a particular interpretation [but] … emphatically not precision of interpretation itself' (xii). There is no one correct answer, but this does not mean that anything goes. Moreover, learners should not merely analyse texts, but should use them as a starting point for creative activities, as 'the experience of poetry, and its educational relevance, depend on the reader assuming an author role' (xi). This may entail, for example, writing alternative poems and looking at differences between original and imitation.

Many practical books for EFL teachers (see for example Maley and Moulding 1985) and some mainly for English-L1 learners (such as Pope 1995) take a more or less Widdowsonian approach. Both these books are to be praised for attempting to demystify literature and for encouraging learners to express themselves, to value their own feelings and responses, to improve their language through risk-taking strategies. But both books (further discussed in section 2.4.9), and many others of the same kind, are perhaps at fault in not even considering the possible qualitative difference between recognised literature and students' (or textbook writers') own efforts, which is surely the other side of Widdowson's coin.

## 1.4 THE BASIC POSITION AND LITERARY THEORY

This is how Bernard MacLaverty's novel *Cal* begins:

> He stood at the back gateway of the abattoir, his hands thrust into his pockets, his stomach rigid with the ache of want. Men in white coats and baseball caps whistled and shouted as they moved between the hanging carcasses.
>
> (MacLaverty 1984)

As we read these very simple sentences, we immediately, almost automatically, begin to think, to ask questions, and to look for possible connections. Who is the 'he'? Possibly the Cal of the title of the book, though we can't be sure. What is he doing at an abattoir, apparently painfully hungry – looking for food? But why isn't he buying a pie in a butcher's shop or getting a takeaway, in that case? We may guess that he is poor, perhaps looking for employment. We may make inferences about his state of mind – perhaps that he is timid or unwilling to venture further. The baseball caps and white coats tell us that the setting is contemporary. And so we proceed to the next sentence ready to go on building up the world of the book, ready to confirm or revise our ideas as the text leads us.

This is a process which many language and literature teachers constantly make use of to develop reading and inferencing skills, sometimes actually introducing their own gaps into the text by missing out words, or in another way by the use of jumbled texts. We try to encourage our students to become active readers, to become engaged with the text, rather than retreating into passivity.

We now take for granted the idea that reading is an active process of engagement with a text. This idea has not, however, always been so commonly assumed: indeed, it was only in the 1970s, with the work of Iser in particular, that the critical movement which came to be known as Reader Response Criticism began to be widely recognised. In almost all literary debates, three elements relevant to interpretation are acknowledged: the text, the author and the reader. It is not the fact of the existence of these three elements that is at issue, but their relationship and the relative importance assigned to each. Reader Response critics, in contrast to their academic predecessors – the so-called New Critics – who had focused primarily on the text as an object, were interested in the relation between reader and text. They examined, often in minute detail, both the relationship between text and reader in terms of the process required by a particular text, and the place of the reader as the interpreter of the text. First they wanted to find out, by close examination of particular texts, how the reader is 'implied' or constructed in the text itself, and second, how real people read texts (the reading process) and what they make of them (the interpretation). To some extent developments in reader response criticism reflected the broad move in the sciences and social sciences (including the new discipline of sociolinguistics) away from the myth of objectivity towards the recognition that the observer (or reader) is inescapably involved in and has an effect on that which he or she observes.

The exploration of the reading process is associated particularly with the name of Iser (though the earlier work of Ingarden and Jauss is also significant in this context). Unlike most of the New Critics, who dealt almost exclusively with poetry, Iser worked largely on prose narratives; he tried to show how the text actually forces readers into becoming active, into creating the text that they are reading, arguing that every text contains numerous gaps, omissions and what he calls indeterminancies, where the reader has to fill in the gap or interpret what is indeterminant. This is precisely what we were doing as we read the opening sentences of Bernard MacLaverty's novel quoted earlier.

A rather more radical view of the role of the reader was that developed by Stanley

Fish (1980). His argument is that meaning lies, not in the text, but in the reader, that we should be concerned with the structure of the reader's experience rather than any structures available on the page. His view is that a poem (or any other sort of text) does not possess its meaning (or even multiple meanings) immanent in itself, but that the reader may read out of it whatever meanings he or she wishes. Taken to the logical extreme, this seems a recipe for interpretative anarchy; Fish, however, sets some boundaries to this dizzying prospect of endlessly multiplying interpretations by positing the notion of the interpretive community, which is, in effect, as far as he is concerned, the academic community. This in turn, of course, begs a number of further questions about readership (surely other people besides academics read novels and poetry) and authority. Nonetheless, in terms of our own pedagogic situation, we could adapt Fish's view of the interpretive community to mean the group of students in any classroom. That is to say, we are not seeking to encourage a solipsistic individualism in reading, but to develop individual responses, followed by a sharing and to some extent an accommodation of our varying interpretations.

Perhaps the most satisfying from the teacher's point of view is the approach typified by the work of Ricoeur (1981). Ricoeur sees the process of interpretation in three stages: first comes a thorough and detailed description of the text, its linguistic features and its broader structure, with attention to content as well as to form; this is carried out in as objective a manner as possible. Then follows the actualisation of the world of the text, that is, creating the text by engaging creatively with it in the process of reading. Finally, there is the stage in which the text is reflected on and existentially and personally appropriated. 'The work thus draws us into it, distancing us from ourselves, but only to deepen our self-understanding by reflecting aspects of and possibilities for ourselves that we might otherwise never encounter' (Kerby 1993: 92).

Many of us would recognise these three stages both in our own reading and in our teaching, though we might not follow Ricoeur's order. More probably, as Widdowson (op. cit.) suggests, we might read, respond provisionally and then perform the descriptive first part in a less rigorous way than Ricoeur appears to favour, but making close reference to the text in support of our particular interpretation. A lively example of how different ways of reading can be practised in a classroom situation is described by Verdonk in his stimulating account of a poetry seminar in a Dutch university (1989). He introduced his (fairly advanced) students to three different stylistic approaches to reading poetry, which they themselves then put into practice on a number of very different poems. Verdonk argues that this approach develops the ability to 'reflect on language', an ability which he is convinced has been somewhat neglected in the recent emphasis on a narrow interpretation of language for communication: 'the average student has learnt to talk quickly and very easily, which is in itself a joyful phenomenon, but I am afraid that this success has often been obtained with the sacrifice of the ability to reflect on language with patience and sensitivity' (242).

## 1.5 REASONS FOR OR BENEFITS OF USING LITERATURE

This section lists the main reasons for teaching literature offered in books for teachers plus two added by ourselves. These are not necessarily 'good' reasons – in our opinion or perhaps even those of the original writers – but we need to take account of all reasons, good or bad, which learners, teachers or those in authority might consider important. (The opinions and priorities of these three groups can be similar, but they are very often very different.)

The books from which we quote are nearly all aimed at  Type B teaching. This is not an accident, as it is in such teaching that there is likely to be a real choice between literature and alternative topics. Some of the reasons are obviously relevant to Type A as well, but in this type issues of reason and benefit are inextricably linked with issues of definition, the 'canon' and so on, discussed later in this chapter.

The first reason is labelled 'cultural enrichment' by Collie and Slater (1987). They explain:

> It is true that the 'world' of a novel, play or short story is a created one, yet it offers a full and vivid context in which characters from many social backgrounds can be depicted. A reader can discover their thoughts, feelings, customs, possessions: what they buy, believe in, fear, enjoy; how they speak and behave behind closed doors.

The second reason, at least 3000 years old, may be called rhetoric. People study literature because it is supposed to provide a model of 'good' writing. In earlier times in Europe, and even now in some other parts of the world, large chunks of 'classical' writing were and are learned by heart, and the speech and writing of educated people was laced both with direct quotations from older authors and with imitations of their style: Milton, for example, writes a kind of 'Latin in English'. Modern EFL teachers are generally cautious about this 'reason' because it may encourage memorising without understanding, and Collie and Slater (op. cit.) point out:

> We would not wish students to think that Elizabeth Barrett Browning's 'How do I love thee?' is the kind of utterance whispered into a lover's ear nowadays!

Nonetheless, rhetoric is alive and well – it is widely taught to native speakers in the USA – and Collie and Slater continue:

> Reading a substantial and contextualised body of text, students gain familiarity with many features of the written language … which broaden and enrich their own writing skills.

A third traditional reason for teaching literature is the idea of mental training. This idea was promoted by the critic F. R. Leavis (1943):

> It trains, in a way no other discipline can, intelligence and sensibility together, cultivating sensitiveness and precision of response and a delicate integrity of intelligence.

Leavis has been very influential, and this rather supercilious view (or perhaps a distortion of it: see 1.9.2 for a more balanced account) is still held by many English teachers. Widdowson (1975) attacks it very effectively, however, pointing out that almost any academic subject can develop these general intellectual qualities, and we must seek more specific justifications for the study of literature.

A fourth and common reason for studying literature is that it is difficult. This reason is not usually admitted in so many words, but a look at school and university curricula in many countries, from Germany to Pakistan, seems to reveal an assumption that at a certain point learners come to the 'end of language', and that the only way to keep stretching them, and sorting out the sheep from the goats, (what sociologists call the gate-keeping function), is by asking difficult questions about Shakespeare. Modern writers have attacked this assumption that advanced language equals literature study, and have pointed out many alternative possibilities, including advanced general English (idioms, non-literary styles), English for business and so on, but if you do have, say, an advanced European university class, you may have to accept that literature teaching has complex institutional foundations, and that you are not allowed to make it too easy.

A much better reason is that of authenticity. Duff and Maley (1990) point out that 'literary texts offer *genuine samples* of a very wide range of styles, registers and text-types at many levels of difficulty' (our italics).

Sixth, literary language is often especially memorable. This applies especially to songs and poems, of which Maley and Moulding (1985) say:

> What is more, poems are often very easy to remember. They stick in our minds without conscious effort. One reason for this is that they frequently repeat patterns of sound or words.

The same authors suggest that poems, especially on tape, 'help us to *assimilate the rhythms* of a language' (our italics). We will call this the seventh reason, though it could be a subtype of the second. The eighth point is well made by Duff and Maley (1990):

> Literary texts are *non-trivial* in the sense that they deal with matters which concerned the writer enough to make him or her write about them. In this they are unlike many other forms of language teaching inputs, which frequently trivialise experience in the service of pedagogy. This 'genuine feel' of literary texts is a powerful motivator, especially when allied to the fact the literary texts so often touch on themes to which learners can bring a personal response from their own experience. (Our italics)

The same authors provide the ninth idea, especially relevant to Type B teaching:

> The fact that literary texts are, by their very essence, open to multiple interpretation means that only rarely will two readers' understanding of or reaction to a given text be identical. This ready-made *opinion gap* between one individual's interpretation and another's can be bridged by genuine interaction. (Our italics)

The final reason for teaching literature is that of convenience. This can be a good reason or a bad reason. It is a very bad reason indeed in some countries, where the EFL textbook consists only of extracts from classical literature, with no vocabulary or grammar, no exercises, no questions, nothing else at all. It can be a good reason if, having thought carefully about learner needs, objectives and methodology, you find a text which seems appropriate, and you realise that finding a text is not the end of your preparation, but only the beginning.

## 1.6 PROBLEMS IN TEACHING LITERATURE

This section offers some preliminary ideas on why literature-in-a-foreign-language learning and teaching can be difficult, and on the general categories of problems likely to be faced. Some of these ideas will be expanded in later chapters. We will not, generally speaking, offer solutions at this stage.

The very concept of problem is, however, itself problematic, ambiguous and elusive. The main type of ambiguity is perhaps that between perceived and actual problems. These are loaded labels and some might prefer to distinguish between problems as perceived by the learner, by the teacher, by an observer or by various authorities. Both ways of seeing have their own validity: there is a sense in which I may understand some of my learners' problems better than they do but, on another level, when one perceives something as a problem the thought becomes the fact. Another obvious difference is between short-term problems ('what does this word mean?'), medium-term ('how am I going to cope with this novel?') and long-term ('how am I going to become a good literature student?'). There are also issues of factual knowledge, skills and emotional attitudes, of teacher behaviour and learner behaviour, of what an individual does, thinks and feels and what a group does, thinks and feels. We will not attempt to resolve or eliminate such ambiguities and multiple meanings, but ask readers to bear in mind that they intersect with, and complicate, some of the specific problems mentioned in the next section.

The first problem is that of remoteness. Texts can be remote from learners in all sorts of ways – historically, geographically, socially and in terms of life experience. Modern readers may find it impossible to understand medieval or early modern concepts of honour or chastity, for example. The many hundreds of millions in tropical countries for whom English literature is still largely British have obvious difficulties with references to the weather, the seasons, and many more subtle points. Oscar Wilde and Victoria Sackville-West are not always totally accessible to the 'working class'. And when teaching older children or even young adults, it is easy to forget how much is still outside their experience.

We do not suggest, of course, that we can never enjoy stories from outside our own world – the popularity of James Bond, for example, immediately disproves such an idea. On a very different note, there is anecdotal evidence that many African and Indian children, for example, find Shakespeare more accessible than many British pupils do. But in school and university many learners, much of the time, are 'turned off' by the remoteness of what they have to read.

Problems two and three, which we shall take together, are those of difficult language and odd language. The former hardly needs comment: like other learning materials, literary texts can be so difficult that learners don't understand them, or understand them only by dint of time-consuming and wearisome dictionary work. But literary language is not only (often) difficult, it is also often 'odd' or 'deviant' in various ways – see section 4.4. And to interpret the text, readers not only need to work out the 'meaning', but to recognise that this is not the normal way of expressing it. If you are a non-native speaker of English, or if you know another language at an advanced but non-native level, you will probably be aware that when reading the 'best' literature you sometimes miss effects created by unusual language.

The fourth problem is the lack of functional authenticity. Literature is written mainly to entertain, to move, to amuse and to excite. Other functions may include political or religious persuasion, enjoyment in sharing ideas, personal therapy or catharsis for the writer. It is never, as far as we know, written for people to take it apart and write essays on it. This can be a serious problem in a communicative approach, when as far as possible we want learners to read, listen, write and speak as they would in 'real life'.

The last sentence gives us a clue to the next problem, that of imbalance between the 'four skills'. Most modern second/foreign language teaching emphasises listening and speaking, unless there are specific reasons (such as future careers) for concentrating on the other skills. At most, reading and writing should in normal circumtances be roughly equal in importance to the oral skills, but millions of teachers throughout the world, faced with a literature-dominated curriculum, are forced to change this order: reading comes first, writing second, while listening and speaking are far behind. Other factors, such as large classes, can of course play a part. An interesting example of the problems this causes may be seen in the German school and university system. In our experience at least, the best English is often spoken by the school leaver, after nine years of English; after about six more years of English, the university graduate speaks far less well – we think you can guess why.

The next couple of problems are in our opinion the most serious of all. They are the likely imbalance of knowledge and imbalance of power between teacher and learner. Especially when working with older literature, the teacher often has a mass of information – biographical, historical, cultural, linguistic – and the learner has almost none, so the teacher feels almost forced into 'lecture mode', simply telling the learners what they should know and even think, perhaps even translating parts of the text. This may sometimes be the only way to get learners through exams, but it clearly conflicts with one of the first principles of communicative methodology, that learners should talk about themselves and what they think. It also usually means that the teacher controls in detail what happens in the lesson – which books are read, which passages selected for intensive study, what kinds of questions asked – and this again conflicts with the modern idea that learners should have some control over their own learning. Thus literature work is often very bad practice for using English in real life to buy, sell, complain, make friends and so on.

The final problem is that in literature teaching there is often no sequencing; there are no staging posts. When we teach other aspects of English, especially grammar, we usually do what teachers of maths or chemistry (for example) do – we introduce the complexities gradually: *play*, then *is playing*, then *has played*, then *has been playing*, and so on. We may expose learners to more difficult language out of sequence, in accordance with Krashen's ideas (1985), but we do have a sequence to fall back on. In literature teaching, we often 'throw them into the deep end', and expect them somehow to acquire the mysterious intellectual qualities mentioned by Leavis. Some do, some do not, and all we are doing is widening the gap between the 'successful' and the 'failures', without diagnosing the problems of the latter and working out a systematic course of treatment. We said we would not offer solutions in this section, but to clarify what we mean by staging posts, we shall give just one. If your learners have difficulty in writing and speaking about metaphor, you could devise a work-sheet on metaphors in everyday language, and make sure that everyone has the necessary terminology for discussing them, before doing the same thing in a literary text which presents many other difficulties.

## 1.7  USE OF TRANSLATED TEXTS

Should texts be studied only in the language in which they are written? This seem-ingly innocuous question raises strong feelings and a host of sociolinguistic issues.

One answer, which takes us beyond the main territory of this book, is that millions of people do and probably always will study, and read for pleasure, texts originally written in a foreign language they have never studied, using translations into their, the readers', native language. No one would seriously suggest that access to Ibsen or Dostoyevsky should be granted only to those who have mastered Norwegian or Russian. In Britain, educated people used to, and some still do, tackle French, German, Latin and sometimes other literatures in the original, and we would encourage this where possible, but certainly not insist on it, especially when the 'subject' is literature rather than language. Much can be learned from studying literature in translation: several British courses known to us include Kafka, Balzac and others under the heading 'English literature'. A more subtle variation on this occurred in a recent book and television series, which dwelt on the wonderful irony of Gregor Samsa being turned into a beetle 'one *fine* morning' in the first sentence of Kafka's *Die Verwandlung*: in fact the phrase comes solely from a bad translation – the original is simply '*eines Morgens*'.

Also rather outside our territory is the situation in some developing countries where schools and universities have courses in 'Literature in English'. In East Africa, for example, students whose home language is Swahili may on such courses en-counter Flaubert or Marquez in English. The rights and wrongs of this are general issues of language planning and educational policy in these countries, not specifically of literature teaching, and we do not wish to make any judgement here.

There are, however, many cases where learners read texts in the 'wrong' language for no obvious reason, or for possibly inadequate reasons. For many decades, French teachers in British schools, relying mainly on grammar-translation and Latin-like textbooks, occasionally used 'readers' to lighten the diet, and perhaps the most popular of these was *Émile et les Détectives*. This turns out to have started life as *Emil und die Detektive*, written in German by Erich Kästner, but translated and translocated to Paris. Similar absurdities can be found in most European countries. This is not mainly a criticism of teachers, who understandably use what is available, but perhaps of those at other levels – heads of departments, advisers, inspectors, trainers, examiners or materials writers – who influence such choices.

Yet another situation is when a class is studying language X, and a text originally written in language X, but studies the text in their own language. This may happen either officially, as when some school-level 'classical studies' exams, taken alongside Latin and Greek, assume that texts have been read in English; or semi-officially, as when British university French lecturers advise their students to read short texts in French but long works (Montesquieu, Diderot, Gide and Malraux, for example) in English (though one may gain marks by memorising a few French quotations and using them in examinations).

We are uneasy about the wide use of translations. The first reason for this is that many people, even the highly educated, seem incapable of remembering when they are dealing with translations, and how this should affect their judgement. The approach we take in this book depends largely on close study of texts, responding to both form and content and appreciating the connections between them. For most serious literature, some of these connections are 'lost in translation'. A translator who is also a good writer may create new structures of formal interest, and very occasionally even rival the original, but then we have a new literary work – *nachgedichtet* is the expressive German term. Fitzgerald's version of *The Rubáiyát of Omar Khayyám* is the classical example in English: students can certainly study this with profit, but they are studying Fitzgerald much more than Omar. More usually, not even this compensation is available, and the translation is a poor second best.

The main argument against using translation, though, is that it does little to foster the various processes which make up foreign language learning, from vocabulary expansion and development of grammatical competence to the skills of skimming and scanning, guessing and inferencing. To the French lecturers who believe that their students simply lack the language level, and perhaps diligence, to tackle *L'Esprit des Loix* or *La Condition Humaine*, we would suggest either that they choose easier (especially shorter) texts, or that they help students with a package of notes and self-study questions, allowing them to omit certain parts, teaching them how to skim others for general meaning, and focusing on carefully chosen passages for detailed study. It is unrealistic to ban students from buying and using translations, but this should not be expected of them, and with carefully designed teaching may not be felt necessary.

Successful learners of a foreign language usually get to a stage where they can read long texts – perhaps not 'serious' works from earlier centuries, but certainly modern light novels – for pleasure and with hardly any recourse to a dictionary. We would like to think that teachers can encourage this process (see section 2.4.1), though we acknowledge that there is no guaranteed recipe, and many people do not even read novels in their own language.

The educational practice of studying literature in translation is firmly established, and nothing we write will alter this. All we suggest is that, especially in situations where practical competence in foreign languages is the or a main objective, greater use of alternatives should be considered.

## 1.8 LITERATURE IN THE CONTEXT OF LANGUAGE TEACHING: TWO CASE STUDIES

Before going on to the next section, which offers a more detailed account of the historical development of critical approaches to the reading and teaching of literature, it may be helpful to consider particular examples of the use of literature in a language teaching context.

### 1.8.1 Malaysia: literature as a resource for language teaching

During the 1990s, the University of Strathclyde in Scotland was host to a large number of teachers of English from Malaysian schools and universities. The university teachers were PhD students, concerned with developing literature teaching at university level, while those from schools were seconded by the Malaysian Ministry of Education to undertake an intensive two-year degree in TESOL (Teaching English to Speakers of Other Languages). The department at Strathclyde had been asked to focus specifically on one of the major concerns of the Malaysian Education Department, namely the development of literature teaching in secondary schools.

The history of English teaching in Malaysia, with the recent emphasis on literature teaching as a crucial element in the drive to improve standards in English language, has been well documented (Edwin 1993). The overseas training programme is linked with a much wider programme within Malaysia itself which aims to provide teachers with both a knowledge of literature in English and the pedagogical application of that knowledge. Very few of the teachers who participate in this programme have an academic background in literature, despite being competent and experienced teachers of English, and the majority are initially apprehensive, feeling themselves ill equipped for their new task. What is evident is that a kind of (misplaced) fallout from the critical approaches of Arnold and Leavis is still having its effect; some of the teachers say, almost in so many words, that they feel they lack the special sensitivity and capacity for response that they believe must be innate in students of literature. They are frequently deeply sceptical of the suggestion that it is possible to learn to read literature (as suggested by Verdonk in the article already cited), and that they themselves can engage in this learning programme. On the other side there are those who 'love' literature and read it eagerly and with strong emotional and aesthetic responses, but tend to find a more analytical language-based approach rebarbative because it goes against the grain of their ideas of how literature *should* be read. In the view of both groups, literary response is (a) primarily affective, and (b) dependent on personal psychological qualities, and there is not much anyone can do about that. In addition, some of the Malaysian teachers are highly critical of Western culture and Western values, which they feel may be mediated through a study of its literature. They rarely express this criticism openly but for a few it may play a significant part in producing a negative attitude to what they are doing, and it is important that those who teach them are aware of this and are willing to make use of opportunities to bring such cultural questions to the surface in a supportive and non-confrontational way rather than pretending that they do not exist.

The attempted solution to these problems of dealing with literature has been that in the first year of the course the Malaysian teachers take the regular first-year General English course alongside British undergraduates, during which they read a fairly conventional and canonical set of texts including short stories, novels, plays and a selection of poems. They attend literature tutorials, which are sometimes in the form of workshops and sometimes general discussions, and they write conventional literary essays. In their first year they also attend a course generally taken by second- or third-year undergraduates called 'Ways of Reading'. This is explicitly analytical in approach, being based largely on linguistics and related theory, but it is also considerably influenced by language teaching methodology and is culturally eclectic in its choice of texts for study. All students on this course take part in a weekly workshop exercise involving small groups, which is carefully structured and is managed by the students themselves, with a lecturer present to facilitate the feedback at the end of the session. The assignments are all practical rather than discursive in form, and the influence of language teaching methodology is apparent in this, since, rather than asking for traditional discussion, they require students 'to do things with texts', for example using cut-up texts to create new ones or changing texts around, using a variety of media. In their second (and final) year, the Malaysian teachers take two courses designed specifically for their needs, which have a pedagogic focus: the first is concerned with the use of literature in a (primarily) language-centred classroom situation, referring to and developing the ideas they have already met in their first year, while the second deals with the development of a curriculum for teaching literature. By the time they are a few weeks into the second year, the majority are making connections for themselves with their first-year work and recognising and drawing with increasing confidence on the expertise that they have developed. The key words are indeed 'confidence' and 'expertise': by the end of their course most of them would agree that it is possible to learn (and therefore also teach) ways of reading literature which are relevant to their cultural and educational situations.

There has as yet been no overall evaluation by the Malaysian Government of this teacher education project (which is very large and involves a number of British universities), so it is not possible to do more than comment anecdotally on the results of which we have heard, mostly in the form of letters from 'our' teachers. Those who write – a self-selected group, obviously, but there always are a few from each cohort – do seem to be using literature in the context of language teaching, almost all for the first time: some are developing their own worksheets and materials, others who are perhaps less confident are drawing directly on materials developed during their time at Strathclyde; several are employed on writing self-access materials, putting extensive reading schemes into operation and running workshops for other teachers. A few from each group have been moved into teacher-training posts. The project has now come to an end in its present form, so an evaluation of it by the Malaysian Ministry of Education should soon be under way and it will be interesting to see the results.

### 1.8.2 Bulgaria: literature in a cultural studies programme

Bulgaria has had for many years, in addition to the ordinary secondary schools, a highly developed system of special language-medium high schools in which (since the changes of 1989, when Russian ceased to be one of the languages taught in school) the languages available have been English, German and French. Under this system, the first year is spent almost entirely in learning the specific language of the school, and thereafter that language is to a great extent the medium of instruction throughout it. This produces a very high level of proficiency, which until recently was achieved almost entirely by means of a teacher-centred 'grammar and translation' methodology, together with (so we are told by the present-day teachers) a somewhat authoritarian classroom atmosphere. During the last ten years there has been in Bulgaria, as in other former Communist countries, an increasing tendency in classroom culture towards a more equal and open relationship between teacher and students and with this a shift to more 'learner centred' and 'communicative' styles of teaching; in broader cultural terms, too, there is an increasing interest in the place of 'cultural studies' within a language-teaching programme. There is a significant relationship between the recent political shifts, these changes in class-room culture and the new interest in critical cultural studies in relation to language learning.

Since the early 1990s the British Council has been instrumental in setting up a network of Bulgarian English Language teachers in the language-medium schools who are interested in developing the teaching of cultural studies in relation to the language programme. Strathclyde University was invited to share in this develop-ment by means of a postgraduate course in 'Teaching British Cultural Studies'. The course was delivered by a combination of in-country teaching sessions and workshops, distance learning and a three-week summer school at Strathclyde. As a result of this, we are also involved in the development of a Bulgarian syllabus for cultural studies in secondary schools.

This is a very different situation from that of the Malaysian teachers whom we described earlier. The majority of the Bulgarian teachers have a degree in English philology, which includes a considerable background of English literature, although in fact in their teaching very few draw on literary texts outside the compulsory tenth year coursebook literary extracts, which include passages from novels and plays in addition to poems, short stories and essays. The dominant approach to these texts in the coursebook (new coursebooks are being written, but it will take time for them to get to Year 10) is that of extract followed by comprehension questions, which make the unexpressed assumption that these texts can generally be regarded as referential: that is, that they are fairly straightforward reflections of social reality and can be read as such in a fairly straightforward way. Bulgarian teachers, many of whom have a highly sophisticated appreciation of literary theory, are themselves increasingly aware of this as a problem and recognise the necessity of viewing texts as constructed, as representations rather than mere reflections of a culture. But what does this imply for classroom practice?

In an attempt to address this problem, one of the modules in the course on teaching cultural studies was entitled 'Literature and Location'; it focused on Scottish literature, driven in this choice not so much by nationalist preoccupations as by the practical arguments for selecting a reasonably manageable group of texts, which would be both varied and interesting and yet have some overall coherence in terms of their relationship to location and culture. What we did not foresee and therefore found doubly interesting was that, while they explored issues of national and group identity in Scottish literature, several of the teachers were inspired to engage in a new and fresh way with their own national literature, and it was this dialectic between the two cultures that produced some of the most interesting work in this module.

Let us use an example to illustrate this. One teacher, who had a particular interest in poetry, took up the notion of 'homeland'. She explored the significance of this concept with her students and together they made a collection of contemporary Bulgarian poems on the subject. How was the notion of 'homeland' constructed in these poems? For example, did the name of the country appear in them? Was any particular geographical location significant? Was dialect used? What metaphors were developed? Was there a difference between poetry written by poets still resident in Bulgaria and poetry by emigrants? Did poets perform their own work in public, on radio or television? Having in this way developed a set of questions from their own reading of Bulgarian poetry, they turned to Scottish poems, asking these same questions of Scottish texts and exploring particular issues further: for example, differences in metaphors, the use of Scots as opposed to Standard English dialect, the 'high' and 'popular' cultural functions of poetry. The way this teacher set about her literature project was by encouraging her students in the first place to stand back from their own cultural texts, which they tended to accept without question as a 'given' part of their environment, and to view them afresh by asking questions of them, by refusing to take them for granted. They then turned their attention to the Scottish poems with a developed set of questions and an interest in discovering comparisons and contrasts. This kind of approach moves through a sequence of raising awareness of aspects of one's own culture which entails a process of defamiliarisation of the obvious and familiar, to asking questions of the other (or 'target') culture in order to understand – as far as possible – that which is obvious and familiar to those who inhabit that cultural context. And in so doing, it inevitably demands a close and increasingly sophisticated attention to the nuances of the target language.

## 1.9  NEW CRITICAL, LEAVISITE AND RELATED APPROACHES

With these two examples to provide a context, we now consider some of the questions around how we read literature, which have arisen from and continue to shape the institutional study of the subject, but which also have wider ramifications involving attitudes to the use of literary texts within a language-teaching context. The debates that we are concerned with here are largely Anglo-American in origin and tend to be pragmatic and text-based rather than theoretical in their approach to literature. We are certainly not attempting anything as ambitious as an overview of literary theory at this point.

### 1.9.1  New Criticism

We will take New Criticism first, as a broadly inclusive term. New Criticism, incidentally, reached the height of its popularity in the 1940s and 50s, so it is a fairly old sort of criticism by now and has been superseded in critical discussion by a dozen other -isms, such as New Historicism, feminism, reader response, post-colonial criticism and so on. Some of its formalist insights endure, however, and one legacy of particular relevance to those teachers and learners whose primary interest is in language, is the emphasis its practitioners accorded to the 'close reading' of a text.

New Criticism developed in relation to the establishment of literature as a subject of academic study in universities, which in the British context happened in the early years of the twentieth century and – importantly for its later development – in Cambridge in the years following the 1914–18 war. The name particularly associated with Cambridge is that of I. A. Richards, who developed the approach known as Practical Criticism with his students – an approach which is probably to be found more frequently these days in language-based classrooms than in any other (see, for example, the approach adopted in the poetry chapter of this book, Chapter 4). Practical Criticism means that a reader/student is given a text to read as it stands, without being provided with or looking for background information, and is asked to understand and interpret it as fully as possible by means of clues which are given in the text itself; by so doing it is argued that the reader develops particular skills and techniques of reading, together with an increasing awareness of how texts work internally. Valuable longer-term effects are associated with this practice, such as developing a capacity to evaluate what we read and learning to use language coherently and expressively to say what we want to say about a literary text. In many ways, this still remains the basis for much use of poems or short stories in language-teaching contexts.

The practitioners of New Criticism in the USA took Richards' ideas further, particularly in developing in a more theoretical fashion the notion of the text as an object in itself without any necessary reference to its origins or history, or to the situation of the actual reader. They argued first that the poem (it was mainly poetry that they dealt with – indeed, one of the problems with this way of reading is that it does not work so well with longer texts such as novels) stands on its own, that is, a critical reading of it is not dependent on knowledge of its author or the circumstances of its writing or production; and second, that it is a unity in itself and cannot be reduced to paraphrase – or, at any rate, that to paraphrase is a profoundly reductive exercise, in the process of which the true poem is lost. The unity of the poem seems, from this point of view, to be an undisputed given, and the critic's task is to show how, often very precariously and with much difficulty, this unity is achieved in the poem by means of paradox, ambiguity and irony; these are all poetic devices of tension, which, when skilfully deployed, produce a sense of delicately achieved balance. The *a priori* assumption of such a critical approach is that the literary text is a coherent unity, which is produced by a kind of internal textual conflict leading to an internal textual resolution.

This was in many ways a reaction against the background assumptions of those 'traditional' approaches which imply that the meaning of a text is contained not so much within the text itself as in its relation to other factors such as the historical period, the author's beliefs, and so on. New Critics raised the status of the text as text, that is, as significant in itself without reference to its context, but together with this they implicitly rejected any concern with its social and ideological relations. In doing so, these practitioners failed to recognise their own ideological premises, which were fundamentally those of liberal humanism, together with the assumption that certain values are universal. These particular issues underlie much of the cultural debate on whether or not to use literature in the language classroom; but it is clear that alongside the concern with cultural opposition and difference an emphasis on what is shared by human beings continues to animate the practice of most teachers and learners.

### 1.9.2  The influence of F. R. Leavis and the 'Leavisites'

Like the New Critics, Leavis directed his critical attention to the close reading of texts; unlike them, he dealt with a broad range of genres, including prose narratives, drama and epic poetry as well as their special favourite, the short lyric poem. The lasting positive impact of Leavis' work, at any rate from our point of view as teachers of language and literature, probably lies in four areas:

1. The continuation and development of the close-reading method;
2. The way he encouraged his students to reach their judgements: a typical question being 'This is so, isn't it?' rather than a flat authoritative statement; by so doing, he intended to invite students to either agree or disagree, with qualifications 'Yes, but ...' or 'No, but. ...'. In other words, for him judgement was achieved by means of collaborative discussion;
3. His conviction that literature was important to life; that it could touch its readers deeply with the power to change their ideas and attitudes; and
4. His lifelong struggle against what he perceived as the stranglehold on education of the social, institutional and cultural establishments of his time (he lived from 1895–1978).

F. R. Leavis and his wife Q. D. Leavis were both deeply concerned with the nature of 'great literature' and the development of the literary canon, although their pre-ferred term was 'the tradition', in accordance with T. S. Eliot's usage. Though revolutionary at the time (they were writing quite specifically in opposition to what they perceived as the socially and culturally snobbish elite of the Bloomsbury group) and enormously influential on the succeeding generation of critics, their work on 'the tradition' appears to many readers now to be highly elitist and to be, indeed, a narrowing down of literature rather than opening it up to a broader understanding.

The irony is that the kind of reading Leavis sought to develop and his own struggle with the powerful institutions of his time produced a new kind of elitism, dependent on a highly culturally specific sensitivity of response to particular significant texts, which inevitably led to a form of cultural and aesthetic snobbery that was both negative and long-lasting in its effects. This development could be seen to be respon-sible, to a large extent, for the lack of confidence among some of the Malaysian teachers participating in the literature programme we described earlier (the sense that their literary sensibilities were unequal to the highly specialised task of literary appreciation), a feeling of inadequacy that is not confined to that particular group but is widely shared by teachers who are not literary specialists.

### 1.9.3  Raymond Williams and the development of cultural studies

The final influence on critical reading that we consider here is the work of Raymond Williams. Like Leavis in many ways, he, too, came from a non-establishment back-ground but eventually became a Cambridge academic and the founder of an in-terpretative school of reading. As Leavis was a member of the post-1914–18 wave of new thinkers, Williams belonged to those who returned to higher education after the Second World War. Williams challenged the notion of 'high literature' as a collection of almost sacred texts (which Leavis' criticism had reinforced) and the sense that 'imaginative literature' existed in a privileged enclave of value. His own work, growing very much out of his own experience of belonging in different ways to a variety of specifically English subcultures, was concerned to show how literature and 'high' art in general were part of a whole system of meanings, social, economic and political, and fulfilled a great variety of functions besides that of educating the individual sensibility. He set the study of literature within the broader inter-disciplinary context of 'cultural studies' and also, through his interest in popular forms, opened up the catchment area of literature far beyond the Leavisite great tradition. While one result of this shift of view is that a whole range of popular texts are now being seriously – and, it must be admitted, in some cases extraordinarily ponderously – discussed and written about in university departments, it also means that those who study literature are becoming much more interested in what non-specialists (for example, those who read for pleasure rather than for professional reasons) choose to read, and why, and in what contexts.

Clearly, the implications of this expanded notion of literature have been taken on board by practitioners in the literature-for-language context (see for example Maley

1989) as well as by those working in the field of cultural studies. You will find in Chapter 8 a reference to how one such popular text (a Mills and Boon novel) might be employed in the classroom.

## 1.10  DEFINITIONS OF LITERATURE

So far we have been using the term literature with apparent confidence that we are all in agreement as to its meaning. It may be worth at this point pausing to consider the question addressed by Williams as to what we do in fact mean when we use the word, and what possible meanings it has had at different times and in different cultures.

'Of all the definitions contained in this volume, the one for literature is easily the most fluid.' So begins the article on literature in a recent encyclopaedia of contemporary literary theory (Makaryk 1993: 581). Indeed, it is probably not possible, or even desirable, for our purposes to look for a watertight definition which is at once wide enough to include all we might want to include and also sufficiently precise to exclude all that we might feel should be excluded. A more helpful way of approaching the question may be to consider literature as a functional rather than an ontological term (Ellis 1974); that is, a term which is concerned with what something does (or with what we do with it) rather than with what it could be said to be in itself. Such an approach implies that our definition of literature is under constant revision, an issue that we return to when we consider the canon.

In Western culture, at least since the eighteenth century, the word literature has been closely associated with literacy; the term has tended to imply something written and read rather than spoken and heard. Does this mean that we exclude oral cultures and traditions from our consideration when we talk about literature? Does it also imply that a play only turns into literature once it has been printed and distributed for reading? Is performance poetry recognised as literature? These questions indicate something of the complex relationship between ways of valuing certain cultural objects and the modes of production and consumption of those objects by society. For our purposes in this book, our main sources are almost inevitably written texts, though we do refer to oral material; we hope that those of our readers whose cultures include an oral tradition will supplement and develop our examples wherever possible. (An extended treatment of oral literature based on an analysis of linguistic features can be found in Fabb 1997.)

Literature has sometimes been seen as special or different from other written forms in that it is 'creative' or 'imaginative' verbal production. The first term implies an assumption about the origin of literature, that it is defined somehow in relation to its source, to its author and to the author's understanding of what he or she is doing. Most contemporary critics would argue that while the author's intention is part of the whole picture, it is not definitive. The creator of the text is assumed to have consciously intended to communicate something, but there is usually some unconscious or unintended meaning in the text as well. As in spoken utterances, the writer 'is both conscious and unconscious creator of the text' (Spolsky 1994: 145). Moreover, while a writer may quite acceptably regard his or her work as creative, that does not guarantee its status as literature and the author may not even be interested in producing a 'literary' work. For example, 'creative writing' in schools and language classes does not, as has already been said, necessarily produce work that would be valued as literature by either the writer or the reader. On the other hand, while the term creative does not of itself guarantee literary status, we may wish to retain it as an important quality in work that we do consider to be literature – although it must be acknowledged that this is still a very fuzzy distinction in that there is a creative element in many kinds of writing – journalism, for example, and even, perhaps, academic textbooks!

To turn to the second term, what is meant here by imaginative? If it implies a distinction in subject matter between fiction and fact, it is a difficult distinction to sustain; the sermons of John Donne or Daniel Defoe's *Journal of the Plague Year* or Boswell's *Life of Johnson* are all regarded as part of the canon of English literature, yet none of the genres they represent could be described as purely fictional. On the other hand, imaginative could refer to the quality of feeling that is expressed through certain kinds of writing. We might describe this rather loosely as a Romantic view, where the primary understanding of literature is writing which 'embodies' in language a profound and sincere emotion. Authentic poetic language gives a body to the 'spirit', which is the meaning. As expressed by Wordsworth and Coleridge in particular, this approach offered a complex and subtle exploration of the organic relationship between form and content in poetry, which over time developed at a less subtle level into the view that the value of literature arises primarily from the quality of the emotion, its truth or sincerity, rather than from any special or extraordinary use of language. Literary value then seems to reside somewhere in the relationship between the inner experience of the author, the 'truthful' expression of that experience in language, and the sympathetic reception of that expression by the reader. But if we are looking for a workable definition of literature, this approach raises a problem in that it seems to make assumptions about the enduring and shared nature of particular emotions and values which may not in fact be borne out by the actual experience of readers.

However, the term imaginative might very well point to something about the form rather than the content, to the argument that the distinguishing feature of literature is the use of language that is in some way particularly vivid or striking. If we compare the line 'Time has turned the bloom to gray' (Emily Bronte: 'Long neglect', 1837) with the statement 'She looked much older', most of us would say the first has literary quality while the second doesn't. The Formalist school of criticism argued that literature is that form of writing which draws attention to itself by in some way distorting the ordinary use of language, by 'making it strange'. The first line of Langston Hughes' poem 'Harlem' (1951) is a good example:

What happens to a dream deferred?

where the alliteration emphasises the oddity of the conjunction of 'dream' and 'deferred'. The Formalists were concerned not with the subject matter of literature or the emotional content or the value systems that it might express, but with its linguistic form. The problem here is that while their definition of literature is applicable to certain kinds of poetry, or to highly wrought prose such as the writings of Sir Thomas Browne or Modernist novels such as *To the Lighthouse*, it is difficult to extend it to, say, novels written in the realist tradition, like George Eliot's *Middlemarch*, which are generally regarded as a highly significant part of literature in English. In its focus on language, it is very valuable in highlighting an important aspect of literature, but it excludes too much to be useful as a definition.

Literature may also be regarded as writing that fulfils certain socially and culturally approved functions; in the West it has traditionally been expected to be both pleasurable and thought-provoking, to fulfil both aesthetic and moral functions. This may indeed be a common feature of literature in a variety of cultures. In Western society until the eighteenth century the moral function of literature included a strong didactic element; with increasing social fragmentation, that didactic purpose has largely disappeared and is, indeed, now generally regarded with suspicion – although it could be argued against this that there is a powerful didactic element in the work of Brecht to take an obvious example, and in the politically committed theatre groups which have been influenced by him, such as 7:84 in Scotland, whose play *The Cheviot, the Stag and the Black, Black Oil* (1974; 1981) presented a very direct political message. Particularly with a multi-cultural group of learners, it can be interesting and illuminating to consider the different and evolving functions of literature in different societies, at different periods and in different social and political contexts: literature may be celebratory or subversive; idealistic or ironic; reinforcing the norms of society or critical of them. Certain forms may also fulfil certain quite specific social functions, such as the marking of occasions by, for example, formal poems at weddings or funerals or by the praise songs of certain African traditions.

These three broad views may be characterised as oriented towards (1) content; (2) form; and (3) function. A further and overarching notion is that of value. The existence of the canon indicates that there are 'official' views on what constitutes good or bad literature, or at least what is 'high' and what is 'low'. Literature teachers are almost inevitably constrained to some extent by canonical considerations which influence the choice of texts on a syllabus and the public exam requirements, but language teachers who choose to draw on literature in their classrooms have much greater freedom and can range from pop lyrics to Shakespeare – though they will still almost certainly exercise judgements of value in some form, even if only in terms of what might be described as the criterion of enjoyability.

## 1.11 THE CANON

The word 'literature' is derived from Latin, where it signified (a) writing; (b) grammar; and (c) wide reading, erudition, or what might now be described as 'cultural literacy' (Hirsch 1987), this last meaning implying a broadly accepted notion of normative value or a canon of literature. So from very early times the notion of literature has been bound up with socially and culturally constituted notions of value. The term 'canon' comes from the classical Greek word for a measuring rod and could also mean a list. The first use of the term to signify an authoritative list of books is found in the early centuries of the Christian era, where the Biblical canon designates those writings that are officially regarded by the church as Holy Scripture. So the notion of a canon of literature carries implications both of value and of some kind of official or publicly constituted authority.

One of the most debated questions of recent critical discussion is that of the canon: how it has been formed, what it represents and to what extent it is open to alteration and development. Our consideration here is confined to the canon of 'English literature', but readers will no doubt be aware of similar issues in their own literary culture. For many this has become a somewhat sterile and tired debate, but its effects are still felt in literature departments and are apparent in the literature syllabuses that many of us have to teach. The English literary canon as we know it now found its clearest formation around the end of the nineteenth and beginning of the twentieth century and it reflects the values of the dominant ideology of that period in Britain, which were nationalist (and implicitly imperialist), socially and educationally middle to upper class and almost entirely male oriented. The development of the canon was also importantly related to pedagogical and institutional concerns, in that it was during this period that English literature was beginning to emerge as a subject of study in British universities. Many of the recent objections to the canon have come from post-colonialist and feminist writers and critics – not to mention English language teachers – who argue that it is elitist and unrepresentative of the work and experience of subordinated and minority groups and of popular literature. Certainly, it reflects a particular 'high' view of art. (These criticisms, incidentally, are also levelled at other canonical formations, such as those of painting and sculpture.) Some critics argue for revisions and extensions of the canon to such subgroups: they refer, for example, to the canon of women's writing or the canon of Indian writing in English. Others wish to revise the existing canon to reflect a more pluralistic set of values, a task of revision that would presumably have to be ongoing to encompass new varieties and productions. Others argue for the abandonment of the idea of a canon altogether, though it could be difficult to abandon what is now so deeply entrenched a notion. A more workable solution may be simply to recognise its existence and the important questions it raises about how we value literature; in particular, the complexity of the relationship between ideology, value and historical context. We do not, fortunately, have to reach any conclusion on this relationship here, but it is important to recognise that many literature syllabuses require students to engage with works which are on the syllabus simply because they are canonical and that this may pose (and should, we believe, encourage) specific questions about ideology, relevance and the social significance of literature. Chapter 5, which is concerned with teaching novels, considers ways of working with one such problematic canonical text, Conrad's *Heart of Darkness*.

# Chapter 2

# What can teachers and learners do with literature?

## 2.1 INTRODUCTION

In this chapter, we attempt to classify the kinds of activities involving literature which might occur in a foreign-language classroom (or in homework or other preparation or follow-up activity out of class). Some types, especially varieties of close linguistic analysis, are discussed at greater length in Chapters 3–7.

As already suggested in section 1.5, there is a potential disparity between what those in authority want to happen or think is happening, what teachers want or think, and what learners want or think. Teachers may openly disregard what authorities (at any level) have directed them to do, or they may consciously or unconsciously subvert it, or they may use the gaps left by curriculum guidelines to introduce their own ideas, or they may convey different messages simply by being themselves. Similarly, learners rarely do exactly as they are told: even when they are not deliberately disobedient, and do not lack any of the knowledge and skills which a teacher's plan pre-supposes, they will almost inevitably interact with a text – even if only inside their heads – in ways which are not completely predictable, nor even completely observable or testable during or after the event.

Our list of activities, however, will be based on teacher intention, that is, what is 'supposed to happen', as revealed mainly by the teacher's instructions. This is the only practicable basis for a general description of lessons, although it can and should for some purposes be supplemented by data on what learners actually do, know or want (see Chapter 9).

## 2.2 TRADITIONAL APPROACHES

In this section, we briefly describe four types of activity which modern language-teaching methodologists tend to think of as old fashioned, and to contrast unfavourably with newer methods. Some of our descriptions will include negative comment, and by and large we tend to view these activities less enthusiastically than most of those in section 2.4, but no black-and-white contrast would be sensible, and the following caveats should be borne in mind:

- Most 'new' methods, or something like them, were present in many 'old' classes;

- Many 'old' methods are still found, indeed very commonly, today;
- 'Old' methods may be justified in all sorts of ways, not least by learner expectations and what learners and teachers are comfortable with;
- In any case the opposition between new and old methods is an unreal one. Allwright (1991) has written of the 'death of the method', and he and others have shown that what happens in classrooms cannot be explained by a finite number of methods, but only by the interaction of many variables, only some of which can be directly observed (see section 9.3), and many of which go beyond linguistics and literary theory into highly subjective realms of personality and emotion.

### 2.2.1  Rote learning and summary of content

This may include learning the basic plot of novels or plays for instance, or facts about the writer's life, relevant history and politics. Especially at school level, this can simply be the memorisation of facts given by the teacher: Dickens' Mr Gradgrind, who wanted only facts, is alive and well as the twenty-first century dawns. At university, one of the present writers (BP) spent much of his 'study year' in the middle of a German degree, in Germany as prescribed, not actually talking to Germans but making thirty-page summaries of 600-page novels, a procedure actively encouraged by his tutors, while his German counterparts studying English were and still are often encouraged to produce an *Inhaltsangabe*, or summary of content, though admittedly only as one stage in a longer process of analysis.

Some readers may argue that rote learning and summary of content are entirely distinct. Indeed they are, in principle, but in practice they often go together because assessment is by examination taken without reference books, and learners believe, rightly or wrongly, that they will get a degree in German or certificate in English if they demonstrate enough factual knowledge 'under examination conditions'.

### 2.2.2  Reading aloud

For many British readers, this procedure has associations with nineteenth-century and early twentieth-century schooling, and lessons read about in novels and biographies – archetypically Latin lessons, but also French and German, as well as English. The popular belief – supported by, among other things, our own classroom research and teacher interviews – is that reading aloud still happens in British schools, but is no longer the staple diet, and may sometimes even be seen as an emergency stopgap or the last resort of a tired teacher. In our own lessons, one of us at least (BP) has tended to be rather dismissive of this method, expecting learners to read texts as homework, or, failing that, silently in class; but many learners have learnt English for many years, to very advanced levels, by the 'read aloud first' method and are uncomfortable with change, so compromise has been essential and further rethinking may still be necessary.

One point about reading aloud is that it is a specialist skill – most people do it badly even in their own language. To put it provocatively, if students are good enough to read a text aloud, they probably do not need to! Other arguments are that this is not how most people read literature in the world outside the classroom, and that it introduces unnecessary complications and 'red herrings', for example, the problem of how words are pronounced. It does not develop skills such as gist extraction, rereading short sections to confirm meaning, or even skipping forward over boring passages.

If students expect to study long texts by reading aloud in class, we think there is an overwhelming case for re-educating them, as gradually as necessary, but sometimes teachers might be advised to read aloud themselves, or use tapes of other competent speakers, to avoid some of the problems mentioned above.

All of this applies in full only to novels, short stories, essays and similar non-oral genres. There is obviously a much stronger case for students hearing all drama, and most poetry, again with judicious use of teacher and tape, including videotape where available – or, best of all, attending a live performance.

### 2.2.3 Translation

Translation, the teaching of translation and the interface of both of these with literature, are wide topics to which whole books are devoted, and we can only touch on them here. The use of translated texts as an object of study was considered in section 1.7. In the present section, we discuss translation as process, and in particular those activities in which a class goes through a book – usually the complete work, sometimes selected passages – translating it sentence by sentence. In the archetypal form of this activity (at least for Britain), translation goes with reading aloud, and students are called upon one by one to read out a sentence and translate it. One of us (BP) was prepared for French, German and Latin 'A' Levels by this method in 1965, and it still survives, especially in conservative private schools, with or without modification.

At least two variants are reported by our students from other European countries. In one variant, the teacher does most or all of the translation, sometimes even dictating or translating for the students to write. Another variant, less traditional and less frequent, involves student groups working on translations, the written product being checked by the teacher and/or read aloud to the class.

These methods are certainly not in all cases misguided or unsuccessful; in particular, they may be a logical response to situations where outside authorities force learners to study foreign-language literature without an adequate prior knowledge of the language: the production of 'cribs' or commercial translations, such as the infamous *Kelly's Keys* for Latin, is a part of this depressing but (for some learners) necessary 'solution'.

There is, however, a conflict with the present consensus view on the place of translation in language learning. Broadly, this is that translation is not the best way to learn language, but is an 'add-on skill' which those already proficient in a foreign language can develop for very specific purposes. Good readers do not translate an L2 text, even in their heads, but understand it directly (and behave analogously in listening, speaking and writing). Learners at lower levels should be led towards this way of reading (for example), and away from reliance on translation. The extreme form of this argument, as found in the Direct Method, makes all translation taboo. Nowadays most experts would not go so far, and accept that learners often need some recourse to translation, perhaps at the word level, perhaps at phrase or sentence level, which can either be supplied ready made, usually by the teacher, or found by the learner in dictionaries or notes, or constructed (guessed or worked out) by the learner and then checked; but all such translation is partial and selective, and the aim is that as the learner progresses more and more of texts should be understood 'directly', and the role of translation – written, spoken, even 'in the head' – should be progressively reduced.

### 2.2.4 Reworking of secondary literature

Study of first-language and foreign-language literature at university level (and sometimes at school) has traditionally included reading 'secondary literature' and incorporating parts of it, either verbatim, summarised or otherwise reworked, in essay form: taking lecture notes, and memorising them before exams or using them in essays, is a variant of this. It is difficult to generalise about this activity, as the content of such secondary literature and what students do with it can vary greatly. At one extreme there may be a collection of historical and biographical facts, scholarly findings on text variants, and even received opinions which students are expected, and/or themselves expect, to regurgitate with little change: a lecturer known to one of us told generations of students that Stefan George was a 'major minor poet', and seemed gratified when they told him the same. Other academics claim to be less encouraging towards regurgitation, but unable to prevent it:

> Everyone who sees the work of Honours students of English at a university has noticed with distress their increasing tendency to see books wholly through the spectacles of other books. On every play, poem or novel, they produce the view of some eminent critic. An amazing knowledge of Chaucerian or Shakespearean criticism sometimes co-exists with a very inadequate knowledge of Chaucer or Shakespeare. Less and less do we meet the individual response. The all-important conjunction (Reader meets Text) never seems to have been allowed to occur of itself and develop spontaneously. Here, plainly, are young people drenched, dizzied, and bedevilled by criticism to a point at which primary literary experience is no longer possible.
>
> Lewis (1961: 128–9)

Most university teachers would probably claim that study and use of secondary literature is not an end in itself, but should assist in a wider activity, which is writing about primary texts. Such writing – usually in the form of an essay – should include the students' own direct analysis of the primary text, but the secondary literature is expected to stimulate and enrich this analysis. Teachers seem to be divided about whether use of secondary literature is essential for a good essay, or merely desirable, or an optional extra, or even a crutch for weaker students, and the same teacher may answer this question differently for different essays and student levels.

The content of secondary literature, and the expected content of essays, are very varied, and some activities which could fall under this heading overlap with ideas in later sections. There are, however, a range of core essay types which readers will recognise as traditional. For these, the points made at the beginning of section 2.2 apply: we do not condemn, but feel that alternatives should be explored.

## 2.3 PRACTICAL CRITICISM

This is an often used, though rather unsatisfactory, label for a range of activities which seem to us logically intermediate between those in 2.2 and 2.4. They belong to a tradition which includes F. R. Leavis in Britain and 'New Criticism' in North America, but also dissenting voices within these camps (see section 1.9 for a brief historical overview).

In terms of classroom process, 'practical criticism' usually requires students to give responses to a previously unknown text, using their own ideas more than in the approaches discussed above (2.2), but with an aesthetic and 'literary' bias which distinguishes the approach from those discussed below (2.4). At its worst, it can be a sort of gatekeeping mechanism checking that students share, or can pretend to share, the tastes and values of their tutor. At its best, though, it is a valuable type of activity, and we pass quickly over it in this chapter only because we discuss it (or aspects of it, or something like it) at length in Chapters 3–7.

## 2.4 WHAT ELSE CAN BE DONE WITH LITERATURE?

In this section we consider a range of ideas which are, generally speaking, less traditional, and possibly more in line with the general climate of ideas in 'communicative' foreign language teaching and in the underpinning disciplines. Our claim is not that these activities are necessarily better than those above, or should replace them – though both these things may be true in certain specific cases – but that they can widen the repertoire of teachers and learners.

### 2.4.1 Reading for pleasure (including extensive reading schemes)

Considerable anecdotal evidence and experienced teachers' opinions strongly suggest (though there is no conclusive research evidence) that, in a wide variety of situations, learners who read in quantity – tens or hundreds of books, far beyond what is directly taught and tested – improve more rapidly than those who do not; this improvement usually extends to all areas of language, including speaking. For generations, some dedicated teachers have tried to help some or all of their students by encouraging reading for pleasure, perhaps even lending them their own books. The use of simplified readers is also centuries old: see Kelly (1969: 140–2).

More recently, encouragement of extensive reading has become more systematic. Many EFL publishers produce 'graded readers' – some abridged and simplified and some only abridged – for the EFL market. Probably the largest (over 3000 books) and most thoroughly research-based scheme for using such readers is the Edinburgh Project in Extensive Reading (EPER), based in the Institute for Applied Language Studies, University of Edinburgh, which provides a consultancy service for teachers using graded readers and packages of material, including tests of reading level, work-cards for library readers, teaching guides for class readers and reading cards for beginners.

A rather critical view of the use of simplified readers is provided by Vincent and Carter (1986). They generally prefer using factual texts for 'simple' material, and keeping literary texts unsimplified and 'authentic', or using naturally simple material such as children's literature. A more recent view is Davis 1995, which despite its negative-sounding title is very favourable to EPER and to simplified readers in general.

In our own classes, we have tended to encourage students to find texts which interest them – not generally simplified, but not 'high' literature either, as a self-prescribed course of forty or fifty 'cheap' detective stories or romances can do wonders for some language learners. The key variable is not simplification, nor literary quality, but the reader's personal enthusiasm. Extensive reading can also have a research dimension (see section 9.1.1).

### 2.4.2  Reading for content

It is with some hesitation that we include this among the 'alternative' rather than the 'traditional' approaches. Of course, the latter also often involved a considerable concern with content, though as a sort of substitute for analysis – writers of essays were warned not to 'tell the story'. There is, however, a certain kind of 'modern' literature class in which questions such as these are common:

- 'What was life like in Dickens' London?'
- 'What picture of Africa do you get from the stories of Achebe and Okri?'
- 'What would it be like to be one of Chaucer's pilgrims?'

These questions are often, though by no means always, for oral rather than written discussion.

The rationale behind such questions, in part at least, seems to be that they help to widen cultural horizons, to reduce the imprisonment of learners in the worldview and values of their own time and place. The teacher may be looking for answers on a variety of levels – a simple remembering of facts, various levels of interpretation, comparisons with other texts and with students' own lives – and may be less concerned with 'right answers' than with the 'right attitude', perhaps conceived as a willingness to explore, relativise, suspend or refrain from moral and aesthetic judgement or recognise multiple moral and aesthetic standards, so that the study of literature will enable class members to understand and empathise with each other.

We certainly see a place for teaching of this kind somewhere in the curriculum; it accords at least in part with our general approach and with the spirit of Bremer's poem (see section 1.3). We have two reservations, however. First, we believe that cross-cultural awareness raising also belongs in other parts of the curriculum, especially history, geography and social studies, and that works of literature can be used there; in lessons devoted to (first and foreign) languages these ideas can be reinforced, but should not dominate to the extent that content squeezes out form, and the distinctive contribution to education of these different curriculum subjects is reduced. The other danger is that of attempted indoctrination: just as compulsory religious education in Britain has probably helped to create many atheists, it seems possible that a heavy-handed political correctness which pays lip service to a party line of intercultural respect might produce a generation of hypocrites. The willing study of good literature, guided by genuinely culturally open teachers who inspire by example, can encourage tolerance and respect, but one cannot dictate outcomes in any simple way.

As well as the cross-cultural subtype outlined above, there are other subtypes of reading for content. Sometimes it is atheoretical – teachers can think of nothing better – but sometimes there is a wish to foster general cognitive skills. Our opinion about these is similar: acceptable in small doses, but not really contributing to the distinctive educational outcomes which may be expected or desired from language and literature study.

### 2.4.3  Reading solely as foreign-language practice

We are thinking here of lessons (and associated homework) in which learners study a literary text, or more usually an extract, look up unknown vocabulary, answer questions about it, and perhaps do exercises on vocabulary and grammar relating to it. The possible range of such questions and activities is wide, from summary and paraphrase to 'write the story from the point of view of X', but the main features distinguishing this from other activity types are that the status of the text as literature is not important – the activities could equally well be done with a journalistic or non-fiction text – and that there is little or no concern with stylistic effect.

Our readers may be expecting another slightly negative verdict here (all right in moderation, but …). In fact we have considerable patience with such activities, because they often conform to learner expectations, can introduce a lot of literature 'by the back door', and yet avoid putting pressure on learners by forcing them to don the mantle of literary critics before they are ready.

There are dangers, though; some mirror previous discussions, together with one additional danger: that an exclusive diet of short texts and extracts can distort literature, discourage extensive reading and militate against learner independence. Teachers of English in Italy, whose students often read literature only as extracts in state-approved textbooks, are often especially aware of this problem. We therefore suggest that the approach should be used only as part of a balanced diet.

### 2.4.4 Linguistic analysis

This is a major feature of our courses at Edinburgh and Strathclyde and, we believe, one of the major activity types which are appropriate in many literature courses for foreign language learners. It involves looking very closely at the language of literary texts, including mainly local or short-range features such as deviance, regularity, polysemy and mimesis, and also features of discourse organisation or narrative structure which typically operate over longer stretches of text. All this is normally combined with some comment on or speculation about the purpose, effect or meaning of such features. (For opinions for and against interpretation and focus on meaning in literary analysis, see Newton 1990.)

In some ways, this approach is a logical extension of Leavisite approaches, involving as it does close attention to text detail and (usually) little or no concern with extrinsic factors. In other respects it may be seen as antithetical to Leavis, as (pseudo-?) scientific and reductionist in opposition to the more humanistic and 'illuminating' Leavisite approach. Such arguments are largely sterile: good critics and teachers will try to get the best of both worlds, and good critical writing can make the difference seem unimportant. Our enthusiasm for linguistic criticism, though, is based on two factors.

First, it removes the appeal to a specially cultivated sensibility, and to reasons beyond rational argument. At their worst, Leavisites and New Critics remind us of Molière's (tongue-in-cheek) dictum '*Les gens de qualité savent tout sans avoir jamais rien appris*' ('People of quality know everything without ever having learned anything'). Linguistic criticism predicates, not that all responses are equally valid, but that any analyst who has made correct linguistic statements about a text – for example, about the normality or otherwise of syntax, the register from which vocabulary comes or the types of cohesion found – and who has linked these to suggested purposes or effects, deserves to be taken seriously, and cannot be refuted merely on grounds of taste or sensibility.

Second, the approach is particularly useful in a foreign language, because it is largely in addressing the kinds of question implied in the last paragraph – is the syntax 'normal'? Where does the vocabulary come from? and so on – that a student can become more aware of, and take steps to solve, his or her problems as a non-native reader.

A fuller discussion of this approach, interwoven with and sometimes shading into 'practical criticism', occupies most of Chapters 3–7.

### 2.4.5 Personal response

This is a rather loose term and could be applied to many categories of classroom event. In this section we are concerned only with two. In the first, students are asked what books or parts of books (this includes novels, stories, plays and poems) they want to study, and after starting a book they are asked how much they like it, and what they want to do now: that is, finish or abandon it, read it in more or less depth, continue it in class or finish it on their own, write or talk about it in different ways, go on to more works of the same type or to something totally different. Students are encouraged to give more details of their reaction, and of features in the text which caused this reaction, but only if they want to, not simply as a 'display answer' to prove their academic knowledge or skill. The sort of response hoped for might be something like this:

> I like the way Alasdair Gray [in *Poor Things*] told the same story from different points of view. As a woman, I thought he showed a real understanding of how women are often more practical and down-to-earth as well. I also liked the bits about Glasgow, perhaps because I'm from a big city too. I'm interested in his other novels, especially *Lanark*, from what you've told us and what I've read, but I'm afraid of starting *Lanark* because it's so long and perhaps difficult. What advice would you give? Could we [the students] agree to read it at home and study selected extracts together in class?

This is an invented (though fact based) and perhaps unrealistically 'perfect' response. In many classes, students expect the teacher to tell them what to read, and will say little about what they really like. Such habits and attitudes can be changed only slowly. In such cases, and indeed generally, careful preparation by the teacher is necessary: if the teacher just says 'What do you want to read next?' students may be unwilling or unable to answer, or to make sensible choices, and may also feel that the teacher is not doing his or her job. Some kind of guidance is therefore necessary – perhaps a shortlist of books to choose from, with summaries and comments, perhaps a trial lesson (or half-lesson) where a short extract is studied before a class decide to read a whole book, perhaps some video clips from a film of the book or a slide show about the place or time. Often work can be divided, with different groups within a class each reading (part of) candidate texts and reporting back. Where there are external constraints such as an examination syllabus, the class should be told of all possible choices, of their physical availability for buying or borrowing, and of the teacher's own reasons for recommending some texts and advising against others.

There are at least three advantages in encouraging this type of personal response. One is that it improves the chances of studying the right book – one that students will enjoy, read fully and understand. The second is that, having chosen to begin or continue a book, students are likely to have more emotional commitment to it: even if they find themselves not entirely understanding or enjoying it, they will have reason to persevere. The third is that, if students know that their opinions about a book are considered important and actually make a difference to what happens, both the act of reading and the act of talking about the book should be more real, authentic and communicative, and hence more likely to promote language learning (and perhaps also learning of facts and literary skills).

The second type of personal response which interests us may be seen as exploring the question of 'Has anything like this ever happened to you?', though this precise form of words would not normally be used (see below). Strictly speaking, a 'response' can only occur after (part of) a work has been read, but in this approach students can talk about their own lives and feelings before as well as after reading. For example, the reading of a story about a compulsive gambler could be preceded by a question such as 'Do you buy lottery tickets?'

Considerable caution is necessary in the selection and presentation of questions for personal response activities. Many, perhaps most, important events and feelings described in literature are potentially extremely painful or embarrassing, and it would be quite inappropriate even in the most relaxed and uninhibited class to ask directly 'Have you ever done/felt this?' In the example above, this question is asked only about the relatively 'safe' (at least in some cultures) topic of gambling. Questions about family relationships are, rightly, not personalised in this way, but in a supportive classroom learners could bring in personal experience in exploring such questions.

Another example is from Collie and Slater (1997: 232):

> The students were asked to complete the following sentences in any way that they felt appropriate:
> A good father …
> A bad father …

This again can develop as personally or impersonally as students wish.

### 2.4.6 Games and 'fun' activities

Although many teachers use the concept of 'game' in their own lesson planning and in certain activities for their students, the boundary between games and other activities is very fuzzy: a few things clearly are games, a few others clearly not, but there is a large intermediate category which could be classified as game or not-game, either by simple naming or by adding or subtracting presentational features such as point scoring, competing groups and time limits. To call something a game may make it more or less successful, or have no effect, depending on learners' culture, previous experience, and perhaps even gender – in one group of eleven-year-olds we knew, the (usually lazy) boys tried much harder in 'games', and the girls often let them win.

Among the more centrally game-like games are vocabulary matching, where words from a text are written on slips of paper, the definitions on other slips, and both are distributed to students, who have to find a match; crosswords and similar puzzles; charades, where learners have to 'demonstrate' a literary work or character (for instance) by gestures without speaking; or 'Just a Minute', which involves talking about a given topic for sixty seconds without hesitation, repetition or deviation.

Many other games fall into other categories in this section, including prediction (see Collie and Slater (1987), especially Chapter 3, for many examples), and most of all 'creating one's own text' (see below).

Literature also offers an almost limitless opportunity for discussion games, of a type familiar to most foreign-language teachers. Rather than list all possibilities, we refer the reader to Penny Ur's *Discussions that Work* (1981), which is not about teaching literature, but gives the most satisfactory typology of discussion activities in the foreign-language classroom, plus practical advice to teachers using them. Almost all of Ur's types could be applied to literature; we give just a few examples here, the categories being Ur's, the examples ours.

**Guessing games** (p. 27): two students act out a dialogue loosely based on a scene in a recent book, but not taken verbatim from it, and omitting names and other giveaway details; the rest of the class guess the intended book and scene.
**Connections** (p. 33): one group think of a connection between two characters, places, and so on, in different books; the others guess.
**Interpreting pictures** (p. 40): this could be based on the jacket illustrations of a book, a still from the film of the book, or a drawing made by students themselves. The task will be to identify characters and events and explain facial expressions and other details.
**Detecting differences** (p. 51): someone narrates an incident in a recently studied text, making small but significant changes. Ideally, the speaker should represent one of the characters, trying to establish an excuse for his or her behaviour or an alibi. The rest of the class cross-examine the speaker and try to prove inaccuracy or inconsistency.
**Choosing candidates** (p. 73): you are in a balloon with Iago, Cassius and Lady Macbeth – which one do you throw out? There are of course endless variants.

All of these types, especially the discussion games, have a place in a teacher's repertoire. They can help to gain or regain the interest of apathetic students, and can bring life and real learning to otherwise 'dead' sessions at the end of a day or week. They can also be problematic, though, and we know of several cases where very 'serious' students have protested that games were taking time away from 'serious' study, from learning new content: objectively, such complaints may be ill founded, but if students are discontented they will not learn.

Even in the spectrum of game-like activities, the ones mentioned so far are not those we would recommend for most extensive use. They tend to emphasise factual knowledge of the text, with only limited interpretation. Furthermore, most can be used only after a text, or quite a lot of it, has already been read and understood, and it is not always clear what they add to literary understanding (though they can enhance language skills, confidence, and so on). The kinds of 'game' we most favour are those involving prediction or creating one's own text, and we will describe and justify some of these in sections 2.4.7 and 2.4.9. As they are not always called games, we have classified them separately, but readers who wish to treat them as a sub-category of games are invited to renumber the sections accordingly.

### 2.4.7  Prediction and related guessing activities

The activity of prediction is now a commonplace in FLT reading classes, for both literary and non-literary texts. Learners may be asked to guess what a story is going to be about, first on the basis of the title alone, then after a few paragraphs, then again at regular intervals throughout a text. The question may be general – what will happen? – or very specific. Both teachers and learners often seem to enjoy this, perhaps because it relates to a basic human need to know the future, perhaps also because if one guesses wrongly one has not failed or lost face. The likely benefits are at least threefold – heightened awareness of general literary conventions, closer attention to details of plot, and an increase in real language and in personal involvement. The main dangers are that, like all good activities, it can be over-used and become too routine, and that it might lead to an exclusive focus on plot, or 'what happens next', at the expense of other interesting features.

The following is an example of 'related guessing activities': learners are given the beginnings and endings (say one to three pages) of, for example, eight novels, retyped in identical print and with proper names omitted. All sixteen texts are mixed up, and learners have to guess which ones go together. This is more similar to prediction than to guessing what other students mean as in 2.4.6, because it requires close engagement with a text, and may sometimes be more challenging and productive than prediction exercises in that it requires focus on form as well as content.

### 2.4.8  Performing a literary work

This very important activity type is discussed at length in Chapter 7.

### 2.4.9  Creating one's own text

This brings us back to the second aspect of the Claus Bremer poem (section 1.3), the idea that response is creative, and thus to a class of activities which is becoming more and more important in the teaching of literature.

One can 'create one's own text' in many different ways. At one extreme, one can write a completely original text; in the middle, there are almost infinite possibilities for adaptation, parody, pastiche, summary, translation, transfer to a new genre (novel to play for example), sequel and so on. At the other extreme – and this should logically come first, as being closest to Bremer's idea – every act of reading is the creation of a text, a point recognised both by psycholinguistics and by Reader Response theory (see sections 1.3 and 1.4).

Creative writing is now a familiar topic in teaching institutions, though at school level it is far more common in North America than Britain. In this book, we are not interested in courses or approaches which give primacy to writing, and either ignore reading or use it only as a source of ideas and models, but this still leaves us with a wide range of approaches which either give similar weight to reading and creative writing, or which are ultimately more concerned with reading but use creative writing as an important means to their ends.

The best-known book of this type is Maley and Moulding's *Poem into Poem* (1985). This consists of a series of topic-based units, each of which follow the same pattern, described by the authors (p. 2) as follows:

- First there is a section called *Warming up*. It prepares you for the theme of the poems which follow. You may be asked to do activities in connection with a picture, make notes on a recorded conversation, or perhaps read a brief prose passage. These activities all involve discussion with a partner or in groups..
- You will then listen to the first *Poem* as you read it. This is followed by activities aimed at helping you to understand it.
- The same procedure follows for the second *Poem* (and in Unit 1 for the third and fourth *Poems*).
- A section on *Writing* usually follows. This contains activities leading you to produce your own poems, usually in groups. This also involves discussion of your own and other groups' work.
- Finally there is a poem for you to read and listen to on your own, with no work attached – simply for your enjoyment.

One problem which some teachers have with this book is that many of the texts are not literature in the narrow sense. They include songs, poems specially written by EFL teachers, and others redolent of the school magazine. Maley and Moulding would presumably justify this in terms of accessibility – those who disagree can still use their approach, while applying it to more recognised and (arguably) more substantial poems.

Another book in this area is Rob Pope's (1995) *Textual Intervention*, which assumes much higher levels of linguistic and literary competence than does *Poem into Poem*, and seems equally suitable for native and non-native speakers. It includes both non-literary and literary texts, but the former seem to be largely for comparison, and the book is largely about literature in the widest sense. It starts from the premise that:

> The best way to understand how a text works (…) is to change it: to play around with it, to intervene in it in some way (large or small), and then try to account for the exact effect of what you have done. (p. 1)

Though briefly mentioning the literary theory of deconstruction (Derrida and others), Pope acknowledges that what he advocates is only distantly related to this and is or can be much simpler, a practical experimental approach. His suggestions for 'intervention' can entail producing 'parallel, opposed and alternative texts' (p. 2).

In some suggested activities, students are asked to change a text in any way they like, in others to change specific aspects, for example genre, speaker or addressee. They may for instance adopt another character's viewpoint – even that of an 'extra-textual character', such as the worker who made objects referred to in passing; 'translate' a rather formal poem into conversational tone; describe or speculate on what else was happening at the historical time of a novel, but was not mentioned; write a socialist or feminist response to a poem; convert a nonsense poem into a film script.

The range of possibilities is seen in its most concentrated form in Pope's suggested rewritings of Descartes' 'I think, therefore I am' (pp. 31–9), which include:

'I think – therefore I *am*!!' she said, with a glint in her eye, iron in her soul and a plastic lemon squeezer in her hand. (p. 34)

René thought he was Descartes, but his mother called him Cyril. (p. 35)

Thinks (thought bubble): 'I AM!' (p. 37)

Pope's book can at times seem very self-indulgent, but its saving grace is an insistence on coming back to the reasons for and the effects of change.

We feel, though, that both Maley and Moulding and Pope are in danger of going too far in their laudable desire to wean students from an excessive reverence for established literature. The healthy impulse towards equality of respect for all individuals, ethnic groups, genders and so on, can lead to a rather sterile insistence on equality of all kinds and a refusal to make any evaluations. We suggest that, having taken a text apart and convinced themselves that they can write alternatives of real value, learners should be encouraged to go back to the original and explore with open minds whether it is still 'better', more 'special', more 'satisfying'. If they do, this should not of course be linked to any negative self-evaluation, first because the reader creates the text, second because their own masterpiece is due next week!

Although the categories in Maley and Moulding and Pope are in principle wide enough to cover all 'own text' activities, there are two subvarieties which it might be more helpful to classify separately.

The first, already mentioned in passing, could be called 'editing for performance'. Sometimes it involves change of genre, mostly poem or novel into play, sometimes it involves summarising and perhaps paraphrasing. The basic task is to create a version of a text for (normally) informal performance within a lesson, which is interesting to the audience (normally one's classmates), which fits in with the restricted time of the lesson and space of the classroom and conveys the spirit of the original. The difference from Pope's suggestions is only one of emphasis – learners are not 'trying to be clever', and are expected to be only as creative as necessary, but there is freedom for personal taste as well.

The second additional type is guided simulation based on a play, preferably one that the class is going to see later. In this case a lot of the creative work is done by the teacher, who produces 'scene cards' describing the main events of the play and 'role cards' telling the students acting particular roles who they are, including background, personality, relationship to other characters, and tips on stage business. (These cards do not have to follow the real play exactly, and our experience suggests that the activity works best if some facts are withheld or changed.) The simulation is performed, often several times by different people, and those not acting give reactions, comments and advice. Then the real play is seen, and the two are compared: learners usually find some things better in their own version, but the main idea is not to say 'which is better' but to explore the logic of each interpretation, as in principle both are equally valid.

# Chapter 3

# The language of literature and ways of 'teaching' it

## 3.1 INTRODUCTION

The four chapters which follow this one will look in turn at poetry, short stories, the novel and drama, especially at the language each employs, and at the kind of teaching of these areas which emphasises or includes close linguistic analysis. To prepare the ground for this discussion, the present chapter explores some general concepts to which we shall refer from time to time in these chapters. We have been selective, excluding from this chapter the more basic and well-known concepts such as grammar and vocabulary, and also concepts such as rhythm and focalisation which are most relevant to one particular genre. What is left is a somewhat heterogeneous collection of concepts, linked mainly by the fact that they influence our understanding of texts on a global level.

In sections 3.2–3.6 we look at the concept of language variety, at literary language and learner language ('interlanguage') considered as varieties, at the interface between these varieties and the implications for teaching and learning. Sections 3.7 and 3.8 look at pragmatics and intertextuality respectively, and 3.9 draws these two concepts together in a second 'implications' section. For ease of discussion, we use mainly English in our examples: most of what we say could be applied to other languages too, though there are many differences of detail and some of substance, especially when we move beyond European culture: a good source of examples, especially for Chinese, Japanese and Arabic, is Baker (1992), Chapters 5–7.

## 3.2 VARIETIES OF LANGUAGE

Literary English and English learners' interlanguage are both varieties of English. The branch of English which studies varieties is called stylistics – see Turner (1973) and Haynes (1995) for popular accounts. Like most linguists, we use the term stylistics in a very wide sense: it includes, but is not restricted to, the analysis of literary style.

We cannot hope to list all the varieties of English, but the following taxonomy (based on Benson (1993) and indirectly on Crystal and Davy (1969)) includes some of the general kinds of variety with which teachers may be concerned. In most cases, we give an example, that is, a named variety of this type, and then an example of the example, for instance a fragment of English which belongs – or rather, may belong: see below – to this type. (Our examples are necessarily sometimes stereotypes, and no racist or similar assumptions are implied – where they are based on real data, this was often deliberate self-parody, especially in A2 and A3).

## A.  Varieties by user

1.  Geographical variety (dialect), e.g. Scots: 'Will I get you a wee drink?'.
2.  Geographical variety (accent), e.g. Cockney: 'The 'air on the 'ead not the hair in the hatmosphere'.
3.  Borrowing from a foreign language, e.g. Yiddish English: 'More chutzpah yet I need?'
4.  Occupational variety, e.g. lawyer's English: 'We have restricted our fees to £500 000.'
5.  Social class and education, e.g. 'working class' (?): 'the boys done sodding brilliant'.
6.  Social group, e.g. hippies: 'Cool, man!'
7.  Individual age, e.g. teenage English: examples are evanescent.
8.  Historical age, e.g. general archaic: 'swain', 'quoth', 'olde'.
9.  Variety by gender, e.g. female language, which typically has less swearing and more question tags and compliments.

10/11.  Language used *by* and *to* children, e.g.: 'moo-moo', 'mummy bring'.

12/13.  Language used *by* and *to* foreign learners (see section 3.4).

## B.  Varieties by use

1.  Speech versus writing, e.g. 'Further to our recent enquiry'; versus 'Hello ... er, I rang you last week, ... er ...'.
2.  Degree of formality, e.g. 'Show me the way to go home' versus 'Indicate the way to my abode'.
3.  Degree of intimacy, e.g. 'Dear Mr Smith' versus 'My dearest darling John'.
4.  Specific fields, e.g. religion: 'And lo, He did come down from the firmament ...'.
5.  Specific physical settings, e.g.: pub, interview room.
6.  Miscellaneous types, e.g.: newspaper (journalese), advertising, instructions, recipes, bureaucratic language, academic writing.

Three general points may have occurred to the reader:

1.  There is no definite, finite number of varieties. Many if not all can be subdivided, apparently almost *ad infinitum*. There is something called Yorkshire English, but there are different subvarieties for different parts of Yorkshire, even (though less than in the past) for individual villages. There is something called legal English, but this can be subdivided in many different ways. There

is something called interlanguage (see section 3.4), but this varies enormously depending on the user's first language, level, and so on.

2. Study of variety might seem to imply a concept of 'normal' or 'standard' language, but this is problematic to say the least. We might agree in some cases – perhaps, say, that *before* is 'standard' and *ere* is 'non-standard' – but we might not agree, say, on what is a 'standard' accent or dialect or a neutral level of formality, and we would be (or ought to be!) very reluctant to classify either spoken or written language as more standard than the other.

3. A sample of language, considered in isolation, cannot necessarily be assigned to a particular variety. The shorter the sample, the less likely that we can classify it, precisely or perhaps even at all. The question may be 'is it "standard" or belonging to a particular "non-standard" variety?', or it may be 'I know it is non-standard but which variety is it?'

To illustrate the first part of point (3), let us take the putative variety called 'legal English'. There are certain words, phrases and perhaps other linguistic features which can be classified as 'legal', but a particular extract from, say, a courtroom transcript may contain none of these. It may be unrecognisable as legal English, or recognisable only from content and not from its form.

To illustrate the second, consider the utterance: 'If it were true, it were a fault.' This is clearly not standard English, but what kind of English is it? Most readers would probably say 'literary English' or 'old-fashioned English' – it looks like a line from Shakespeare's *Julius Caesar* with an adjective omitted. But it could also be, and has been attested as, interlanguage: *were* for *would be* is a common German error, and *fault* seems to echo the French *faute*. (Of course, fault is also a good English word, and may be exactly what the speaker means, though the meaning of mistake – in fact a mistake for mistake! – would occur first to many EFL teachers, showing that non-standardness may not be visible from form alone).

Ambiguities of stylistic categorisation such as the above are the rule rather than the exception, and all the varieties listed earlier should be considered as overlapping circles, each with smaller circles within them.

Faced with these multiple sources of ambiguity, we will not attempt a watertight description of language variety in general, or of literary language in particular. In our ideas about teaching in this book, we have attempted to keep narrower and wider views of literary language in mind – (a) language which is more or less peculiar to literature, or to some kind of literature; and (b) the language of literary texts as a whole, including that which is shared with other varieties and with standard or neutral English. At times throughout the book, and especially in this and the next four chapters, we focus on (a), as most competent teachers must also sometimes do. The general aim, however, is of course to help learners to cope with (b).

## 3.3 'LITERARY' LANGUAGE CONSIDERED AS A VARIETY

EFL learners who have difficulties with literature, especially with the 'classics', often complain that 'the language is difficult' or 'it's not normal English'. Their teachers, similarly, sometimes tell them that certain words (and, more rarely, grammatical patterns) are 'literary', or, more narrowly, 'poetic'. Is there really a special kind of English called literary English or poetic English? In other kinds of EFL, such as English for lawyers, English for doctors, and so on, teachers seem able to identify more or less adequately a variety called legal English or medical English, despite the problems mentioned in section 3.2. The word 'register' is often used for a variety of this type: it can include occupational varieties, and perhaps those of specific hobby groups, of journalism, even of hippies or gangsters, but not usually dialect, for instance, or archaic language. Is there a practically identifiable register of literature and/or poetry in English? Such registers are generally agreed to exist in many non-European languages, for example in Arabic (Yazigy 1994), and it also seems clear that, at the very least, English used to have such a register. Take the following extract from a poem (in Gray 1966):

### Ode on a distant prospect of Eton College

> Say, Father Thames, for thou hast seen
> Full many a sprightly race
> Disporting on thy margent green,
> The paths of pleasures trace;
>
> Who foremost now delight to cleave
> With pliant arm, thy glassy wave?
> The captive linnet which enthral?
>
> What idle progeny succeeds
> To chase the rolling circle's speed
> Or urge the flying ball?

(Thomas Gray)

The reader might like to attempt the following assignment of tasks and questions in relation to this poem. (Some suggested answers are in Appendix 2.)

### Assignment 1

1. 'Translate' the above poem into modern everyday English. (Where you don't know, guess.)
2. What did you have to change:
    mainly grammar words?
    mainly content words?
    both equally?
3. What effect does such language have on a modern reader?
4. Could you find modern equivalents, or would you say 'They don't write them like that any more'? Why? How do you feel about this?

In twentieth-century English poetry we cannot, on the whole, identify a separate register. There are still a few special 'poetic words', such as *ere* and *yon*, but good poets use them sparingly and in fact many avoid them completely.

This does not mean that register is unimportant in modern poetry study. Modern poets (and other writers) have no registers of their own, but they do not hesitate to borrow other people's! In fact, most would regard the whole of English as their territory, and many of the subtle effects of literature depend on the reader recognising that something is borrowed from a particular kind of English. (Specialists sometimes use the term re-registration for this kind of borrowing). A well-known example is the following extract from 'Naming of parts' by Henry Reed (Reed 1946):

> Today we have naming of parts. Yesterday,
> We had daily cleaning. And tomorrow morning,
> We shall have what to do after firing. But today,
> Today we have naming of parts. Japonica
> Glistens like coral in all of the neighbouring gardens,
> And today we have naming of parts.
>
> This is the lower sling swivel. And this
> Is the upper sling swivel, whose use you will see,
> When you are given your slings. And this is the piling swivel,
> Which in your case you have not got. The branches
> Hold in the gardens their silent, eloquent gestures,
> Which in our case we have not got.

Again, we offer tasks and questions for immediate completion: some possible answers are again in Appendix 2.

### Assignment 2

Divide the poem into parts which seem to be written in different varieties. There may be two parts, or more. The boundaries may be at the end of a sentence/line/stanza or in the middle. The parts may be discontinuous, so for example you may want to identify 'Part A', then 'Part B', then 'Part A' again.

1. Where did you put the boundaries?
2. What label would you give to each part?
3. What features – of grammar, vocabulary, etc. – justify your labels?
4. Can you explain why the varieties alternate in this way?
5. How effective, for you personally, is this alternation?

Other special features of poetic or literary language are considered in later chapters. These include deviance (roughly defined as the breaking of rules), polysemy (intended ambiguity), mimesis (correspondence between form and content) and many kinds of regularity, together with more elusive features such as density and context independence. These are features of a very different order from those which are typical of, say, legal English, but share something with them at a rather abstract level:

at the risk of over-simplifying, we might say that each one in isolation is 'optional', 'it comes and goes' – just as particular legal texts, or even more so bits of them, may not be obvious 'legal English' in some or all ways, similarly (in fact with greater probability) passages of literature may not be obviously 'literary' in every single one, or sometimes in any, of the ways that literary English is described in this book.

## 3.4 LEARNER LANGUAGE (INTERLANGUAGE) CONSIDERED AS A VARIETY

This section will offer only a brief account of interlanguage, only as much as necessary for the later discussion. Much fuller accounts are available elsewhere: the subject is a major preoccupation of Applied Linguistics departments, especially in the English-speaking world. Ellis (1985) is a very clear, though rather dated, introduction.

Interlanguage is the variety of language X – let us again use English for exemplification – spoken by learners for whom it is not a native language. It covers a wide range, from very fragmentary communication of the 'Me Tarzan you Jane' variety, to language which is almost indistinguishable from the native 'target', as when you listen to someone for several minutes before being sure that they are not native.

Interlanguage has much in common with 'child language', the forms we use before achieving adult mastery of our first language or joint first languages, with 'motherese' or 'parent talk', the language used *to* children, with pidgins and creoles, and with 'foreigner talk', which despite its name is the language used *to* foreigners, not *by* foreigners, It may also have something – though much less – in common with other varieties including archaic and literary language. The interlanguage used by one particular learner normally develops over time – otherwise teachers would be out of a job! – but it very often also 'fossilises' or reaches a plateau after which very little change occurs, especially in grammar. Interlanguage is a rule-governed system, not just a series of random 'misses' of the 'target', and patterns can be found in its developpment in grammar, in phonology and in vocabulary.

Most applied linguists claim (with various qualifications) that interlanguage follows a particular route, which teachers cannot change: for example, that the third person '-s' in English is learned late in the sequence, and that attempts to teach it earlier will fail or will result only in short-term 'pseudo-learning'. These claims clearly have a basis in truth, but teachers sometimes find the details unconvincing, based as they are on experimental studies remote from classroom reality. Ellis (1984) stresses the great differences between interlanguage development inside and outside the classroom.

## 3.5 THE INTERFACE BETWEEN INTERLANGUAGE AND LITERARY LANGUAGE

Though interlanguage and literary language are very different kinds of phenomena, they do have things in common on various levels, in their inherent form and in their interaction in the process of teaching and learning. One of us (Parkinson 1990a) has written about one aspect of this:

> The deviant nature of poetic language poses three kinds of problems for those studying poetry in a foreign tongue.
>
> The first is the very basic one of understanding the text. Poems are usually, though not always, more difficult to understand even on the level of 'basic message' than are most prose texts. Few things are more frustrating than to look through all the dictionaries in search of the meaning of some strange word in a poem, only to find that the poet has invented it, or is using it in some completely idiosyncratic sense.
>
> The second problem is that it is necessary to recognise deviance as deviance in order to appreciate its full effect. [The poem 'love is more thicker than forget' by e. e. cummings – see section 4.4.1] includes the word 'sunly' and the phrase 'the least begin'. Some foreign learners may understand the former as sunny, the latter as the smallest beginning. They have succeeded more than those who just abandon the poem as nonsense, but have clearly missed the point to a certain extent.
>
> The third problem is a psychological one caused by the fact that all foreign learners, whether they like it or not, produce deviant language! It is easy to imagine a learner thinking: 'I've been spending years learning to avoid saying 'he comes not', and now we're getting it all the time in these poems!' If we believe, like many applied linguists, that language proficiency is achieved largely by extensive exposure to models through reading and listening, there would appear to be a real danger in making so many of these models deviant. In fact, the danger to language proficiency in the narrow sense is probably less than we might think: the evidence suggests that learners can exploit deviant language, even that of other non-natives, to add to their general proficiency, and that as long as a large and identifiable part of the input is non-deviant the learner's own output will not be adversely affected. The problem, though, is that learners quite understandably may not believe this, and, on a conscious or unconscious level, may reject the strange input which seems to be interfering with their language learning.

Although the issue arises most obviously in the study of (some) poetry, and most obviously in relation to deviance, it affects all text types and also features such as polysemy, mimesis and regularity.

## 3.6 PEDAGOGICAL IMPLICATIONS I: LITERARY LANGUAGE AND INTERLANGUAGE

Some teachers have used this as an argument for not teaching literature. They are, of course, not always wrong – some literature is clearly too deviant or otherwise unsuitable for some learners at some stages. There is a growing feeling, however, that deviant language and other specifically literary features are often, at the very least, harmless – learners can read cummings without having their grammar ruined – and that literature, despite or even because of its strange language, can sometimes be preferable to apparently more suitable text types. General reasons for using literature have been given in 1.5; the idea that deviance (and so on) can be a positive advantage is harder to justify, and is not essential for our arguments, but readers might like to consider two points: first, that baby talk used by parents, and foreigner talk, both mentioned above, seem helpful or at least not harmful to first- and second-language acquisition; second, that the (or some) alternatives to literature may be distorted or unnatural in less obvious ways, and thus possibly more harmful or less helpful – Oller (1995) has claimed that many FL textbooks rely on 'isolated sociocultural vignettes' which fail certain tests of Peircean semiotics, which we take to mean, roughly, that they are less realistic and therefore less satisfactory as input than, for example, (some) literature.

The problems raised by the 'interlanguage interface' should not be dismissed, but they are not arguments for not using literature, only for using it carefully. Suggestions on how this may be done are given in other chapters, especially Chapters 2 and 4, but a few points are worth restating or anticipating here:

1. Encourage learners to look for global meanings, and to develop strategies such as skimming, scanning and guessing. If they see their learning as including the development of skills, especially the skill of reading, rather than simply acquiring vocabulary and grammar, they are more likely to view positively the challenges provided by difficult texts.

2. Spend some time on the 'paraphrasable meaning' of a text, including the basic, everyday meaning of words. Do not launch into complex and subjective issues of response and criticism when students – perhaps all of them, perhaps only the weaker ones – still feel insecure on this basic level.

3. Be prepared to discuss how something could be said in modern or 'standard' English. In the case of archaic language this is largely a placebo and should not be overdone, but may be necessary from time to time to avoid any feelings that 'we are learning incorrect English'. In the case of other deviant language, the discussion may be more directly beneficial – see again section 4.4.

## 3.7 PRAGMATICS

The term pragmatics was introduced by Morris (1938), who defined syntax as the study of the relations among signs, semantics as the study of the relation between signs and their denotations, and pragmatics as the study of the relation between signs and their users and interpreters. In other words, semantics is concerned with what words and sentences mean, in an abstract Platonic sense, while pragmatics is concerned with what people mean by them on a particular occasion. The best general account of pragmatics is probably still Leech (1983). More recent books are not wholly satisfactory – Mey (1993), for example, is anecdotal, over-reliant on fiction and lacking intellectual rigour.

There are many ways of using the ideas of pragmatics in discussing and in teaching literature. Cook (1994) emphasises 'schema theory', and offers rather daunting flowcharts to show how a reader's prior knowledge and expectations interact with a text. Sperber and Wilson (1986), building upon but disagreeing with Searle (for example 1969) and Grice (1975), emphasise shared knowledge, inference and the assumption of communicative intention. All these writers will repay study by teachers of literature, but their apparatus is probably too technical for direct use in the average literature class.

At the other extreme, Sell (1991 and 1995a) comes very close to equating pragmatics with what others call knowledge of the world, for example the (alleged) fact that unattended parcels in restaurants have a very different significance in Helsinki than in London. His discussion of a poem by the fictional Adrian Mole, actually Sue Townsend, centres on his own learners' ignorance of the people and places mentioned in the poem – Leicester, the M1, Sarah Ferguson and so on – and he seems to want to give these facts (or his own opinions?) as a prelude to analysis. His approach is undoubtedly practical and likely to satisfy many learners, but perhaps rather obvious, certainly very judgmental (is this unarguably an inferior poem?) and scarcely justifies the label pragmatics.

There is one area of pragmatics which seems to us both conceptually reasonably easy and intellectually reasonably well founded, and therefore ideally suited for fairly direct use in classrooms. This is the idea that real examples of language in use can be classified according to the functions they have, for instance informing, persuading, apologising or promising. Part of the competence of a real language user is functional competence – recognising, for example, that the utterance 'the window is open' may be a request to close it, or that, in a particular context, the utterance 'I've not been to the cricket lately' may be a suggestion that you and I go to the cricket, a request that you pay for me to go, an invitation to start talking about cricket or a request to stop talking about it!

The functional approach, very influential in language teaching for twenty years, has largely lost popularity recently, in part because most of what we say is ambiguous, as in the second example, and not relatively straightforward as in the first. In literature teaching, there is the added problem of displaced function: the writer's purpose in producing a novel or poem, for instance, overlies and (in some cases, to some extent) replaces the original function, just as in re-registration (see 3.3) the original variety is (in some cases, to some extent) cancelled; indeed, Richards (1929) argues that most literature makes only 'pseudo-statements'! Nevertheless, it is important for readers, especially non-natives, to recognise any conventional or prototypical functional 'meaning' which the words in a poem, story, novel, and so on, would typically have outside a literary context, or what non-literary text type and function is being imitated or parodied. This can be done at the level of sentences or other short units within a text, or for a whole text: Kafka's *Bericht für eine Akademie* has the apparent function of a scientific conference paper, and Ionesco's play *La Leçon* has that of a language lesson. These 'joke functions' may be contrasted with many cases in which, as far as one can tell, the writing really does have the functional purpose it would have as prose, as well as its poetic function: Tennyson pays tribute to his friend in 'In Memoriam', Boileau advises us on how to write in *Art Poétique*, Virgil on how to farm in the *Georgics*, and Kleist wishes death upon the enemies of Prussia at the end of *Prinz Friedrich von Homburg*. (We gloss over several difficulties here: author intention is not the same as function, and writers are rarely as simply motivated as this account implies.)

Linguists such as Searle (1969, 1983) and Grice (1969, 1975), who write about the functions of language, sometimes invoke the notion of 'felicity conditions', without which a function cannot be performed: A cannot promise B to do X, for example, if A knows that X is impossible.

One apparent problem with a functional approach to literature is that writers very frequently seem to promise or ask readers, or ask third parties, to do the impossible, thereby violating such felicity conditions. James Thompson's 'Autumn' begins:

> But see the fading many-coloured woods

But we cannot see them, so the command, request, invitation or whatever is not felicitous.

When Aphra Behn says 'Cease! Cease!' to her admirer (in the untitled poem beginning 'What mean those amorous curls …'), apparently meaning 'Go on! Go on!' an analysis in functional terms may help to explain. Other lines from poems particularly susceptible to such analysis – in each case the beginning of the poem is quoted – include:

> Grow old along with me
> > (Robert Browning, 'Rabbi Ben Ezra')

> You understand it?
> > (Iain Crichton Smith, 'Culloden and After')

> I want you to love me
> love me enough
> enough that it hurts
> hurts and you cry
> > (Tessa Ransford, 'Cry out and Say')

> I am the hermit whom you keep
> at the garden's end
> > (Kathleen Jamie, 'Julian of Norwich')

In some of these, there may be ambiguity in function, and even in who is addressing whom, but for teaching it is all grist to the mill – or should it be flowers to the carnival?

We return to pragmatics, with special reference to drama, in section 7.3.


## 3.8 INTERTEXTUALITY

The concept of intertextuality is a very simple one with very complex ramifications and effects. It refers to anything in a particular text which can be fully understood only by reference to one or more other (written or spoken) texts. If I write, in a letter, 'I'm glad you had a good time on Wednesday', the meaning of this is not fully recoverable unless you have read another letter or listened to a conversation, or been otherwise informed about what a certain person did on Wednesday. If I say 'In this chess club, some chess players are more equal than others', you will not fully understand this unless you have read, or seen performed, or possibly have second-hand knowledge of, George Orwell's *Animal Farm*, in which a similar but not identical sentence appears. The idea of full understanding may be challenged: perhaps we never understand anything fully, but even what passes in common parlance for this is not possible without knowing about certain intertextual references. Furthermore, intertextuality is potentially an infinite topic, as our reaction to every text we meet is potentially informed by every previous text: for reasons of practicality, we confine ourselves in what follows to the more clear-cut connections, on which some consensus is likely among suitably informed readers or listeners.

Even outside the realm of literature, intertextuality is almost everywhere in language, though some writers and publications use it far more consciously and obviously than others. *Guardian* headlines are a reliable source, and a random sample (from 11 January 1997 and 18 January 1997) yielded dozens of examples beginning as follows:

1. The Cape Escape.
2. The day of the royal jackal.
3. America hails the porn king.
4. Sing something simple.
5. The exiled rule of Henry the Fist.
6. Welcome to a dragon on the wagon.
7. It's a spin to tell a lie.
8. Out of sight, into hindsight.
9. Dogger days.
10. Pushing the plug.

Advanced non-native readers may care to list the associations called up by these headlines and to compare them with a native speaker's list and/or with our own partial answers in Appendix 2. This is a good illustration of why language learning is so difficult!

Even within a language community, though, intertextual allusions may be and often are missed. For the present writers, for example, many comedy shows on television fall completely flat, as they depend for their effect almost entirely on references to other shows which we do not watch and celebrities whom we do not know. Similarly, a British teenager steeped in the culture of commercial television and forced to study older English literature will miss most of the intertextual references to Greek and Latin authors. We all miss a lot: no single reader of Joyce's *Ulysses* is likely to capture even half the references, and Kenneth Branagh, who recently completed a film of Shakespeare's *Hamlet*, admitted in an interview that, even with intensive study and rehearsal and the help of leading experts, he had not absorbed all the ideas and references.

The major categories of intertextuality are as follows:

1. Direct quotation, either in something like the original sense, or 'twisted' in some way.
2. Quotation with small changes, as in many of the *Guardian* examples above.
3. Using a name, a common noun, or a short phrase in a way which recalls its use in another text. Sometimes the function seems phatic and reassuring, as when friends use TV catchphrases in greeting and leavetaking. At the other extreme, a word or phrase may be totally subverted by being placed in a different context: the Latin sentence *Dulce et decorum est pro patria mori* [It is sweet and fitting to die for one's country], used for centuries as a high-toned moral exhortation to and praise of soldiers, becomes part of a chilling condemnation of war in Wilfred Owen's poem '*Dulce et decorum est*' (reprinted and discussed in Widdowson 1992: 123–6).
4. Parody and pastiche. Parody is most typically a deliberately crude imitation of a single writer's style for comic effect. Pastiche is usually less crude, more serious, and more likely to have literary merit in its own right. It is also likely to be imitative of a general style of writing, rather than one individual writer or work. An outstanding recent example is A. S. Byatt's novel *Possession*, most of which is a very slightly tongue-in-cheek, but nevertheless faithful, skilful and affectionate, imitation of a certain kind of nineteenth-century 'poetic' style.
5. Reference to specific facts in another text, as in the 'Wednesday' example above.
6. Writing which is clearly within a closely defined literary tradition, and assumes knowledge of that tradition. At its widest, this could apply to any writers, but we are thinking more specifically of traditions such as *amour cortois* (courtly love) in the Middle Ages or preciosity in seventeenth-century France. In modern literature, genre fiction (Westerns, detective stories, science fiction, and so on) provides good examples: a devotee of science fiction may find meanings beyond the referential meaning in, say, FTL (faster-than-light) travel or hyperspace.

## 3.9 PEDAGOGICAL IMPLICATIONS II: PRAGMATICS AND INTERTEXTUALITY

Although pragmatics and intertextuality are very different concepts, they come together quite naturally in learning and teaching; they provide the two main answers to the learner's question: what, besides language in the narrow sense, do I need to know?

Teachers can help with pragmatics and intertextuality in at least six ways. First, they can simply give answers. They can tell learners that, for example, the opening lines of Larkin's poem '*Vers de Société*':

> My wife and I have asked a crowd of craps
> To come and waste their time and ours

are a (changed) example of a typical exponent of the function of inviting in a certain social stratum of English society at a certain epoch, or that Walter von der Vogelweide's use of the words '*frowe*' and '*wîp*' for women represents a reaction against the artificiality of courtly love, as expressed in earlier poems. Students often welcome such spoon feeding, and in some cases it is the only reasonable solution, but good teachers will want to help students to help themselves as soon and as extensively as possible.

This entails teaching strategies to cope with problems of pragmatics and intertextuality. Not surprisingly, these are in essence the same strategies used to cope with other kinds of language problems:

1. Using appropriate reference material, including footnotes and endnotes;
2. Asking native speakers;
3. Making intelligent guesses, and checking these where necessary;
4. Learning to live with uncertainty, and recognising that even native speakers are sometimes uncertain about pragmatic meaning, unaware of some intertextual allusions and so on;
5. In the longer term, where appropriate, reading more widely, in literature and perhaps in history and other fields, to understand the background to a body of writing.

Many of the examples discussed in Chapters 4–7 also raise and, we hope, illuminate, issues of pragmatics and intertextuality.

# Chapter 4

# The teaching of poetry

## 4.1 INTRODUCTION

Many students on literature in foreign-language courses initially find poetry more problematic than novels, short stories and drama: they have less experience of it, and feel less confident in talking and writing about it. Reasons given vary widely, and we start with two sample cases.

A Swedish student recently told us that in his country poetry was upper class and he was working class, thereby destroying our illusion that Sweden was a classless society. Even after a six-month course, the student found it hard to select a poem for a free-choice essay assignment, as all those he looked at were either 'too difficult' – he felt unsure what they 'meant' – or 'too easy' – the meaning was 'too simple', so there was 'nothing to write about'. It emerged after much counselling that he saw poems as a kind of crossword puzzle, with a 'solution' waiting to be found. Because his teachers had not dealt adequately with this problem, much of their teaching had apparently been ineffective (though we prefer to think that the effect was only delayed, as the student produced a good essay when the barriers were cleared).

Our second case was a French student who, although she wrote poetry herself, felt that she knew nothing about it! Her own poetry was in the style of French Romantics such as Lamartine and Hugo, and she was particularly disconcerted by twentieth-century poetry, which seemed to her banal in subject matter and chaotic in form. She also objected to linguistic analysis, which seemed to her contrary to the spirit of poetry: for her, writing about a poem could only be writing about how far she shared the writer's emotions, and appreciated the beauty of their expression. This was how she thought and felt at the start of the course: we do not claim a complete 'conversion', but she did become more tolerant of and even sympathetic to a wider range of poetry, and of ways of talking and writing about it.

The rest of this chapter provides a conceptual structure, supported by examples, for organising the teaching of (or exploration of) poetry with learners not unlike the above, aiming to lead them towards oral and written linguistically-based criticism. It can be used with any language or level, although our main experience is with learners of English whose language level is fairly high but whose knowledge of poetry and of linguistic theory is limited. This is a book about teaching, not about literary or linguistic theory as such, so we have deliberately used simple and partial versions of some theoretical concepts, though we have tried to avoid serious distortion.

Students are encouraged to look at poems in three ways (or three stages, though we make it clear that these are not wholly sequential and separate):

1. Paraphrasable meaning: where possible (and it will not always be possible) indicate what the poem is 'about' – events, descriptions, emotions, and so on – using different words.
2. Linguistic features: a systematic description of the language of the poem, based on the concepts of regularity (including rhyme, and so on), deviance, polysemy and mimesis, though not all of these will be found in every poem.
3. Personal reaction, including an account of how this has changed in the course of rereading and analysis, and an attempt, where possible, to find objective (if partial) reasons for subjective reactions.

Areas not mentioned in this list, such as biography, history or politics, are by no means taboo. We welcome student ideas in these areas, and introduce them ourselves, where we find it helpful, but the particular focus of our course, as of this chapter, gives primacy to (1) to (3) above.

## 4.2 PARAPHRASABLE MEANING

When people read (or rarely, hear) a poem for the first time, they often ask, or want to ask, 'what does it mean?'; they feel either that they have understood nothing at all, or only part of the meaning. This can happen to native and non-native speakers, children and adults, both in the classroom and in the outside world.

Poets, 'experts' and teachers all have a tendency to be unhelpful when faced with questions of this kind. Standard responses include 'a poem should not mean, but be', 'if I could have said it differently/more simply/in prose I would have done so', and 'if you want a message, go to Western Union', or the Scottish variant, 'if you want messages, go to Sainsbury's'. ('Messages' means shopping in Scotland.) Teachers are liable to throw the question back at students, although in many different ways, from the academic 'analyse it word by word, using reference books' to the progressive (?) 'just open your soul – what does it mean *to you*?'

All these responses may be justified and may seem in accord with reader response ideas mentioned elsewhere (section 1.3). And yet, for at least 95 per cent of poems, there is a part of the meaning which is more objective, less a matter of interpretation and personal response, and likely to be agreed in some cases by virtually all native speakers, in others by all native speakers of a certain educational/cultural back-ground. Unless non-native speakers can get access to this part-meaning, they will usually not be able to deal with the other, more subjective elements of meaning in a way which satisfies them or anyone else (though occasionally a 'misunderstanding' can have a poetic and/or personal value in its own right). One of the teacher's jobs, then, is to help non-native learners to get access to this first level of meaning, either simply by informing (for example, giving meanings of words), or, usually better, by helping them to find out for themselves.

For this partial meaning, we have used the term paraphrasable meaning: it is that part of the meaning which can be put into different words, in answer to the question 'What is the poem about?' The term is not widely used, and some may disagree with it; we acknowledge that it is not intellectually watertight, but believe that it has heuristic value, as a way of beginning to understand the poem and to talk about it, though we would explain, even to very elementary students, that all such meanings are 'only a part, perhaps a small part', of how we should understand and 'appreciate' a poem.

Nash (1986: 74) reaches a similar conclusion:

> The consciousness – sometimes embarrassed, sometimes humorous – of what is defective and awry in paraphrase creates a sharp focus on the text (...) we set about trying to identify what we have missed (...). Paraphrase may have no critical status, may be utterly ludicrous as an account of what the poem is and does, but it can still be the step that initiates a sophisticated response to language.

We find that the concept of paraphrasable meaning is readily understood, and can be used, especially for homework preparation, from the first week of teaching a new (non-beginner) class. Like other concepts considered later, however, it should be returned to and 'deepened' at regular intervals, perhaps by considering poems where the paraphrasable meaning seems instinctively to be 'most of the meaning' (for example in some ballads), others where it seems (almost) absent (for instance non-sense poems), and yet others where one wants to talk of meanings in the plural – see below under polysemy (section 4.5).

## 4.3 REGULARITIES AND PATTERNS

After exploring paraphrasable meaning, our learners are asked to look for examples and types of regularity in a poem.

Regularity in this sense is effectively a synonym of pattern, and both words can be used with learners. To introduce the concept, learners can be asked to think about patterns in wallpaper, leaves, fractal designs or whatever, and helped to decide what makes a pattern. Answers will probably include:

- Exact repetition
- Approximate repetition or similarity
- Repetition with change, e.g. turning through 90°, enlarging
- Other mixtures of similarity and difference?

This can then be applied to language, first non-literary – what are the patterns in the way you talk with your friends, or in a TV programme? – then literary. Soon, of course, the need will be felt to subdivide into sounds, grammar, vocabulary, and so on, but all of this should come as far as possible from the learners, rather than being imposed as an arbitrary structure.

### 4.3.1 Phonological regularity

*4.3.1.1 'Traditional' categories: rhyme and metre*

Explanation of phonological regularity can begin with traditional categories such as rhyme, assonance, alliteration and metre. It may be possible to say, for example, that a poem is written in iambic pentameters, and in the rhyme scheme of a Shakespearean sonnet (ABAB–CDCD–EFEF–GG). This first stage of analysing might also include noting clear cases of alliteration, for example, the same consonant sound starting three successive content words: 'the furrow followed free' (Coleridge 'The Rime of the Ancient Mariner'), and of (within-line) assonance, such as the same vowel sound in three successive stressed syllables: 'briony-vine and ivy wreath' (Tennyson 'Amphion').

It is beyond the scope of this book to give a descriptive account of rhyme, metre and so on. Many hundreds of books do this, but we recommend especially Leech (1969), which combines theoretical soundness with accessibility to learners. A good second book might be Davies Roberts (1986), whose idiosyncratic approach should not be accepted uncritically, but will certainly stimulate analysis. Really advanced learners can, at their own peril, tackle the multiplicity of more technical analyses, often challenging accepted categories: for example, Cureton (1993) divides poems metrically, not into stanza, line, foot and syllable, but into section, stanza, part, line, lobe, tactus and pulse, each level either duple or triple. Such analysis, though open to many pedagogical objections, seems to us many times more useful than that of Hobsbaum (1996), an unreconstructed Leavisite: his highly subjective, largely unargued analyses may or may not be 'true', or at least convincing to his fellow sophisticates, but they offer no way into systematic analysis to those who are trying to 'learn the trade', and are of the stuff that made many working-class English grammar-school children, to say nothing of foreigners, despair of English literature teaching throughout the mid-twentieth century.

Returning to Leech, we do find it worthwhile to draw attention, even with elementary students, to 'rhyme and its cousins', our name for the six possible types of correspondence between the last stressed syllables in two or more lines (Leech 1969: 89). In the table below, we have added our own explanations, and used underlining instead of bold type:

| <u>C</u>VC | great/grow | send/sit | 'alliteration' – same first consonant (cluster) in final syllable |
| C<u>V</u>C | great/fail | send/bell | 'assonance' – same vowel in final syllable |
| CV<u>C</u> | great/meat | send/hand | 'consonance' – same final consonant (cluster) in final syllable |
| <u>C</u><u>V</u>C | great/grazed | send/sell | 'reverse rhyme' – combines alliteration and assonance |
| <u>C</u>V<u>C</u> | great/groat | send/sound | 'pararhyme' – combines alliteration and consonance |
| C<u>V</u><u>C</u> | great/bait | send/end | 'rhyme' – combines assonance and consonance |

Three caveats are necessary in using Leech's scheme:

1. Learners must understand that sound, not spelling is decisive: great/meat, for example, is definitely not rhyme, though it can be described as 'eye-rhyme', in addition to being consonance.
2. There are many cases where the ends of two lines seem phonetically similar, but do not fit any of Leech's categories: for these, the term 'approximate rhyme' may be considered.
3. As Leech acknowledges, the terms 'alliteration', 'assonance' and even 'rhyme' can be used in ways which fall outside this scheme. To minimise confusion, we suggest using (where necessary) 'end-of-line assonance' (and so on) to distinguish this from other types.

The six categories in Leech's scheme are not all equally important. After rhyme itself, end-of-line consonance is by far the most frequent, especially in modern poetry. Some poets use it all the time, in preference to traditional rhyme, which can seem too unsubtle, facile, playful, and out of step with the times:

> *In meinem Lied ein Reim*
> *Käme mir fast vor wie Übermut.*
> (In my song a rhyme would seem to me almost like over-exuberance.)
> Brecht, *Schlechte Zeit für Lyrik*
> (Bad times for the lyric), lines 15–16

It is, therefore, one of the few categories which often merits direct teaching at an early stage.

More generally, although learners like to be given lists and rules for rhyme, metre and so on, and often have such lists and rules, usually inaccurate, from previous teaching, it is best to start, wherever possible, with poems and not with analytical categories. Learners should be encouraged to read poems aloud, often several times and in different ways, and to recognise that rhyme and metre are things which they can hear for themselves, and to which labels can be applied later. The kind of guidance questions to be used are fairly obvious, for example:

- Which lines seem to end in the same sound?
- How many beats are there in each line? (*Tap fingers on table.*) Can line X be read in different ways, with different numbers of beats?
- Do the lines reflect the natural way to break up the poem, or should the main pauses be at other points?

Only when everyone in the class has done this with several poems should technical terms be introduced (or, if half known from previous teaching, confirmed, corrected and systematised). Furthermore, the temptation should be resisted to introduce 'every type of X' for the sake of completeness: it is not pedagogically sound to spend time on dactyls, anapaests and amphibrachs if the learners have only met iambic and a few trochaic poems. We do not recommend concealing the existence of other metrical forms, or refusing to answer questions on them, simply not dwelling on them, especially out of context.

This approach is consistent with and analogous to modern ideas about the place of grammar in communicative foreign language teaching: the general view is not that grammar should not be taught, but that it should be taught only after considerable exposure to relevant language, and mainly inductively, with learners forming hypotheses from their own '*Sprachgefühl*' (feeling for language), and checking these against further examples. This is consistent with what we know about learning, and about the functions of the two hemispheres of the brain: right-brain learning, which includes recognising and interpreting patterns, precedes left-brain learning, which includes forming logical explanations.

### 4.3.1.2 Other kinds of phonological regularity

Many poems in English are written without rhyme, or without metre, or both. (Here differences between languages become important: in French, for example, poetry without rhyme is unusual, and often considered 'wrong', see for example Berthon (1930).) Poetry without rhyme but with metre, usually iambic pentameter, is sometimes called 'blank verse' (for instance much of Shakespeare), and poetry without either may be called 'free verse', though not everyone uses this term.

Most good poems which do not have regular rhyme or metre nevertheless have phonological patterning, sometimes strong and insistent, sometimes less insistent and seemingly on the edge of perceptibility. Moreover, poems which do have rhyme, metre, and even alliteration and assonance, often have additional patterns which do not fit, or fit only imperfectly, into any of these categories.

There is a tendency to think that if something does not have a name it is less important. For this reason, we encourage our learners to use the rather clumsy-seeming term 'phonological regularity' for their first ideas in this area on any given poem, rather than seemingly easier and often more familiar terms such as alliteration. The practical advantage of this can be seen by considering learner reaction to the following lines from Larkin's poem 'Toads':

> their unspeakable wives
> Are skinny as whippets ...

Many learners will decide immediately that there is pattern here: the two /s/ and two /w/ phonemes are very salient (though Scots and some others will hear /hw/ in whippets), and combine with other factors (rhythm, length of line) to produce a strong effect. But is it alliteration? Do you need at least three of a particular consonant, or are two enough? And do they have to be consecutive, and if so, in what sense? Learners who wish to pursue this can be referred to textbooks, for example Durant and Fabb (1990: 115–18), who offer several different definitions of alliteration. This, however, becomes an (optional?) second-stage activity, and issues of definition do not interfere with the process of noticing as many phonological patterns as possible.

Similar considerations apply to vowel regularities: learners can simply notice what vowel sounds are repeated, though they may need to be warned about different vowel sounds with the same spelling, and vice versa; transcribing (only) the vowels into phonemic script, where known, will help. They do not need, initially at least, to worry about whether there are enough repetitions, close enough together, to constitute assonance.

The simple counting of repeated vowels or consonants is, of course, of limited value, and learners should try to say something about their distribution within a poem, though this is not always easy. Traugott and Pratt (1980), analysing the following poem (in Sandburg 1950), provide an unusually convincing example: lines 6–8 are held together by consonant repetition, lines 10–13 by vowel repetition, and the former three also have an overlap effect which may mimic the breaking of waves on the shore:

### The Harbor

Passing through huddled and ugly walls
By doorways where women
Looked from their hunger-deep eyes
Haunted with shadows of hunger-hands,
Out from the huddled and ugly walls,
I came sudden, at the city's edge,
On a blue burst of lake,
Long lake waves breaking under the sun
On a spray-flung curve of shore,
And a fluttering storm of gulls,
Masses of great gray wings
And flying white bellies
Veering and wheeling free in the open.

(Carl Sandburg)

Patterns of rhythm, other than those which constitute recognisable metre, are more difficult to pin down. Many critics write persuasively and entertainingly on this subject, as do some poets themselves; here for instance is D. H. Lawrence describing his kind of free verse:

> But all that can be said, first and last, is that free verse is, or should be, direct utter-ance from the instant, whole man. It is the soul and the mind and body surging together nothing left out. They speak all together. There is some confusion, some discord. But the confusion and discord only belong to the reality, as noise belongs to the plunge of water. It is no use inventing fancy laws for free verse, no use drawing a melodic line which all feet must toe.
>
> (Lawrence 1920)

It is impossible, however, to provide a list of rules which learners can use to find patterns. This is partly because each line of a poem can be read in many different ways, and partly because, as there are fewer choices in this area than for individual sounds (over forty phonemes, but only two levels of stress in words, three levels of stress in utterances, and at most five recognisable patterns of rhythm or temporary metre: spondee (--), iamb (∪-), trochee (-∪), anapaest (∪∪-), dactyl (-∪∪)), it is much harder to be certain that apparent patterns are not due to chance. One of the rare totally clear examples is D. H. Lawrence's poem '*Gloire De Dijon*' (in Lawrence 1977) which ends (lines 11–18):

> She drips herself with water, and her shoulders
> Glisten as silver, they crumple up
> Like wet and falling roses, and I listen
> For the sluicing of their rain-dishevelled petals.
> In the window full of sunlight
> Concentrates her golden shadow
> Fold on fold, until it glows as
> Mellow as the glory roses.

The first fourteen lines have hints of rhythmic patterning but no more, but the last four lines are perfect trochaic tetrameters (-∪-∪-∪-∪), the last two reinforced by an (approximate) rhyme.

To coach learners extensively in 'rhythm spotting', just so that they can uncover such rare treasures, is not cost effective or realistic. It is far better to yield to rampant subjectivity and to experimentation here, encouraging learners to say poems aloud in different ways, to use metrical terms such as spondee, trochee, and so on, in describing their subjective readings, but not to expect that clear and relatively objective patterns will emerge: when they do, as in the Lawrence example, this will be a welcome bonus.

All the types of regularity discussed so far could be seen, in terms of our wallpaper example (4.3), as exact repetition. Strictly speaking, there is no such thing, as even two utterances of the same phoneme will always be different, but we can invoke the concept of 'sameness for practical purposes'. The other kinds of regularity all involve things which are different, but somehow perceived as being of the same type. In practice, this usually means that a poem, or part of a poem, is perceived as having a lot of the same kind of vowels, or the same kind of consonants, or both.

The problem, of course, is how to categorise sounds. Learners often want to use labels such as 'hard' or 'soft', or even 'pleasant' and 'unpleasant', but the first pair are hard to define, the second pair probably undefinable. Reactions of this kind should not be squashed – a teacher can ask whether other learners feel the same way – but, over a series of lessons, learners can be encouraged to group sounds according to more recognised phonetic criteria. They should also support their claims by saying something about what sounds are not present, or infrequent. For example, a given poem, or part of a poem, may have:

- lots of plosives (p t k b d g) but not many fricatives (f v s z, etc.);
- lots of voiceless/fortis consonants (p t k f s, etc.) but not many voiced/lenis (b d g v z, etc.);

- lots of long vowels and diphthongs – best considered one category in English – but few short vowels;
- lots of lines beginning with an unstressed syllable and ending with a stressed syllable, but few with the other three logical possibilities.

### 4.3.1.3 The effects and meanings of phonological regularity

Having described the 'what' of sound patterns in a poem, it is natural to want to discuss the 'why' and even the 'so what?': what were a poet's reasons (conscious or perhaps unconscious) for choosing certain patterns, and how do they contribute to the poem's meaning, to its effect, to its beauty, to my personal reaction? Some of these issues are discussed later in this chapter (4.7), but brief comments may be helpful at this juncture.

First, the notion that particular sounds, or even groups of sounds, are inherently beautiful or ugly, or poetic or unpoetic, or have any specific meaning, is not well supported by empirical evidence. Ask a speaker of a language unknown to you to read aloud a poem in that language: it will probably be hard to decide how good the poem is, or even what it is about, and any clues you do get will not be from individual words. Proust claimed that the most beautiful line in French was Racine's 'La fille de Minos et de Pasiphaë', but this is hard to take seriously; those who hate such games might prefer MacDiarmid's claim that the most beautiful line in Scottish poetry is Burns' 'Ye are nae Mary Morison' – a nondescript line, phonetically and in other ways, made beautiful by its context in the poem 'Mary Morison' (see Burns 1990: 308–9). Of course, certain sounds can be associated with beauty – sibilants perhaps, or long vowels and diphthongs; an often-quoted example is Verlaine's 'Chanson d'Automne' (in Jones 1957: 477), the first stanza of which is given below. To assist comprehension we also provide a – rather literal – translation, but the phonological effects discussed are found only in the original.

| | |
|---|---|
| *Les sanglots longs* | The long sobs |
| *Des violons* | of the violins |
| *De l'automne* | of autumn |
| *Blessent mon coeur* | wound my heart |
| *D'une langueur* | with a monotonous languor. |
| *Monotone.* | |

This is indeed beautiful (only in French), but it is not beauty as abstract currency. The sounds reinforce the meaning or mood in this first stanza – languorous monotony! The effect is only fully appreciated by reading on:-

| | |
|---|---|
| *Tout suffoquant* | Quite suffocating |
| *Et blême, quand* | and pale, when |
| *Sonne l'heure,* | the hour strikes, |
| *Je me souviens* | I remember |
| *Des jours anciens* | bygone days |
| *Et je pleure.* | and I weep. |

| | |
|---|---|
| *Et je m'en vais* | And I go away |
| *Au vent mauvais* | in the bad wind |
| *Qui m'emporte* | which carries me off |
| *Deçà, delà,* | here, there, |
| *Pareil à la* | like the |
| *Feuille morte.* | dead leaf. |

In the second stanza, the sounds of *suffoquant* and *blême*, less beautiful to some ears, go with the mood of pain; in the third and last stanza, short vowels, especially in *Deçà delà*, go with the idea of blowing hither and thither like a leaf in the wind. This 'pattern of patterns', where each stanza in a short poem has its own dominant sound-type reinforcing mood or meaning, is extremely common. We suggest that none of these sounds are inherently beautiful or ugly – the beauty is in the matching of sound and mood.

Traugott and Pratt (op. cit.) make a similar point about Sandburg's 'The Harbor', quoted above. In the opening lines, the phoneme /ʌ/, among others, might be thought to suggest ugliness and unpleasantness – *huddled, ugly, hunger*. And yet in the closing lines of the poem the same sound occurs in *fluttering* and *gulls*, associated with beauty and joy. The sound is not inherently ugly, but acquires a temporary negative meaning through its association with negative words, and loses it again in a new context.

These and similar examples suggest to us that only very modest claims can be made about the meaning of the segmental phonology of a poem, that is, the individual sounds and their patterns. This accords with Empson's view in *Seven Types of Ambiguity* (1930: 231):

> [The] most important mode of action (of alliteration, etc.) is to connect two words by similarity of sound so that you are made to think of their possible connections.

This idea can be slightly altered, and put in modern linguistic terms, by saying that alliteration and other sound patterns can create (additional) cohesion within a poem: they help to show what belongs together, but only in combination with other elements, including vocabulary and syntax, can they create more specific meaning. The pedagogical implication is that students should be encouraged to regard alliteration and other devices as clues, perhaps in dividing a poem into sections, perhaps in locating especially important ideas, but discouraged from over-interpretation.

All this applies, we repeat, to segmental phonology: for suprasegmental patterns, especially rhythm and metre, a slightly less modest aim might sometimes be appropriate, and we discuss this further under mimesis in section 4.6.

### 4.3.2 Lexical regularity and patterning

Looking for lexical patterns is a fairly simple and usually popular activity, especially good for non-native students as they can improve their general vocabulary knowledge, and their skill in using dictionaries and other reference books, at the same time as they deepen their understanding of a particular poem. Learners can be asked to make lists of words from a particular semantic field, or a particular register (taboo, slang, scientific, archaic, and so on), or having a particular tone (positive, neutral, negative, intense, cool), or similar in some other respect. Lists should include information on distribution – for example, if most words of a given type are in a particular stanza, this fact should be noted.

A word of caution is needed. If a poem is about topic X – let us say railways – it will hardly be surprising if many words are from the semantic field of topic X: it may still be worth checking, but students should not spend too long on confirming the (perhaps) obvious. Of more interest in many cases are 'covert topics' or 'second topics': a poem seems to be about topic X, but a lot of the vocabulary is from the semantic field of topic Y. In simple cases a native speaker might realise this automatically, but non-natives will be greatly assisted by making lists and checking in dictionaries.

To illustrate this approach, you are asked to study the three Shakespeare sonnets reprinted below, which appear to form one connected sequence. After one or more readings for general meaning, you should list the vocabulary items – at least the nouns and verbs – under whatever headings you find appropriate. When you have done this, ask yourself if these lists change, or amplify, your understanding of the poems.

### Sonnet 33

Full many a glorious morning have I seen
Flatter the mountain tops with sovereign eye,
Kissing with golden face the meadows green,
Gilding pale streams with heavenly alchemy;
5  Anon permit the basest clouds to ride
With ugly rack on his celestial face,
And from the forlorn world his visage hide,
Stealing unseen to west with this disgrace.
Even so my sun one early morn did shine,
10  With all triumphant splendour on my brow;
But out alack, he was but one hour mine,
The region cloud hath mask'd him from me now.
Yet him for this my love no whit disdaineth;
Suns of the world may stain when heaven's sun staineth.

### Sonnet 34

Why didst thou promise such a beauteous day,
And make me travel forth without my cloak,
To let base clouds o'ertake me in my way,
Hiding thy bravery in their rotten smoke?

5    'Tis not enough that through the cloud thou break,
      To dry the rain on my storm-beaten face,
      For no man well of such a salve can speak,
      That heals the wound, and cures not the disgrace.
      Nor can thy shame give physic to my grief;
10   Though thou repent, yet I have still the loss.
      Th' offender's sorrow lends but weak relief
      To him that bears the strong offence's cross.
      Ah but those tears are pearl which thy love sheds,
      And they are rich, and ransom all ill deeds.

**Sonnet 35**

No more be grieved at that which thou has done:
Roses have thorns, and silver fountains mud,
Clouds and eclipses stain both moon and sun,
And loathsome canker lives in sweetest bud.
5    All men make faults, and even I in this,
      Authorising thy trespass with compare,
      Myself corrupting, salving thy amiss,
      Excusing thy sins more than thy sins are;
      For to thy sensual fault I bring in sense -
10   Thy adverse party is thy advocate -
      And 'gainst myself a lawful plea commence.
      Such civil war is in my love and hate,
      That I an accessory needs must be
      To that sweet thief which sourly robs from me.

PLEASE DO NOT READ ON UNTIL YOU HAVE COMPLETED THE TASK.

Our students usually decide that, at a general level, the poems are about the English landscape and weather, or about a friend or lover who has betrayed the poet and been forgiven, or about both: good students usually decide, as have most critics, that the poems have two main meanings (elements or levels of meaning). A lexical inventory will of course reveal many words from these two main areas, for example:

| | |
|---|---|
| Landscape and weather: | mountain, meadows, streams, clouds, celestial, sun, shine, cloud, smoke, storm-beaten |
| Relations between friends: | triumphant (?), love, disdaineth, promise, shame, tears, lovers, sensual fault |

Beyond this, however, several other categories can be identified, with some words falling into more than one category. For example:

| | |
|---|---|
| Medicine: | salve, heal, wound, cure, physic |
| Religion: | shame (?), repent, bear … cross, grieved |
| Money/riches: | pearl, rich, ransom |
| Law: | adverse party, advocate, lawful plea, accessory, thief |

After further examination of the detailed associations of these words, and of course their distribution, one student concluded that 'beautiful nature metaphors can no longer describe this relationship; other kinds of human activity, especially sordid ones, provide better metaphors'. This is of course not the last word in analysis and interpretation, but an example of what kinds of response can be elicited.

A different issue concerning the vocabulary of poetry can be exemplified by this extract from the beginning of a poem by Hugh MacDiarmid 'On a raised beach' (in MacDiarmid 1987):

> ALL is lithogenesis – or lochia,
> Carpolite fruit of the forbidden tree,
> Stones blacker than any in the Caaba,
> Cream-coloured caen-stone, chatoyant pieces,
> 5  Celadon and corbeau, bistre and beige,
> Glaucous, hoar, enfouldered, cyathiform,
> Making mere faculae of the sun and moon
> I study you glout and gloss, but have
> No cadrans to adjust you with, and turn again
> 10  From optik to haptik and like a blind man run
> My fingers over you, arris by arris, burr by burr,
> Slickensides, truité, rugas, foveoles,
> Bringing my aesthesis in vain to bear,
> An angle-titch to all your corrugations and coigns,
> Hatched foraminous cavo-rilievo of the world,
> Deictic, fiducial stones. Chiliad by chiliad
> What bricole piled you here, stupendous cairn?

This poem presents even the native or very advanced non-native reader with a problem familiar to the average non-native: the vocabulary is so difficult that one is tempted simply to give up.

We would not recommend detailed study of this poem in an EFL class, but a brief look at it, in a non-threatening context and with appropriate preparation, could be useful learner training. If students can be persuaded not to look up all the unknown words (and not to give up!) they will find some much easier lines later on, and may be able to arrive at, not only a satisfying general paraphrase of the poem, but a linguistic interpretation which would include classifying of the lexis in the early lines as 'technical terms, difficult even for native speakers, many but not all from the field of geology'.

Our lexical examples so far have mostly been on the level of the individual word, but longer units should not be neglected. Research suggests that native speakers, and good non-native learners, plan their utterances largely in multi-word units, from proverbs and formulaic expressions to looser collocations. Poets sometimes subvert the process by combining words in unusual ways, and this is rightly a main focus of linguistic analysis (see below), but sometimes more 'normal' combinations are important too: in Tennyson's 'Crossing the Bar', the verb phrases 'put out to sea' and 'crossed the bar', as well as the single word 'embark', can be understood as units, and classified in the way shown above, to bring out the lexical–semantic patterning of the poem.

### 4.3.3  Other kinds of regularity and patterning

In practice, we find that systematic hunting for regularity or pattern is very useful in phonology and lexis, but much less so, at least as a separate activity, in other areas. Syntactic and semantic regularities can be found, in fact they are almost everywhere, but often they are best considered either in conjunction with deviance (see below) or as an aspect of other, mainly lexical, regularities.

Patterning on the pragmatic level (see section 3.7) can sometimes be of interest. Writers of the sixteenth and seventeenth centuries, in particular, may sometimes seem to be performing a surprisingly large variety of 'speech acts' within their poems – informing, questioning, commanding, requesting, begging, hoping, expecting, and so on – and students can be asked to list these (including ambiguities), to look for patterns (including sudden changes), and to discuss how genuine the speech acts are – is the poem addressed to a real person, are the requests real requests? How many different speech acts, and how many examples of each, do you find in this well-known poem by Ben Jonson (in Harrison 1937)?

**To Celia**

Drink to me only with thine eyes,
    And I will pledge with mine;
Or leave a kiss but in the cup
    And I'll not look for wine.
The thirst that from the soul doth rise
    Doth ask a drink divine;
But might I of Jove's nectar sup,
    I would not change for thine.
I sent thee late a rosy wreath,
    Not so much honouring thee
As giving it a hope that there
    It could not wither'd be;
But thou thereon didst only breathe,
    And sent'st it back to me;
Since when it grows, and smells, I swear,
    Not of itself, but thee!

Lastly, we mention graphological or graphetic regularity, the arrangement of words on the page. Nearly all poems are arranged in lines, which helps to show that they are intended as poems but otherwise requires little comment. Graphic features over and above this may require more attention, usually but not always in conjunction with phonological analysis. Some of these factors are conventional – the indentation of the last two lines as a Shakespearean sonnet, often combined with a semantic/pragmatic change – others are one-off, as in this Roger McGough poem.

**40-Love**

| middle | aged |
|--------|------|
| couple | playing |
| ten | nis |
| (…) | |

## 4.4  DEVIANT LANGUAGE

### 4.4.1  General

Deviant language, also called deviance or deviation, is language which differs from what is considered normal. Sometimes it can be what a lay person would call 'wrong', as in the poem by e. e. cummings (in cummings 1966) beginning:

> love is more thicker than forget
> more thinner than recall
> more seldom than a wave is wet
> more frequent than to fail …

Sometimes – a weaker form of deviance – it can be merely unusual, for example, 'Jim I saw in Enderby', instead of 'I saw Jim in Enderby'. What counts as normal or unusual is a question to which we shall return later, but the general principle can be understood by students without rigorous definition of this reference point.

Some poetry, including most of cummings, is very strongly, obviously and consistently deviant; other poetry, probably the greater part, contains at least a sprinkling of obvious examples and further debatable ones; some of the rest may seem rather undeviant on casual inspection but, in addition to the 'routine' deviance that 'the lines don't go all the way across the page', further kinds can often be found, expressions which sound 'normal' but probably would not be said quite that way in non-literary prose. (Some literary prose, by contrast, is much more deviant than some poetry, though the 'average' deviance of poetry, so far as these things can be quantified, is probably much higher.)

We now give some examples of types of (sometimes clear, sometimes arguable) deviance found in poetry. In every case, we suggest a label for the deviance, or rather what we see as the main deviance; most examples contain multiple possibilities. In some cases we give (relatively) non-deviant comparison forms – note, not 'translations'; if the poet had wanted to say that he or she would have done so.

Our treatment is not linguistically complete or rigorous, as this is a book about teaching, not about linguistic description, and the list simply exemplifies what kinds of language phenomenon we want to discuss, either as problems which students can be helped to cope with, or as resources to enhance teaching, or more neutrally as features to be taken account of. Our (possible and partial) answers are given in

Appendix 2, but readers are encouraged to write down their own answers before looking at these. The first six examples are from Parkinson 1990a.

*Examples*

(a)  Through purblind night the wiper
     Reaps a swathe of water
     On the screen; we shudder on
     And hardly hold the road.

     (Louis MacNeice, 'The Wiper')

(b)  To be woken by hearing
     The voices of enchanted birds
     And the voices of disenchanted birds.

     (Peter Levi, 'To Speak about the Soul')

(c)  A little reading and a little loving
     A little eating and a little sleeping
     The days went over me half happy
     With friends and books and cups of coffee

     (Francis Scarfe, 'Ballad of the Safe Area')

(d)  Drake he's in his hammock and a thousand miles away
     (Captain art thou sleeping there below?)

     (Henry Newbolt, 'Drake's Drum') (Modified spelling/dialect)

(e)  When the lamp is shattered
     The light in the dust lies dead
     When the cloud is scatter'd
     The rainbow's glory is shed
     When the lute is broken
     Sweet loves are remember'd not ...

     (Percy Bysshe Shelley, 'When the Lamp is Shattered')

(f)  *[Describing a town buried under sand]*
     And where now hedgehog delves
     And conies hollow their long caves
     Houses will build themselves
     And tombstones re-write names on dead men's graves.

     (Andrew Young, 'Culbin Sands')

(g)  And for that minute a blackbird sang
     Close by, and round him, mistier,
     Further and further, all the birds
     Of Oxfordshire and Gloucestershire.

     (Edward Thomas, 'Adelstrop')

(h)   … until he Pops,
      Croaks, passes in his checks and Stops.

      (Hilaire Belloc, 'The Statesmen')

(i)   Another Troy would rise and set …

      (W. B. Yeats, 'Two Songs from a Play')

(j)   I shall not murder
      The mankind of her going with a grave truth.

      (Dylan Thomas, 'A refusal to mourn the
      death, by fire, of a child in London')

(k)   On Wenlock Edge the wood's in trouble
      His first fleece the Wrekin leaves.

      (A. E. Housman, first lines of untitled poem)

Before we turn to specific pedagogic suggestions, it may be helpful to make three general points about deviance.

First, as already hinted, deviance is relative. What seems deviant (British) English may be standard Indian or Canadian English, what is first perceived as 'funny' German may be perfectly normal Dutch, what is wrong in 'general' English may be correct in the (or a) register of economics, chess, particle physics or Citizens' Band radio. Within the literature class, something may be 'wrong' with respect to the target language as normally taught, but right for Dante or Shakespeare or even Joyce.

Second, an appeal to a different norm sometimes completely cancels an apparent deviance, and we can say fairly confidently that something would not be perceived as deviant – it was/is normal in a certain century, or in a certain genre. In other cases, the reverse is true. Joyce's language in *Ulysses*, though it can be explained as his own particular idiolect (an individual's language variety), and even acquires a certain normality for dedicated Joyce readers, clearly depends for some of its effect on its difference from a norm. Most poets and most poems are somewhere between these extremes – good readers recognise certain features as 'routine licences' (see Leech 1969, Chapter 3), or conventions, but they try not to be so blasé that they lose all feeling for the effects produced by the difference from routine prose.

Third, within mainstream literary stylistics, the fashion for 'style as deviance' has waned considerably – its popularity was brief, and a more subtle and multi-layered approach has rightly superseded it. For teaching purposes, however, and especially for teaching non-native speakers, the approach has far more vitality and practical utility than mainstream stylisticians often allow, and it seems to meet a variety of cognitive and emotional needs. For learners, the approach can be empowering: they have a vital contribution to make in the short term, their views are taken seriously, and the feedback should help with their next contribution. For teachers, the approach can be awareness raising, leading to better understanding both of how their learners perceive and of their own (the teachers') unexamined assumptions. For both teachers and learners, it can be confidence building, and provide the security of a shared approach (algorithm?, ritual?) shaping at least part of the encounter with new texts.

### 4.4.2  One possible approach to the teaching of deviance

One of us (Parkinson 1990a) has outlined a possible approach as follows:

> The first stage is to establish as fully as possible the paraphrasable meaning of a poem. This stage is often skimped, as learners and even teachers may believe that a poem has no precise meaning, but in fact poets are generally not less but more precise than the rest of us, and you will often be surprised how much it is possible to establish about who is doing what to whom, when and where, and what people and things look like. Poetic elements add to this meaning, they do not dilute it.
>
> The second stage is to ask 'How would this be said in normal prose English?' This is a valuable speaking/writing exercise, highlighting any remaining problems in the detailed comprehension of the poem, and sensitising the learners to subtle distinctions of register and usage. There may be resistance to the idea of 'reducing' Shakespeare or Eliot to such a translation, but when the exercise is attempted, it soon becomes clear that the translation can never be a substitute, and appreciation of the original is enhanced rather than diminished.
>
> Psychological resistance to deviant language should have been weakened by sensitive treatment of stages one and two, after which even the most anxious learner should feel they have had an 'antidote' to any deviant input. A further brief stage of explicit counselling may, however, be required. Learners can be helped to understand that any advanced language study must involve exposure to a wide variety of native language models, not all of which are to be imitated, and that they must learn how to recognise different language varieties and what to use and not to use in their own speaking and writing.
>
> In the final stage, the class must face the biggest question of all: what is the point of these deviances?

The article then goes on to suggest several possibilities, covered – in a different way – elsewhere in this book.

This brief summary, written a decade ago for a readership of mainly inexperienced teachers, requires some expansion and qualification for present purposes. First, we would now be less prescriptive: the general approach still seems valid, but the stages could be varied, combined, omitted or negotiated. Second, we would stress more than in 1990 that there are often no 'right and wrong answers': research on native speakers doing tasks of this kind, such as Parkinson 1990b, shows that even literary sophisticates can disagree on almost everything – on what is most deviant (even within a single sentence), on how it might be 'translated', and on why the deviant form is used. (Teachers should not be afraid of the word 'wrong'; if a student says that an inversion after 'hardly' is deviant, he or she can be corrected, but this still leaves a lot of cases where other teacher responses are preferable, from 'Yes, I hadn't thought of that' to 'Well, I doubt if a native speaker would see it that way, but they might.')

Third, the second-stage question 'How would this be said …?' would now usually be changed into something more open or plural, such as 'Can you suggest some similar phrases which would be more standard or normal in the kind of English you learn?' Fourth, and most importantly, we would now be less interested in arriving at a single answer from the class, and more in getting a range of answers, of which the teacher's might only be first among equals. Students can be encouraged to design simple questionnaires, to find out what, say, three classmates think, and to contribute a research-style report (see also Chapter 9). For many poems, we still hope to lead the class to many of the insights which we (and/or past students and/or 'experts') have had earlier and which probably led to this particular text being included in the course: the other ideas offered in the class, though, are not to be seen as fumbling attempts to reach this golden truth, but as valuable truths in their own right.

## 4.5 AMBIGUITY AND POLYSEMY

Consider the following poem (in Scott 1970):

### Continent O Venus

She lies ablow my body's lust and love,
A country dearly-kent, and yet sae fremd
That she's at aince thon Tir-nan-Og I've dreamed,
The airt I've lived in, whar I mean tae live,
5   And mair, much mair, a mixter-maxter warld
Whar fact and dream are taigled up and snorled.

I ken ilk bay o aa her body's strand,
Yet ken them new ilk time I come to shore,
For she's the uncharted sea whar I maun fare
10   To find anither undiscovered land,
To find it fremd, and yet to find it dear,
To seek for't aye, and aye be bydan there.

(Alexander Scott)

| | |
|---|---|
| *ablow*: below | *airt*: place |
| *fremd*: foreign | *ilk*: every |
| *kent*: known | *mair*: more |
| *aince*: once | *maun*: must |
| *Tir-nan-Og*: land of youth or Gaelic paradise | *aye*: ever |
| | *bydan*: staying, living |

When discussing the paraphrasable meaning of this poem, students initially tend to split into two main camps. Crudely speaking, some believe 'it's about a country', others believe 'it's about a woman'. After discussion, perhaps rather predictably, most classes tend to agree that 'it's about both!'

In non-literary language, when we say or write something with two totally different meanings it is usually seen as unintentional, and referred to as 'ambiguity'; one of the meanings is seen as the 'right' one, the other as a misunderstanding. Some ambiguities – with *funny, football, German* (and so on) *teacher, golf club, tea, partner*, for example – are fairly common, at least in certain circles, while others – *log tables, time flies* – may be the stuff of urban myth.

By contrast, it is very unlikely that Scott really meant this poem to be *only* about a country or *only* about a woman: the response that it's about both is surely correct in essence, though requiring many qualifications – see our earlier comments on paraphrasable meaning (section 4.2).

More generally, when two or more meanings seem possible in a poem, it can often be argued that both meanings are valid. We are shifting our ground slightly here, by saying valid and not intended. Many volumes have been written about the importance or otherwise of author intention, but we will cut the Gordian knot by saying that, for present purposes, it is not crucial: on the rare occasions that poets tell us – outside the poem – what they 'meant', this is interesting data but not the last word.

The concept of polysemy is related to and overlaps with that of metaphor. In 'Continent O Venus', for example, the double meaning could be 'explained' in various ways, for example:

- The poem is really about a (relationship with a) woman, but this is illuminated by an extended analogy with knowledge of a country: most of lines 1 and 7 are literal, all the rest is an extended metaphor.
- The poem is really about (feelings for) a country, but this is expressed in human, sexual terms: much of the poem is to be understood literally, but there are substantial metaphorical elements, including but not restricted to lines 1 and 7.
- Both the 'woman' meaning and the 'country' meaning are equally valid – nothing is metaphor, or everything is metaphor.

We are not sure if objective arguments can choose a 'winner' between these three positions – especially between the second and third, as the first rather loses out on quantitative arguments. For pedagogical purposes at least, though, we confess a preference for explanations such as the third, for this poem and for many others, especially modern ones. There are poems for which the literal–metaphorical distinction has some value – we might say that in Wordsworth's 'She dwelt among the untrodden ways' the 'springs of Dove' are real, and the 'violet by the mossy stone' a metaphor, though even to this objections can be made. If this game were ever playable, though, its assumptions were surely undermined for ever by the first lines of Shelley's 'To a Skylark':

> Hail to thee, blithe spirit!
> Bird thou never wert –

This is not just a metaphor, it is another level of reality. (Plentiful examples can,

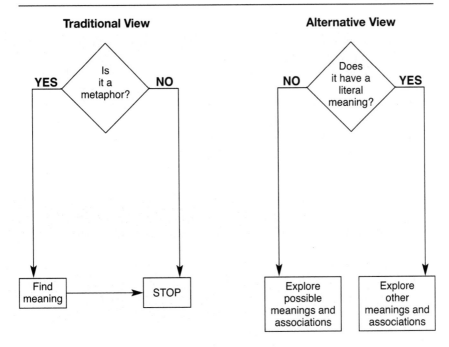

*Fig. 1*

of course, be found from other languages – Mallarmé and Rilke, among others – and arguably from much earlier periods – Ronsard? – though the collapse of clear literal/metaphorical dichotomies has gone further in recent centuries).

Our main reason for preferring explanations of the third type above is, however, pedagogic and practical: debates about what is literal and what is metaphorical are often sterile, and close down discussion rather than opening it out. Explanations in terms of polysemy are more powerful, more stimulating to further and wider explanation. Elsewhere, one of us (Parkinson 1994: 110) has presented the two approaches in terms of two flowcharts (Fig. 1).

## 4.6 MIMESIS

Mimesis is derived from the Greek word meaning imitation, and is used in literary criticism for describing the relationship between form and content; between what is said and how it is said.

Outside the realms of literature, modern linguistics has tended to downplay such a relationship: a central place is accorded to Saussure's dictum that the linguistic sign is arbitrary, so that there is no relationship between the words *galaxy*, *banana* and *love* and the things – the *signifiés* – to which these *signifiants* refer. There are exceptions, such as onomatopoeic words, but these are held to show the power of the general rule. Syntax is clearly less arbitrary (in this sense) than lexis, and some discoursal and pragmatic features even less so, but the basic position remains tenable.

Is the language of poetry less arbitrary, and more mimetic, than other kinds? Are mimetic elements present in only a few poems, or most, or all? Are they on the level of phonology, and/or syntax, and/or something else, and can this be more narrowly defined? How accessible are they to learners at different levels, and with first languages that are close to the target language (such as Germans learning English) or distant (Scots learning Japanese)?

We present the above as questions because we do not have many answers! We believe mimesis is potentially important, otherwise we would not have mentioned it, but it is certainly less universally important, for practical pedagogy, than paraphrasable meaning, regularity, deviance and polysemy, and to insist that every class spend substantial time on mimesis with every poem is to risk demotivation and barrel scraping. The opportunity to find mimesis should always be offered, but zero answers should sometimes be acceptable.

With this caveat, let us look at some of the types of mimesis which learners might (be guided to) find. We suggested above that it is generally unprofitable to look for meaning in individual sounds. On the other hand, it is undeniable that semantic effects can be found in more complex phonological features, including rhythmic patterns and consonant clusters (consonants occurring together, without vowels between them). This was known to classical Greek and Roman writers, and to Pope in this extract from his *Essay on Criticism* (1711):

> True Ease in Writing comes from Art, not Chance,
> As those move easiest who have learn'd to dance.
> 'Tis not enough no Harshness gives Offence,
> The Sound must seem an Eccho to the Sense
> Soft is the Strain when Zephyr gently blows,
> And the smooth Stream in smoother Number flows;
> But when loud Surges lash the sounding Shore.
> The hoarse, rough Verse sho'd like the Torrent roar.
> When Ajax strives, some Rock's vast Weight to throw,
> The Line too labours, and the Words move slow:
> Not so, when swift Camilla scours the Plain,
> Flies o'er th'unbending Corn, and skims along the Main.

The effects of softness, loudness, slowness and swiftness which Pope's lines imitate are not mainly the result of individual phonemes, but are effects of rhythm and metre and the presence or absence of consonant clusters (more than one consonant together without a vowel between). Many similar examples can be found, and all seem to show, like the Sandburg and Verlaine examples earlier, that the 'meaning' of sounds, if discoverable at all, is a matter of cumulative effect, and of interaction between phonology and lexical meaning. If learners feel that the sounds of a poem are affecting their interpretation and response, they should be guided to explore this further mainly by looking for such suprasegmental effects and interactions, rather than by counting the frequency of phoneme types.

Mimesis is usually (mainly) a connection between the semantic and phonological levels, but it can sometimes, additionally or instead, be between the semantic and some other level. The simplest type is perhaps a poem with a non-standard typography/layout which either directly pictures, or more subtly imitates, what is being described. Can you guess the title of the following poem, by a group of Swiss–German schoolchildren (in Reber 1986)?

```
P        P        P        P        P        P        P        P        P
  pta      pta      pta      pta      pta      pta      pta      pta    pta
   tliptliptlip    tliptliptlip    tliptliptlip    tliptliptlip    tliptliptlip
    bliblob      bliblob      bliblob      bliblob      bliblob      bliblob
     pittapitt      pittapitt      pittapitt      pittapitt      pittapitt
      betebetebetebete      betebetebetebete      betebetebetebete
       drimpollillins      drimpollillins      drimpollillins
        plimniblemni plimniblemni plimniblemni plimniblemni
         lepplutopp  lepplutopp  lepplutopp  lepplutopp
          duk   duk   duk   duk   duk   duk
           perlidroms     perlidroms     perlidroms
            tilapitatu      tilapitatu      tilapitatu
             kudabulut kudabulut kudabulut
              ipdes  ipdes  ipdes  ipdes
               pellek  pellek  pellek
                sploat  sploat  sploat
                 sipsipwusch
```

(The answer is in Appendix 2).

Widdowson (1975, 1992) has provided several examples of the relationship between syntax and meaning/effect which are very persuasive and which our own classes, with suitable Socratic questioning, have sometimes replicated and even expanded. An especially good example is the last eight lines of Larkin's poem, 'Mr. Bleaney' (in Lucie-Smith 1970). The poem ends as follows:

> But if he stood and watched the frigid wind
> Tousling the clouds, lay on the fusty bed
> Telling himself that this was home, and grinned,
> And shivered, without shaking off the dread
>
> That how we live measures our own nature,
> And at his age having no more to show
> Than one hired box should make him pretty sure
> He warranted no better, I don't know.

Students can show how the tortuous syntax mirrors the thought processes of Mr Bleaney's unhappy successor as lodger, and they may also find meaning in the non-standard word order and the possible syntactic ambiguity of the if-clause, which may be adverbial or nominal.

## 4.7   INTERSUBJECTIVITY AND PERSONAL RESPONSE WITHIN A LINGUISTIC APPROACH TO POETRY

For most of this chapter, we have been describing an approach which attempts to be relatively objective, perhaps even 'scientific'. We have not, however, dealt with the French student's objection to such objectivity (section 4.1), nor have we made it clear how far linguistic analysis is an alternative to encouraging subjective reactions, and how far the two should be complementary. These are fundamental tensions within all poetry study, and we have no definite solutions and answers, but we now offer a few practical suggestions.

If learners are troubled by the conflict between what is subjective and objective, it may be useful to introduce and to discuss with them the concept of intersubjectivity. This is explained by Cluysenaar (1976) as follows:

> The work of verbal art thus has a structure which is neither objective nor subjective, but intersubjective. The reader who wishes to discuss with others his reaction to a work relies on the fact that his reactions and theirs share certain features. And although some of his, and their, reactions are necessarily restricted or private (hence, of course, the value for individual psychology of word-association tests), these reactions do not form the basis for discussion, since however deeply they may affect the individual, they are not, intersubjectively, 'in' the work. The reactions that do form the basis of discussion are those which the language-system and the culture in which it operates make (or, in the case of an older text, made) a common ground of reference. Sensitivity of reaction varies with individuals, with experience of reading, and with mood and situation. But a solid intersubjective basis remains. If I miss something you can 'show' me that it is there. And that is one of the purposes of most useful literary discussion.

If a learner believes that he or she can be shown, and show others, something new in a poem, this is an important step to successful learning, and it is worth spending a lot of time on learner training to achieve this.

In many foreign language teaching contexts, however, the priorities are rather different from those of Cluysenaar, who was probably thinking mainly of first-language teaching. Intersubjectivity remains important, and belief in the possibility of intersubjectivity even more so, but neither is the last word, and personal reaction beyond the intersubjective retains great importance. Furthermore, although we have mentioned 'personal response' as a separate activity type in section 2.4.5, we do not find that a reason to exclude from this chapter something with the same label, though made different by the different context, but on the contrary feel it essential to include, or at least allow, a 'personal' element within the more stylistic and 'objective' kind of teaching. 'Personal response' is one of the three pillars of the approach, alongside 'paraphrasable meaning' and 'linguistic features'. It is essentially a simple idea, but we find (on teachers' courses) that it can be a source of many misunderstandings, which we shall now try to resolve or pre-empt.

'Personal reaction' can include, but is much wider than, the kinds of reaction mentioned several times in the foregoing sections. For example, the use of rhythm and other devices in a given poem may produce a spoken reaction such as:

> I can feel that I'm on a moving train, very fast, I'm breathless,
> and I can feel the crash coming.

or even, very simply:

> The poem sounds very sad.

Both of these are perfectly valid as personal reactions, but they seem to us very different from responses such as:

> It reminds me of my grandmother.

or even:

> The poem makes me sad.

The first two reactions could be, though need not be, pedagogic answers – what we are supposed to think, what an ideal reader would think and feel. In the last two answers (assuming them to be honest) the speakers have put more of themselves into the response. They might be seen as leading up to, or retrospectively explaining, the most basic kind of personal response:

> I like(d) the poem [a little, a lot, not at all ...].

Modern psychological theory suggests that many kinds of reaction to life's events have a far greater subjective component than generally recognised. Attempts to quantify pain, for example, show that it cannot be put on a simple scale from mild to severe, but has at least two dimensions, one more physical (for example, depending on the strength of electric shock), the other depending on the subject's psychological state. Describing the human variable is not just an optional requirement, but a fundamental part of the equation.

As already mentioned, the three stages are not meant to be rigidly sequential. We are not describing an algorithm, a computer-like set of procedures for teaching, but the setting up (or negotiating) of classroom rules and conventions about what is allowed, expected or encouraged. Specifically, we are suggesting that learners should see it as natural, permissible and even desirable to refer to their personal reactions before, during or after their more objective linguistic comments, though separating the two as clearly as they can.

Extended personal reaction should not be compulsory. It is often claimed that certain learner groups (such as many younger East Asians?) do not like giving personal reactions, and even on the individual level any one of us may feel that we have nothing 'personal' to say about a particular poem: perhaps we are feeling academic and detached today, perhaps at the other extreme our reactions are powerful but too personal to talk about. Any teacher who insists that students always react in detail must be insensitive and clumsy. We believe that teachers are always entitled to ask for a reaction, but should do so in a non-coercive way ('Any particular feelings about this one?'), and should not only accept neutral or non-committal replies, but should from the earliest stages teach students how to make such replies if they so wish ('I think I may need to read it several times', 'I'm not sure how I feel yet').

On the other side of the coin, students must understand that they do not have to be polite or neutral. If their initial reaction is that a poem is bad, or boring, or disgusting, or upsetting, they should feel that it is quite acceptable to say so.

This freedom is rather hard to grant convincingly, and to accept totally, for various obvious and less obvious reasons. It may seem insulting to the poet (more serious in some cultures than in others), and rude to the teacher (or, rarely, classmate) who has 'offered' the poem (a potential problem in any culture). The student may also risk loss of face if his or her negative reaction is later shown to be the result of a poor understanding of the poem, a lack of relevant background knowledge or cultural experience.

We try to meet these problems by laying down some ground rules when we first invite personal reactions from a new class, and repeating those often in the early lessons. The formulation of these varies, but they amount to the following:

1. You don't have to react at all – see above.
2. You don't have to like or 'appreciate' all the poems, and we don't want you to pretend to when you don't. We don't necessarily like all of them ourselves, and they are offered as material for analysis and language practice, not as quasi-religious icons to be worshipped, nor as presents to be grateful for.
3. We accept that anything you say will be an immediate reaction, valid today but perhaps not tomorrow, or even thirty seconds from now. It is quite normal for anyone, even a cultured native speaker, to change their mind about a poem, and we will not think less of you if you do.

In our opinion, very few of those who write about literature fully acknowledge the extent to which some of it is disliked: we nearly all feel that we ought to appreciate everything! (This seems to apply to texts, especially older texts; strangely, the reverse seems to be true of performance, where professional critics and others are possibly too ready to dislike and dismiss.) If we are honest, we have to recognise that large areas of literature are a closed book to many people, even the fairly cultured. John Hegley, whom some consider one of the best living English poets (though, like Betjeman, he claims to write only 'verse'), said in an interview with the *Independent* newspaper (7 December 1996):

> I don't find myself enjoying many of the older poets ... If you don't understand it, it's probably a poem. I've been doing a programme about Seamus Heaney for fifteen-year-olds on BBC schools ... trying to find a way into poetry for them. But I find it very hard myself. I'm thinking of saying to kids, 'Look, it's like those

Magic Eye pictures, you first need to have a special way of looking' – but I haven't found it yet. I know it's there. I know it's not a con. I've got these books of poetry at home … [but] I can't see the pictures. I'm looking forward to the day when I get the trick and I can see them at last.

For a lot of poems, our learners can reasonably hope to 'get the trick' one day. Others may always be locked up to them, and us, and the most we may get is a sort of intellectual appreciation. It is better to face up to this and talk it through than to struggle against half-suppressed guilt feelings.

The fact that one or more students do not like a poem is not normally a reason for immediately abandoning its study. If done regularly, this is time wasting and encourages laziness and querulousness. The exact opposite course, though, that of ploughing on regardless, is even worse, first because students learn little when they have negative attitudes, second because it is insulting and psychologically harmful to ask for people's views and then not to act on them.

There are obviously all kinds of compromises possible, and a teacher can select one of these or, often better, offer the class two or more choices. It may be possible to: 'finish off' a poem quickly, perhaps by looking only at certain aspects; give learners more help, for example a partial translation or ready-made analysis; or not do more poems by the same author, or of the same type.

These three options, though all sometimes justified, may seem to imply failure or defeat. Often, however, it may be possible to respond in terms which are more positive, perhaps in substance, perhaps only in language of presentation:

'Which other authors would you find more appealing?'

'Describe the last poem you enjoyed, and how it was different from this one.'

'Let's go and see a Shakespeare play together – this may help to bring his poems alive.'

# Chapter 5

# Teaching short stories

## 5.1 INTRODUCTION

> The study of narrative appears to be a field in which formalisms are ... more productive than in other areas of literary study.
>
> (Hawthorn 1985: p. xii)

While poetry may appear (at least initially) to be the most problematic of the genres that we are considering in this section of the book, short stories are probably regarded by both teachers and learners as the most straightforward. They have the obvious advantages of being short and self-contained; they generally require less contextualisation than longer fiction, or, in a different way, drama, and they are generally less linguistically complex than poetry. For language teachers on the hunt for texts that generate communicative activities, they are ideal in that they offer opportunities for group discussion, role play and so on. Many teachers will be aware of excellent material already available on using short stories in the classroom (see for example Collie and Slater 1993; Lazar 1993; *ELT Journal* 1990). This, however, tends to be limited to presenting ideas for using individual stories or even just short extracts from stories in the language classroom. What we attempt to do here is to consider how a teacher might set about designing a course of short stories linked in a coherent and principled way so as to provide a framework within which students' skills in reading, comprehending and analysing texts could develop progressively alongside the development of language skills. It should be emphasised that such an approach does not deny the student's right to enjoy and respond to a text in his or her own way and to defend that response – indeed, opportunities can be specifically provided among the activities in any lesson for the discussion of individual response – but learners can become frustrated if their discussion never moves beyond the level of exchanging personal views.

There are various possible concepts which might guide a teacher in developing a short story course: historical period, location (for example, rural, urban), nationality (Canadian, South African), stylistic variety, gender, representativeness of a particular culture, as a way of illustrating varieties of English, and so on. The course described in this chapter has been designed around a narratological framework: each of the stories to be read is both – we hope – of interest in itself and also illustrative of a particular aspect of textual construction. There is no need, however, to regard this as a complete package, intended to be used as it stands. It is much more likely that as a teacher you will find some sections of the chapter that are immediately applicable to your own classroom and others which you may adapt or decide are not relevant to your concerns. The focus will be primarily on the structure of narratives, drawing on two major fields of theoretical work: structuralist narratology on the one hand and sociolinguistic analysis of oral narratives on the other. These two approaches have been chosen at this point because in our experience they can be helpful in meeting a need that both teachers and students often feel for an agreed terminology, a common language, in which to discuss works of fiction. For language-oriented readers in particular (which, after all, presumably includes all teachers and learners of the language) one of the most accessible ways of reading such texts is to develop a fairly eclectic battery of narratological tools, though obviously the degree to which technical language is used depends on the level and purpose of any particular class. These enable communication at the level of a description of what is going on in the text and provide a useful prelude to other approaches. We are not attempting here to provide an account of structuralist narratology for its own sake but a consideration of the ways in which aspects of it may be useful for teaching. The narratology-based ways of reading short stories that are described here are particularly valuable in language teaching in that they require the learner to pay careful attention to specific features of the text: for example, to questions of vocabulary, connotation and register which may be pointers to the existence of different voices in a text; to differences of tense and aspect which may be significant in the presentation of time in a story; or to modality as an indicator of attitude in the narrator.

Most books on narratology are concerned primarily with presenting the concepts, and the texts cited, whether short stories or novels, tend to be used by way of illustration. To some extent this is – inevitably – true of this chapter. It is, however, we believe important when teaching to start with the story itself, encouraging students to explore what they find significant in it, rather than obviously using the story as a peg on which to hang a narratological concept. For example, the questions asked in the chapter indicate the kind of questions one might ask oneself while reading and also ask a group of learners. If in the classroom we employ this more learner-centred exploratory approach, the concepts can be shown to arise from the text and to be illuminative of it. We emphasise this here at the outset because the methodology of presentation in this chapter is much less 'process-oriented' than that of the previous chapter on teaching poetry and also very different from the methodology of the classroom.

There is a great variety of short fiction to choose from, and some useful anthologies are suggested at the end of this chapter. Most of the books that deal with narratology are very eclectic and draw on a very wide variety of texts. This wide-ranging method did not seem to be the most practical in the context of this book so the examples given in this chapter will be drawn in the main from the easily available *Penguin Book of English Short Stories* (Dolley 1967) and the *Second Penguin Book of English Short Stories* (Dolley 1972) though some less canonical stories will also be used. Film, of course, is another medium that uses narrative structures, and in cultures where there are traditions of oral or folk narrative, these may also be used as an additional and interesting resource for comparison.

## 5.2 ARRIVING AT A DEFINITION OF FICTIONAL NARRATIVE

What do we mean when we ask someone to tell a story or say of a work of fiction 'That was a good story'?

A useful exercise with a group of learners is to ask them to tell each other stories; real-life personal narratives, accounts of something that has actually happened to them (if students at beginner or lower-intermediate levels are asked to do this exercise, you would probably allow them to use their own first language). From this experience, they can try to categorise the particular features of organisation which their stories share.

- Do the stories all have a recognisable beginning and end?
- How are these beginnings and endings indicated?
- Are the stories all told chronologically or is the time sequence disrupted in some way?
- Is description included, and if so, of what kind?
- Is the storyteller involved with the story or detached from it – and what are the indicators of attitude?
- How does the storyteller relate to his or her audience?

We can then go on to ask:

- What do we look for in a story (in any medium)?
- What makes for a satisfying story?

The point of doing this kind of exercise is to help learners focus not simply on content – which is easy to do – but on structure.

Taking this exercise a step further, we can look at a selection of short passages to see which meet the criteria that have been established as the requirements for a satisfying narrative. Of the following very short examples, which in your view constitute a story – or part of a story?

A. The king died. Shortly after his death, the queen married his brother. The old king's son killed his uncle.

B. Lavender's blue, dilly, dilly,
   Lavender's green.
   When I am king, dilly, dilly,
   You shall be queen.

C. It was night. He got feverish. Next day by dusk he was really sick. He died.

D. It is a truth universally acknowledged that a single man in possession of a good fortune must be in want of a wife.

E.  A lap-dancer who made thousands of pounds as Britain's most prolific female
    bigamist, was spared from jail yesterday because of an eye injury.

F.  The children meet their grandfather Horned Grebe who helps them across the
    river. Their mother meets Horned Grebe.

*Sources:* (A) Summary of the plot of *Hamlet*; (B) Nursery rhyme; (C) *Frog Legend*
(cited in Koehn 1976: 244); (D) opening sentence of *Pride and Prejudice* by Jane
Austen; (E) Newspaper report *The Scotsman* 27 March 1999; (F) An Obijwe
narrative (cited in Fabb 1997: 195)

As you read each of these, consider whether you would describe it as a narrative or
not. Which of the criteria for narrative that you have already established guide your
decision?

A characteristic that is shared by all six is that they have been organised for us; the
constituent items (the words and sentences) are not random but have been presented
in a particular order. In some cases we may understand them as utterances of one
kind or another; that is to say, they seem to emanate from a more personal source
than simply an unspecified organiser of the text. A voice is speaking, someone is
telling us something – whether what they are telling us is something we would
recognise as a story is another question. Conventionally in literary discourse, this
organising agent or speaker would be termed the narrator. But is this is enough to
establish them all as narratives? What other criteria operate to distinguish between
narrative and non-narrative utterances?

We tentatively suggest that most readers would agree that B and D are not narratives but that A, C, E and F are. So what are the differences between them?

The key difference seems to be that those we accept as narratives present a
succession of events which we as readers are able to interpret as both sequentially
and causally related. Indeed, it seems that readers work quite hard at constructing
narratives, at times making what Barthes (1966: 10) points out is the illogical
assumption that if Y follows X, it has somehow been caused by X. It is possible, for
example, to construct a convincing narrative based on a bank statement! In other
words we assume that a narrative is characterised by both sequentiality and causality
– though there may be genre or cultural differences here: for example, in the
conventions of the magical realist novel, the reader is required to make narrative
connections in a way that would not be required for a classic realist text such as a
novel by Jane Austen. And different cultures may make certain causal connections
that are not operative in others.

If we take a closer look at the examples given, we may see this more clearly. With
A and C, the events do not seem merely to follow one another in time; they seem
to be more profoundly related as cause and effect, even though in C this is not
specifically stated but has to be inferred by the reader. Moreover, they involve particular actors or agents. But what about B, which you have – we are assuming –
agreed is not a narrative? It involves particular agents and contains in lines 3 and 4 a
sequence, thereby implying causality. These, though, are events that are predicted –

that have not yet happened. The inference is that we tend to assume that narrative is concerned with past events. We feel that the narrator must be, so to speak, a step ahead of what is narrated. Even where a narrative is offered in the present tense, as in the final example (F), we assume that it is the conventional narrative present: in other words, it is being told in the present tense but we recognise that the story is dealing with past events. It is not impossible, certainly, to conceive of a story that might be written entirely in the future tense, but if that were the case, we would probably assume that it was a flouting of the normal conventions of narrative for a particular purpose.

D is not a narrative because it does not present an event; it is a generalisation. Such 'universal' statements do not present either the particularity or the temporality that we expect of narrative.

With C, E and F a further question arises, which one might term the 'communicative' status of narratives. E is a narrative in the sense of presenting apparently connected events with implied agents but it specifically claims, by virtue of its context, not to be fictional (although it is of course a constructed version of the events that it describes). With C we have what appears to be a narrative in the terms arrived at above, and the characters and events could be either fictional or factual. F, however, might be difficult to fit into common so-called Western assumptions about the nature of a 'factual' universe and so those who read within that framework will probably assume it is, in some sense, a fictional account – or that the culture from which this 'story' comes has a very different worldview from that of our other examples.

The question implied here concerns the communicative status of the utterance in which the narrative is embedded and its communicative force or implicature (for a detailed discussion of this see Fabb 1997). It illustrates the fact that when we speak of narrative in literary terms we tend to think of it as having its own peculiar communicative function. In other words, the focus here is on the pragmatics of literary narration – the relation between addresser and addressee and the implied contract between speaker/writer and listener/reader. The reader tends to want to know how to approach a text, what expectations to enlist for the reading (cf. the term made familiar by Jauss: the reader's 'horizon of expectations'). It is true, of course, that the relationship between factual and fictional may be an area of both contestation and playfulness between author and reader: canonical narratives of English literature such as *Moll Flanders* and *The Confessions of a Justified Sinner* are presented as 'true' stories; the genres of biography and novel entwine in, for example, Peter Ackroyd's *Chatterton*. In television and film particularly, the mixed genre of faction, neither pure documentary nor pure fiction but a blend of both, is popular and much debated. However, it may be that this is perceived as a type of reportage, fact presented with fictional trappings, but read basically as fact. Indeed, we would suggest that the pleasure of such viewing or reading arises in part from the conscious awareness of the interplay of different genres. This, again, is worth pursuing as a topic for discussion with learners. There may, for example, be cultural differences in the status of different types of narrative.

Finally, we turn to what might be termed the shape of the story. If we compare A, C and F we see a difference between them: we feel the stories in A and C, though rudimentary, are in some sense complete, something significant has happened – in both cases someone has died – which brings this story or this part of a larger story to a point of completion. We have a sense of closure and thereby a sense of the shape of the story. If we compare this with F, we find that here we have two sentences which seem to be connected but do not by themselves tell a story. They give part of a story, they do not exhibit the shape of a complete narrative.

Thus for a set of sentences to be recognised as a narrative, the following features seem to be required (though with the caveat that many, particularly post-modern, stories deliberately disrupt our conventional expectations of narrative):

- A narrator, the one who tells or presents or orders the story (and who may exist at any point on a continuum between explicit personal involvement and almost total impersonality);
- Agency, that is, there are participants or characters of some kind within the story;
- A set of two or more (past) events that are causally and sequentially related (though this does not indicate that the presentation of events in the narrative must be chronologically ordered);
- A 'shape' (a recognisable beginning and end).

And for fictional narratives there is a further requirement, namely that the communicative status of the utterance is culturally recognised as fiction (even in cases where there is a degree of intertwining of fiction with fact) and that the reader orientates himself or herself accordingly.

*To what extent do these features coincide with the list of characteristics that you found emerging from the storytelling exercise suggested at the beginning of this section?*

In the following sections we consider these four shared features of narratives in more detail.

## 5.3 NARRATION AND POINT OF VIEW: THE NARRATOR AND THE FOCALISER. WHO TELLS? AND WHO SEES?

*Stories:* Kingsley Amis, 'Interesting Things'; James Joyce, 'Clay'.

We start with the first item in our brief list of the features of narrative, the narrative voice. The reason for making this our first concern rather than any of the other possibilities is that the distinction between narrator and focaliser seems to be a particularly illuminating and practical instrument for making visible the various strands in narratives and the relationship between the narrator and the characters. Focalisation is a concept that is fundamental to narratological approaches and has been explored in considerable detail by a large number of critics. You may find it used (for example by Rimmon-Kenan and Toolan) to refer to both narrative (or external) and character (or internal) focalisation. In many ways it is similar to the notion of point of view, which could also be taken to refer to both narrator and character in terms of the angle from which they see the event and characters of the fictional world. Here, however, we shall keep the terms narrator and focaliser distinct from each other, that is, we shall be using the term focaliser to refer to the character (or characters) within the fictional world and focalisation to mean the character's way of seeing that world, their perception of it through both their physical senses and their emotional, cognitive and ideological responses.

Our first examples are from stories in which the positions of the narrator and the characters are quite separate, while in the next section we shall consider an example where the narrator is also a character in the story ('You Should Have Seen the Mess' by Muriel Spark). It should perhaps also be made clear here that when we talk about the narrator, we do not equate that voice in the story with the real-life author of the text: for example, in the extract below the narrator is not regarded as the real person Kingsley Amis but as a textual construct.

We have seen that one of the constituting features of narrative is the voice of the narrator, the one who tells the story. But often this narrative voice is subtly modified by, as it were, another centre of consciousness, who is a character in the story, one who sees (or hears or feels or thinks) – in other words, the focaliser of the experience. For example, as you read the opening paragraph of Kingsley Amis' story 'Interesting Things', you will recognise the voice of the narrator, the person who is telling the story. Can you also at times hear a second voice, belonging to the character Gloria?

> 1. Gloria Davies crossed the road towards the Odeon on legs that weaved a little, as if she was tipsy or rickety. 2. She wasn't either really; it was just the high-heeled shoes, worn for the first time specially for today. 3. The new hoop ear-rings swayed from her lobes, hitting her rhythmically on the jaws as she walked. 4. No. 5. They were wrong. 6. They had looked fine in her bedroom mirror, but they were wrong somehow. 7. She whipped them off and stuffed them into her hand-bag. 8. Perhaps there'd be a chance to try them again later, when it was evening. 9. They might easily make all the difference then.
>
> (*The Second Penguin Book of English Short Stories* (ed. Dolley): 308)

Would you agree that some of this is Gloria's thoughts and is expressed in her language? For example, sentences 4 (the single word 'No'), 5 and 6 sound like Gloria talking to herself, while sentences 3 and 7 do not seem to be Gloria, but the voice of the narrator, the one who tells the story. What happens in the last two sentences? Are these couched in the voice of the narrator or of Gloria? One test is to try to turn the possible Gloria-utterances into direct speech or thought; to try putting 'she thought' in front of them. For example: she thought 'Perhaps there'd be a chance to try them out again later, when it was evening. They might easily make all the difference then.'

Does this work?

For the most part, we probably agree that it does, though there is a slight problem with the tense of 'there'd' and 'was', which are those we would expect in indirect rather than direct speech or thought. (These differences will be dealt with in more detail in the section below on speech and thought presentation.)

So what is it in the language of those sentences that leads the reader to think that Gloria is the source of these utterances rather than the narrator? It may be that the first indicator is a slight shift towards informality: 'there'd be a chance', 'all the difference', which seem to indicate speech or thought rather than more formal written narration. And there is the modality of 'perhaps', indicating the character's attitude to a possible future event.

If we go back to sentences 1 and 2, would you describe these as narrator or character or a mixture of both voices? Sentence 1 as far as the comma seems to be the narrator describing Gloria; sentence 2 contains indicators of Gloria's attitude towards what is happening (the modals 'really', 'just' and 'specially'), and also a time indicator ('today') which seems to belong to the temporal perception of the character rather than to the point of view of the narrator. And what about 'tipsy or rickety': does that sound like the narrator or like Gloria? There could be disagreement about the ownership of that last phrase, with reasonable arguments on both sides. It is a good example of the kind of interweaving of both points of view, of narrative voice and character focalisation, that is often found in both fictional texts and in reportage.

*Can you describe the effects that this intermingling of narrator's and focaliser's voices produces?*

Here is another example, this time from 'Clay', one of the stories in Joyce's *Dubliners* (1961). Maria works in a laundry; she is insignificant in appearance and poor but apparently content with her lot:

> 1. She went into her little bedroom and, remembering that the next morning was a mass morning, changed the hand of the alarm from seven to six. 2. Then she took off her working skirt and her house-boots and laid her best skirt out on the bed and her tiny dress-boots beside the foot of the bed. 3. She changed her blouse too and, as she stood before the mirror, she thought of how she used to dress for mass on Sunday morning when she was a young girl; and she looked with quaint affection at the diminutive body which she had so often adorned. 4. In spite of its years she found it a nice tidy little body.
>
> (*Dubliners*: 101)

Here again we are aware of the different voices of the narrator and the focaliser, for instance in sentences 3 and 4, 'diminutive', a Latin-derived word seems to belong to the sophisticated discourse of the narrator, while 'nice tidy little body' seems to echo Maria's way of speaking.

This disjunction between the narrative and the focalising voices is often a source of irony, particularly when the focaliser is limited in some way: when it is a child, perhaps, or a simple person like Maria; for example, we might feel that Maria's view of herself as a 'nice tidy little body' is not borne out by the apparently more objective view of the narrator that she is abnormally small. By nineteenth-century writers such as Jane Austen or Dickens, this use of the character's voice within the narration is often employed in a way that indicates that some kind of moral judgement is being made on a character. We shall consider it in more detail when we look at the presentation of speech and thought and in particular at free indirect discourse.

One way of exploring the effect of this use of focalisation in narrative is by rewriting a passage like those quoted above entirely in the voice of the narrator and considering the differences that this produces.

### 5.3.1  Types of narrator: first and third person narrators

*Stories:* Muriel Spark, 'You Should Have Seen the Mess'; James Joyce, 'Araby'.

Both the stories quoted in the previous section are told by a third person narrator (so-called because references to characters within the fictional world use the third person pronouns), who in both these cases stands outside the story. However, there is another kind of narrative voice. Muriel Spark's 'You Should Have Seen the Mess' begins like this:

> I am now more than glad that I did not pass into the grammar school five years ago, although it was a disappointment at the time.
>
> (*The Second Penguin Book of English Short Stories* (ed. Dolley): 301)

Here we have another common type of narration, the first person narrator, where the narrator is also a character within the story. Where, then is the focaliser in a first-person narration? Here is a later passage from the same story:

> I can honestly say that Willy's place was the most unhygienic place I have seen in my life. He said I had an unusual type of beauty, which he must capture. This was when we came back to his place from the restaurant. The light was very dim but I could see the bed had not been made and the sheets were far from clean.
>
> (ibid: 306)

Clearly what we have here are the perceptions of the 'I' narrator, so we may conclude that in first-person narratives, the narrator and focaliser are the same person.

There may, however, be first-person narrations where there is a distinction between the narrating and the focalising centres of consciousness. For example, a retrospective first-person narrative may have an adult voice (the narrator) who tells the story about the experiences of his much younger self (the focaliser). Charles Dickens' *Great Expectations* is often quoted as an example of this: in the novel, the adult Pip looks back on his childhood and youth in a way that includes both compassion for and judgement of his younger self. The 'I' is at times a detached narrator who stands outside the story and at times the focalising narrator who is a character inside the story. 'Araby', one of the early stories in James Joyce's *Dubliners*, is an interesting example of this retrospective narration, and the clash between the two points of view, the sense that the adult is looking back on and judging his younger self, produces a sense of quite painful irony. The story ends like this:

1. I lingered before her stall, though I knew my stay was useless, to make my

interest in her wares seem the more real. 2. Then I turned away slowly and walked down the middle of the bazaar. 3. I allowed two pennies to fall against the sixpence in my pocket. 4. I heard a voice call from one end of the gallery that the light was out. 5. The upper part of the hall was now completely dark. 6. Gazing up into the darkness I saw myself as a creature driven and derided by vanity; and my eyes burned with anguish and anger.

(Dubliners: 35)

How do you read that final sentence? Does it simply describe the young boy's feelings or are the boy's feelings being interpreted by the adult narrator? And what is it in the language that leads us to our conclusions?

*What are the effects on us as the addressees of a first-person narrative?*
*Do we feel ourselves to be more directly addressed than by a third-person narrator?*
*What kinds of relationship may be established by this mode of narration?*
*Do you trust the narrator?*
*Is he/she reliable? And if not, why not?*
*Is it something in the narrator's situation that limits her/him? Or is it that you distrust her/his judgement?*

'I'-narrators are by no means always reliable, and as readers we discover this from various signals in the text. It may be a matter of information (perhaps we have a child telling the story so there are gaps which we have to fill in ourselves); we may discover at the end of the story that we have been tricked (as occasionally happens in crime novels where the narrator turns out to have been the murderer) and we have to revise our view of characters and events; or we may be aware while we are reading of stylistic pointers in the text indicating that the narrator's point of view and judgements may be problematic. This may become clearer if we consider again Muriel Spark's 'You Should Have Seen the Mess'. The first two paragraphs of the story read like this:

> I am now more than glad that I did not pass into the grammar school five years ago, although it was a disappointment at the time. I was always good at English, but not so good at the other subjects!!
>
> I am glad that I went to the secondary modern school, because it was only constructed the year before. Therefore, it was much more hygienic than the grammar school. The secondary modern was light and airy, and the walls were painted with a bright, washable gloss.

(The Second Penguin Book of English Short Stories: 301)

As we read, we make inferences from the text and rapidly build up a mental image of the narrator. We (probably unconsciously) ask ourselves questions such as: what sort of person is this? What age is she? Is she sophisticated or naïve? What is her attitude to education? What are the things she really cares about? And as a result of this process, we may go on to ask: do I trust her judgements?

We are likely to infer that she is young, either still at school or recently left and that she is much concerned with cleanliness. She also gives the impression, even in these two short paragraphs, of being unsophisticated, not only by what she says but by how she says it, by her style; for example, her use of double exclamation marks. She seems to have learned about the importance of cohesion in her school English classes without learning to be particularly skilful in its deployment in her writing (note the careful but clumsy use of 'therefore' in sentence 4). Her choice of vocabulary is quite striking: why does she say 'constructed' and 'hygienic' instead of 'built' and 'clean'? What about the choice of register in 'bright, washable gloss'? The style is giving us pointers about the narrator and even at this stage raising questions in our minds about her lack of sophistication and the limits of her experience, which may affect her capacity for making reliable judgements.

The story ends like this:

> One night, when I went home, I was upset as usual, after Willy's place. Mum and Dad had gone to bed, and I looked round our kitchen which is done in primrose and white. Then I went into the living room, where Dad has done one wall in a patterned paper, deep rose and white, and the other walls pale rose, with white woodwork. The suite is new, and Mum keeps everything beautiful. So it came to me, all of a sudden, what a fool I was, going with Willy. I agree to equality, but as to me marrying Willy, as I said to Mavis, when I recall his place, and the good carpet gone greasy, not to mention the paint oozing out of the tubes, I think it would break my heart to sink so low.

(ibid: 307)

Do you think she has changed at all?

It could be that she has been through an experience in her relationship with Willy that has unsettled her neat and ordered view of the world and which might have changed her had she allowed it to do so. The syntactic complexity of that long last sentence is uncharacteristic of her style and in marked contrast to the preceding sentences of the paragraph. It seems to reflect her sense of being pulled in different directions, a reading which is further emphasised by the contrast of the descriptive words *white, new, beautiful* with *greasy* and *oozing*.

And if you compare this paragraph with the beginning of the story quoted earlier, has your judgement of her reliability as a narrator altered at all?

### 5.3.2  The narrator and the narrative level

*Stories:* Graham Greene, 'The Destructors'; D. H. Lawrence, 'The Horse Dealer's Daughter'; Ernest Hemingway, 'The Killers'.

Narrators may be involved in the story they are telling at a variety of levels. They may stand quite outside the story they are telling, i.e. they are extradiegetic narrators (the terminology used to describe the various types of narrators develops from the Greek term diegesis, meaning story). You can probably think of many examples of such narratives: the James Bond novels, the classic realist novels of nineteenth-century

British literature, the novels of Tolstoy. The majority of the short stories in the Penguin collection are of this type.

On the other hand, we may find examples of the intradiegetic narrator, where there are two levels of narrative: an inner story told by a character who figures in the outer or framing story. The inner story is told by the intradiegetic narrator and the outer or framing narrative by the extradiegetic narrator. Conrad uses this formula in the novels where the character Marlow is a narrator; *Heart of Darkness* is a very clear example. Though less often found in short stories, Chekhov's story 'Gooseberries' contains an extended narrative told by one of the characters about his brother.

*What do you think might be the effects of this kind of framing? What kind of comment might it offer on the inner story?*
*Does it distance the reader?*
*What difference might it make if it were removed and the narrative made to function at a single level?*

The second pair of terms relates to the degree of the narrator's involvement in the story. A narrator who does not take part in the story is known as heterodiegetic and one who does take part is homodiegetic. The conventional 'omniscient narrator' is both extra- and heterodiegetic, that is, he remains outside the story. What kind of narrator do we have in Graham Greene's story 'The Destructors' (*Second Penguin Book of English Short Stories*: 254–70)? The story begins with this paragraph:

> It was on the eve of the August Bank Holiday that the latest recruit became the leader of the Wormsley Common Gang. No one was surprised except Mike, but Mike at the age of nine was surprised by everything. 'If you don't shut your mouth,' somebody once said to him, 'you'll get a frog down it.'
>
> (ibid: 254)

How would you (from admittedly brief acquaintance) describe this narrator? Is he inside or outside the story he is telling? What kind of knowledge does he have of his characters? How do you as a reader relate to this narrator – with trust or with suspicion? We can see that he has inside knowledge about Mike: he knows Mike is easily surprised and he can tell us what 'somebody' once said to him (p. 254).

In a later paragraph we read:

> Old Misery – whose real name was Thomas – had once been a builder and decorator. He lived alone in the crippled house, doing for himself: once a week you could see him coming back across the common with bread and vegetables, and once as the boys played in the car-park he put his head over the smashed wall of his garden and looked at them.
>
> (ibid: 255)

Here the narrator shows background knowledge of his characters (Old Misery's real name and his habits), which seem to show that he has a kind of overview of the events and people of the story. The statements are declaratory, they seem to be giving us facts about the characters from an authoritative source. These features of authority and inside knowledge are characteristic of the so-called omniscient narrator.

A homodiegetic narrator may tell his own story in the first person (as in *Great Expectations* or 'Araby'), or may be a subsidiary character telling a story about other people in which he is only slightly involved or involved only as a spectator. In David Dabydeen's *The Counting House*, a novel about bonded labour in Guyana during the nineteenth century, the first two sections are narrated in the third person while the third section is told in the first person by Miriam, a character who has already appeared in the novel and is now telling her own story. Or, in a perhaps better known example, Stevenson in the long short story *Dr Jekyll and Mr Hyde* presents a narrative in which we have for most of the time a third-person narrator but with inserted homodiegetic narratives by Dr Lanyon and Jekyll himself. So why are these different forms used? What is their effect? (If you are not familiar with these particular examples, think of novels or short stories that you do know where this technique is employed.)

One of the concerns of Dabydeen's novel is to give a voice to those whose voices have not been heard in the official narratives, the coolies and ex-slaves on the Guyanan plantations, and so the formal act of employing Miriam's first-person voice seems to become a significant political act within the compass of the novel. Stevenson, on the other hand, tells a story that deals with the themes of secrecy, repression and different forms of enclosure, and the actual forms of stories told within stories in the narrative imitate or echo some of these central themes.

Narrators vary in terms of their relation to their narrative; they also vary in their degree of perceptibility in the story. How perceptible do you find the voice of the narrator in these examples?

1. He turned uneasily aside, the retreating steps of the horses echoing in his ears. Then with foolish restlessness, he reached for the scraps and threw them to the terrier that lay against the fender. He watched the dog swallow them, and waited till the creature looked into his eyes. Then a faint grin came on his face, and in a high, foolish voice he said:
   'You won't get much more bacon, shall you, you little b – ?'
   (D. H. Lawrence, 'The Horse Dealer's Daughter'
   (*The Second Penguin Book of English Short Stories* (ed. Dolley)): 151)

2. 'I'll have a roast pork tenderloin with apple sauce and mashed potatoes', the first man said.
   'It isn't ready yet.'
   'What the hell do you put it on the card for?'
   'That's the dinner', George explained. 'You can get that at six o'clock.'
   George looked at the clock on the wall behind the counter.
   'The clock says twenty minutes past five', the second man said.
   'It's twenty minutes fast.'
   (Ernest Hemingway, *The Killers* 1965: 57. Originally published 1928)

What differences did you find between these two in the relation of the narrator to the narration? How would you characterise the differences? What is the tone of each example? A pair of terms that is often used is 'overt' and 'covert'. Is one of these examples overt and one covert?

The first passage includes several value-laden words that refer to the character's feelings ('uneasily', 'restlessness', 'foolish'), indicating that the narrator seems to be in possession of privileged inside knowledge of his character, which he then shares with the reader. In the second passage the narrator appears to remain outside the characters' thoughts, merely describing what could be seen by any observer rather than interpreting it for the reader. The first could perhaps be described as involved with the narration (more visible, more overt) and the second as detached from it (less visible, more covert). As a reader, do you find that you respond differently to the narration in each example? Returning to the story we considered earlier, 'The Destructors', where, from the evidence of the paragraphs quoted, would you place the narrator on the overt–covert continuum, and for what reasons?

### 5.3.3 The presentation of speech and thought

We looked earlier at the relation between the narrator and the focaliser. In this section we will look at this issue in more detail as it appears in the presentation of the voices of narrator and characters: whether they are quite separate from one another or intertwined to varying degrees.

A character's words may be presented in various ways:

1. 'I'll have a roast pork tenderloin with apple sauce and mashed potatoes', the first man said.
2. The first man said that he would have a roast pork tenderloin with apple sauce and mashed potatoes.
3. The first man gave his order.

You will recognise the first two as examples of direct and indirect (or reported) speech. But how do we describe the third example? We would probably agree that it is a kind of reported speech in that the narrator here is reporting that the first man said something and giving us the gist of what was said. This is generally termed a narrative report of speech act (NRSA) (Leech and Short: 1981, Rimmon-Kenan: 1983, Short: 1996).

*If we think in terms of control exercised by the narrator over the character, which of the three would you say is the most controlled and which is the least?*

There is another way of presenting the character's speech which is known as free indirect speech (FIS). Here is a short extract from James Joyce's 'The Dead' describing the supper party conversation:

Mr Bartell D'Arcy, the tenor, a dark-complexioned young man with a smart moustache, praised very highly the leading contralto of the company, but Miss Furlong thought she had a rather vulgar style of production.

(Dubliners: 198)

The first part of the sentence gives us the narrator's summing up of Mr D'Arcy's speech but the second seems to be an echo of Miss Furlong's actual words, an extract, if not the whole of what she said. A direct speech version would have read:

I think she has a rather vulgar style of production.

And an indirect speech version:

Miss Furlong said that she thought that she had a rather vulgar style of production.

It is often argued that the effect of this kind of interweaving of the voices of the characters with that of the narrator is to intensify the ironic detachment of the narrator from those he is describing. Certainly it is a technique that Joyce uses a great deal in *Dubliners*.

The next example is the extract from 'Clay' that we considered earlier in the section on focalisation. This gives us an example not of what the character says, but of what she thinks. Here we have the complete paragraph:

1. But wasn't Maria glad when the women had finished their tea and the cook and the dummy had begun to clear away the tea-things! 2. She went into her little bedroom and, remembering that the next morning was a mass morning, changed the hand of the alarm from seven to six. 3. Then she took off her working skirt and her house-boots and laid her best skirt out on the bed and her tiny dress-boots beside the foot of the bed. 4. She changed her blouse too and, as she stood before the mirror, she thought of how she used to dress for mass on Sunday morning when she was a young girl; and she looked with quaint affection at the diminutive body which she had so often adorned. 5. In spite of its years she found it a nice tidy little body.

Here we look more closely at the relation between narrator's and focaliser's voices. Overall we would probably agree that the narrator is, so to speak, in charge but that there is quite a lot that sounds like Maria's own thoughts or words. In sentence 4, Maria's thoughts are introduced by an appropriate verb: 'she thought of how'. Sentence 1, however, is more problematic. Suppose the sentence read:

Maria was glad when the women had finished their tea and the cook and the dummy had begun to clear away the tea-things.

All that has happened is that the verb is no longer inverted and the exclamation mark has been removed. But what is the effect of these small changes? Instead of echoing the forms of Maria's thought, the sentence has returned entirely to the control of the narrator. We do not hear Maria's characteristic tones to the same degree, we do not feel as if we were experiencing the world through her point of view.

This kind of interweaving of the voices of narrator and character is known as free indirect thought (or FIT). Where, in terms of narrator control, would you place free indirect speech/thought in relation to direct speech and the forms of indirect (or reported) speech that were considered earlier? The classic view of speech presentation (see for example Short 1996 pp. 292–3) is that direct speech presents the clearest division of responsibility between narrator and character: we know exactly which set of words belongs to which voice as they are clearly separated from each other, traditionally by the use of quotation marks. There is little apparent influence of narrator's voice over the character's. However, in indirect speech the character's words have in some way been taken into the narrator's voice; they are mediated by the narrator. In free indirect speech there is an interweaving of the two voices: at certain times the narrator may be dominant, at other times the character. It seems less completely controlled by the narrator than the forms of indirect speech, but neither does it provide the character with the freedom offered by direct speech.

You will find an example of different kinds of speech and thought presentation in the exercises in Appendix 1.

## 5.4 CHARACTER

In this section we shall consider two ways of looking at participants, or what are traditionally referred to as characters, in narratives. The first is a formalist or structuralist approach which is concerned primarily with what the characters do, with characters as agents. It focuses on the recurring functions that are performed by characters in a variety of different narratives. The second emphasises a more humanist or mimetic view of character, and focuses on textual features that distinguish characters from each other both within a single narrative and between different narratives.

### 5.4.1 Characters as functions of narrative

Many narratives can be seen to be built from a set of common components – a bit like building blocks that can be assembled to make different structures. If we think of particular genres of narrative (thrillers, Westerns, romances of the Mills and Boon variety) we recognise recurring types of character who can be defined as functions in the story as well as in some cases being quite individually developed characters. (The term function is taken from Vladimir Propp, who in the 1920s carried out a pioneering and extremely influential structuralist analysis of Russian folktales.) Take the romance, for instance: what are the typical characters of this genre? There are, of course, the heroine and the hero, but there is generally also a villain of some sort and a confidante or helper of the heroine. Sometimes, too, there is a figure whom Propp terms the 'donor', who gives a gift of some kind (for example, secret information) to the hero or heroine. Can you carry out a similar analysis of the functions in the genre of the detective novel? Or for a film such as *Star Wars*? It's important to remember that in this sort of analysis the functions are not gender-specific (for example, a villain may be male or female), nor indeed are they necessarily confined to an individual; the heroine requiring rescue may be a group of people or a whole nation; the villain may be an invading army of aliens. Moreover, a particular character may perform more than one function: a commonly cited example is that of Magwitch the convict in *Great Expectations*, whose initial appearance is in the role of villain, but who later functions as the donor of wealth to the hero, Pip. You might also consider the functions of Angela, the daughter of Lord Moping in the story by Evelyn Waugh quoted below. She sets out on a mission to obtain for Mr Loveday a short holiday from the asylum in which he is confined and thereby becomes responsible for the death of a young woman whom he murders.

Looking at narratives in this way offers interesting possibilities of cross-comparisons, both within the same genre and across genres: stories, or stories and films, oral and written narratives. It also suggests ways of analysing the structure of newspaper or television reports of news stories.

### 5.4.2 Characters as textual constructs: the presentation of their particularity

We return here in some respects to our earlier concern with the relationship between narrator and character. How much knowledge does a particular narrator show of the characters in a story? By what means are characters presented in stories? Some possibilities are: direct speech; description of physical appearance; insight into thought or feelings; past history; by various forms of analogy such as the use of proper names. Other methods can be added and you could compile your own list.

Here are some examples of different ways of characterisation. Can you describe how the characterisation is presented in each (there may, of course, be some overlap between the examples)?

1. As he passed in the way of the cheval-glass he caught sight of himself in full length, his broad, well-filled shirt-front, the face whose expression always puzzled him when he saw it in a mirror, and his glimmering gilt-rimmed eye-glasses.

   (Joyce, 'The Dead' *Dubliners*: 218)

2. For Fanny was beautiful: tall, erect, finely coloured, with her delicately arched nose, her rich brown hair, her large lustrous grey eyes.
   (Lawrence, 'Fanny and Annie' *The Penguin Book of English Short Stories*: 211)

3. Despite all the pallor and grubbiness, however, she looked so young and delicious to Maurice – especially so much younger than he had expected, no older perhaps than he was – that he was unable to speak and he felt the giddiness and trembling of the legs which lust always brought to his repressed body. Her eyes seemed to him extraordinarily sensual under their drowsing, half-closed, red lids; her white cheeks were nevertheless plump about their high pommets and her heavy lips were half-opened in a Greuze-like pout. She

looked altogether like some eighteenth-century print of a young dying harlot
– ostensibly a morality, in fact a bait for prurient eyes.

(Wilson, 'After the Show' *The Second Penguin*
*Book of English Short Stories*: 282)

4. He kept his studio as neat as a pin. Everything was arranged to form a pattern,
a little 'still life' as it were – the saucepans with their lids on the wall behind
the gas stove, the bowl of eggs, milk jug and teapot on the shelf, the books and
the lamp with the crinkly paper shade on the table. An Indian curtain that had
a fringe of red leopards marching round it covered his bed by day, and on the
wall beside his bed on a level with your eyes when you were lying down there
was a small neatly printed notice: GET UP AT ONCE.

(Mansfield, 'Feuille d'Album' *The Second Penguin*
*Book of English Short Stories*:170)

5. 'Now then, what the Turk do it matter to us about Farmer Lodge's age, or
Farmer Lodge's new mis'ess? I shall have to pay him nine pound a year for the
rent of every one of these milchers, whatever his age or hers. Get on with your
work, or 'twill be dark afore we have done. The evening is pinking in a'ready.'

(Hardy, 'The Withered Arm' *The Penguin*
*Book of English Short Stories*: 26)

6. Lord Moping habitually threatened suicide on the occasion of the garden
party; that year he had been found black in the face, hanging by his braces in
the orangery; some neighbours, who were sheltering there from the rain, set
him on his feet again, and before dinner a van had called for him.

(Waugh, 'Mr Loveday's Little Outing' *The Penguin*
*Book of English Short Stories*: 293)

The first example, we suggest, uses physical appearance (including clothing and what
might be termed 'props' – the gilt-rimmed glasses) to indicate character. It also says
something about Gabriel's own feelings about himself, perhaps suggesting that there
is an insecurity there, a dichotomy between how he feels and how he appears. The
narrator is able to see inside the character and tell us what he is thinking and feeling.

In the second, we have a description of a young woman. It seems unproblematic
in the sense that the narrator seems to assume that the reader shares the categories of
beauty that the narrator suggests. There is a kind of confidence and authority in the
use of terms of description: they are employed without qualification or hedging.
Compare this with the third example, which shows the response of one character to
another, and so manages to tell the reader something about both. Maurice sees the
girl as desirable despite (partly because of?) her grubbiness. We realise, too, that the
girl is in some way presenting herself to his gaze – and so we also make our inferences
about her. The cultural references (to Greuze and eighteenth-century art in general)
are also part of the presentation of the characters, for Maurice (as we learn earlier in
the story) is a young man consciously and snobbishly aware of his education in high
culture.

The fourth example (from a story specifically concerned with the ways in which people can misread character) shows how environment can be shown to be an indicator of character. The young artist of Mansfield's story can only be understood as a character in the privacy of his own room, and that environment is consonant with his idea of himself as an artist – it provides a 'still life' for him.

In the fifth we see how direct speech can indicate character. What do we learn about the speaker? He speaks a rural dialect (the fact that it is rural rather than urban is indicated by the subject matter); he also speaks with authority as the employer of the workers he is addressing, using the imperative without any mitigating forms of politeness.

In the last example, there is a comic analogy between the name of the character and his situation: he is moping and he attempts suicide. Analogy of this sort seems to be a feature of comic narrative in particular, or comic portions of longer narratives. It is often found in novels by Dickens (Mr Gradgrind in *Hard Times*, whose name refers, even onomatopoeically, to his views on education) or by Fielding (for example, Mrs Slipslop in *Tom Jones*, who is slipshod and sloppy in both appearance and morals).

These examples do not complete the typology of characterisation but they give some indication of its scope and variety and may encourage you to find more instances as you read.

## 5.5 THE ORDERING OF NARRATIVES

In our consideration of the common features of narratives at the beginning of this chapter, the third and fourth concerned the relation of events to each other in terms of sequence and causality and the overall shape of the narrative, in particular beginnings and endings. In this section we shall be considering two rather different perspectives on these questions of narrative ordering: the first is based on work on oral narratives of personal experience by the American sociolinguists William Labov and Joshua Waletzky, while the second draws on an influential study of text time in literary narratives by the French structuralist Gérard Genette. Our main concern is with the distinction between what is told and how it is told; that is, between the supposed chronological order of events on which the narrative is based and the way it is presented in the text. This difference has been indicated by various pairs of terms and the ones that we will use here are 'story' (that is, what happened) and 'discourse' (how it is told).

### 5.5.1  Telling stories: the oral tradition

We suggested earlier that asking learners to tell each other stories is a valuable activity in the context of studying short stories, whether the learners are primarily students of literature or of language. If, having told each other their stories, they then discuss the structuring of these oral narratives, they might wish to compare their own findings with those of Labov and Waletzky. It may well be that there are considerable differences in the way different cultures (and subcultures) tell and evaluate stories. Particularly with a multi-cultural group of learners, this may present opportunities for comparative work, both in relation to content – what is regarded as tellable in the sense of constituting a story that has a point to it? – and in relation to structure: is faithfulness to chronicity valued, or are elaboration and extravagant embroidery seen to be the marks of a good storyteller? How are different ways of performance in the act of storytelling rated by different cultural groups? Is gender a significant factor in either style or subject matter? What stylistic varieties may be presented in performance?

Labov (1972) presents the sequence of progression of an oral narrative which we reproduce below:

1. Abstract
2. Orientation
3. Complicating action
4. Evaluation (this may occur at any point in the narrative)
5. Resolution
6. Coda.

So what do these items represent?

The *abstract* is a kind of preliminary summing up, giving the listeners an idea of what the story is about; it is therefore separate from the main narrative. The *orientation* tells us about who was involved, and when and where it all happened; it provides the context. The *complicating action*, together with the *resolution*, constitute what might be called the plot: together they tell us what happened. The *evaluation*, which as we have pointed out, may occur at any point, is a kind of justification of the story, telling the hearers why it is interesting. The *resolution* gives the end of the story (which is very often the main point of it and may include the punch line, if there is one). The *coda* indicates that the storyteller has finished the story part and is coming back to the present situation; it is a bridging device.

Labov has many strands in his argument about the structure of oral narratives; the one that we shall focus on is the distinction he makes between the storyline or narrative clauses and the non-narrative or free clauses. This distinction highlights a feature of oral narrative, that is, the requirement for the storyteller to relate at frequent intervals to his audience, to keep in touch with them and sustain the sense of a shared experience, as well as telling the actual story. The aspect of teller–hearer relationship seems to be crucial for a successful performance.

For teachers of literature this seems to offer at least two possible areas for exploration with learners. The first is to focus in reading on the issue of the narrator–narratee relationship within a text. We may ask: how is the story told? Do Labov's constituents hold good for it? Is the relationship between teller and hearer sustained in the way that Labov suggests? (for example in *Heart of Darkness*, Marlow, the intradiegetic narrator, addresses his listeners directly at intervals with a comment on the story or on their response or lack of response). The second area is to consider how the relationship is expressed and sustained at another level, that between the narrator and the reader of a short story or novel. Is a level of communication established that operates above the narrative, or, to draw on Labov's terminology, is there evidence of anything like an abstract, evaluation or coda?

If we skim rapidly through the beginnings of each of the stories in the two Penguin collections, it is difficult to find anything that immediately offers itself as an abstract; the stories tend to start in the middle of events. (Why do you think this should be so?) The possible exceptions are, first, the epigraphs to the two stories by Kipling, both of which focus on a significant aspect of the story to be told, and thereby illustrate rather neatly the signalling function of the epigraph, the way in which it may flag important issues in the following text, and, second, the first short paragraphs of 'The Bucket and the Rope' by T. F. Powys (*The Second Penguin Book of Short Stories*: 105–12):

> A bucket once lay upon its side in a little shed, that was a short way down a by-lane, near to the village of Shelton.
>
>     This bucket, a large one, had been kicked over by a man who had hanged himself up by the neck, by means of an odd piece of rope that he had tied to a strong beam.
>
>     The man's name who had hanged himself was Mr Dendy, who rented a few pleasant fields that he used to plough happily, and, besides keeping a few good cows, he fattened some nice pigs.

The remainder of the story presents a conversation between the bucket and the rope, speculating on the reasons for Mr Dendy's suicide.

If this could be seen as an abstract, and if, as seems to be the case, abstracts are very rare in short stories, what do you think is the purpose of employing it here? How does it affect the way we read the rest of the story?

If we go on to evaluation, there may be more candidates. For example, Kipling's 'At the End of the Passage' (*The Penguin Book of Short Stories*: 82–102) includes a number of brief asides such as the following:

> There are very many places in the East where it is not good or kind to let your acquaintants drop out of sight even for one short week.
>
> (83)

> The resonant hammering of a coffin-lid is no pleasant thing to hear, but those who have experience maintain that much more terrible is the soft swish of the bed-linen, the reeving and un-reeving of the bed-tapes, when he who has fallen by the roadside is apparelled for burial ...
>
> (101)

What marks these out as different from a passage of narrative?

Most obvious is the use of the present tense indicating that this is different from the surrounding narrative, that is, in Labov's terms it is made up of free clauses. There is also the sense that the reader is being addressed directly, that an additional level of communication is being established between the narrator and the reader. This is a feature of Kipling's fictional style which may bear some relation to his work as a journalist in India, where he was addressing a British audience who would often expect comment and explanation as well as description. Recognition and discussion of this stylistic feature with students could lead on to comparing the structuring of newspaper stories and comment with literary texts and oral narratives.

The last of the non-narrative (or free clause) elements is the coda. Labov describes codas as 'bridging the gap between the moment of time at the end of the narrative proper and the present. They bring the narrator and the listener back to the point at which they entered the narrative' (Labov 1972: 365).

It is worth skimming rapidly through the endings of short stories this time to see if this coda element can be found in them. A surprising number of the endings do in some way hark back to the beginning (or possibly to the title) in order to complete the story. Compare, for example, the first and last paragraphs of 'After the Show' by Angus Wilson (*The Second Penguin Book of Short Stories*: 271–300):

> All the way home in the taxi and in the lift up to her flat on the seventh floor Mrs Liebig kept on talking. Sometimes she spoke of the play, making comments to Maurice in the form of questions to which she did not await the answer …
>
> (271)

> All the way back in the taxi from *The Pajama Game* Mrs Liebig hummed 'Fernando's Hideaway'. 'That was a good show,' she said. 'Something to take away with you.'
>
> (300)

While we are dealing here with a different return after a different 'show', the parallelisms of language point to parallelisms in the events and in a sense they return us to the place we started from.

You might want to try out an analysis of a short story based on Labov's approach. Hemingway's *In Our Time* is a collection of linked stories set in America with intercalated very short stories (each one is a paragraph long, roughly 150 words) about the First World War that provide a kind of counterpoint to the main narrative. A possible exercise is to read through all the very short story sections to decide which of them we feel are satisfactory narratives and why: which features (voice, agency, ordering of events, address to the reader) are significant in determining our response? Is Labov's distinction between narrative and free clauses relevant for these stories? You might try writing a very short story yourself (and also ask your students to do so), a so-called 'postcard fiction' that would fit on one side of a postcard. A comparison of the different stories would offer material for a discussion of what is needed for such a short story to work successfully.

## 5.6 THE ORGANISATION OF TIME IN LITERARY NARRATIVES

Labov and Waletzky explicitly focus on stories that recount the events of the story in the same order in which those events originally happened. It is not always the case, even with highly effective oral narratives, that stories are told in this way, and certainly in literary narratives the ordering of events may be very complex. This is particularly true of longer texts such as novels but short stories may also exhibit considerable complexity. The organisation of time in literary narratives is a particular focus of Genette's work and we shall follow his categories here in our focus on the ordering of events and the relation between text time and 'real' time.

### 5.6.1 The ordering of events

The ordering of events is another aspect of the relation between 'story' (what happened) and 'discourse' (how it is told). Are the events of the story presented chronologically or does the story move to and fro between past, present and (less commonly) future? The scope for reordering of events is somewhat limited in short stories and is perhaps more commonly a feature of novels. There are of course exceptions, particularly in science fiction which may be specifically concerned with issues of the relation of space and time. *The Prime of Miss Jean Brodie* is an example of an apparently traditionally narrated novel that shifts frequently to and fro in time, moving from present to past to future in flashbacks (analepses) and flashforwards (prolepses). It tells the story of a group of Edinburgh schoolgirls and their influential teacher Miss Brodie. Three 'future' events in particular are frequently alluded to by means of generally very brief prolepses: the death of Mary Macgregor in a hotel fire, Sandy Stranger's reception into an enclosed religious order and the betrayal of Miss Brodie by one of her own pupils. However, a kind of modified reordering of time is often presented even in short stories in the form of extended passages of memory or, it could be argued, in analepses that develop out of memories. Somerset Maugham's 'The Force of Circumstance' starts a few months after Doris' marriage to Guy; she is waiting for him while he dresses for dinner:

> That was why she had fallen in love with him, perhaps, for no amount of affection could persuade her that he was good-looking. He was a little round man, with a red face like the full moon, and blue eyes. He was rather pimply. She had examined him carefully and had been forced to confess to him that he had not a single feature she could praise. She had told him often he wasn't her type at all.
> 'I never said I was a beauty,' he laughed.
> 'I can't think what I see in you.'
> But of course she knew perfectly well … Once, sitting on his knees, during their honeymoon she had taken his face in her hands and said to him:
> 'You're an ugly, little fat man, Guy, but you've got charm. I can't help loving you.'
>                                                        (*The Penguin Book of Short Stories*: 130)

And on the next page the story returns to the present and to Doris sitting on the verandah and hearing 'Guy clatter down the steps to the bath-house'.

At several points in this story we find passages like this one, where we have not merely Doris' memories presented in the form of free indirect thought but also small snippets of direct speech, little re-enacted scenes which have something of the quality of an analepsis and which in a film would possibly be presented as a flashback. In our experience, recognition of the function of linguistic forms such as the tense of 'had fallen' as an indicator of a time shift affecting the following paragraph is a reading skill that learners need to be helped to master, for it is not always obvious to the comparatively unpractised reader where the transition from text-present to text-past appears.

### 5.6.2 Summary and scene

Chronological time may be disrupted or rearranged but reordering events is not the only way in which time can be re-presented in narratives. Time can be speeded up or slowed down, condensed or expanded. Events can be summarised or presented in such a way that they seem to occupy as much time in reading as they would in being acted out. This distinction is sometimes referred to as 'summary' and 'scene'. How would you describe the following extracts (all the stories are in *The Penguin Book of English Short Stories*): as closer to summary or closer to scene, or as a mixture of the two?

> 'Guy, I have something I want to say to you,' she murmured.
> His heart gave a sudden thud against his ribs and he felt himself change colour.
> 'Oh, my dear, don't look like that, it's not so very terrible,' she laughed.
> But he thought her voice trembled a little.
> 'Well?'
> 'I want you to do something for me.'
> 'My darling, I'll do anything in the world for you.'
> He put out his hand to take hers, but she drew it away.
> 'I want you to let me go home.'
>
> ('The Force of Circumstance': 151)

> 'What are you two whispering about?' said Hummil suspiciously.
> 'Only saying that you are a damned poor host. This fowl can't be cut,' returned Spurstow with a sweet smile. 'Call this a dinner?'
> 'I can't help it. You don't expect a banquet, do you?'
> Throughout that meal Hummil contrived laboriously to insult directly and pointedly all his guests in succession, and at each insult Spurstow kicked the aggrieved persons under the table; but he dared not exchange a glance of intelligence with either of them. Hummil's face was white and pinched, while his eyes were unnaturally large. No man dreamed for a moment of resenting his savage personalities, but as soon as the meal was over they made haste to get away.'
>
> (Kipling, 'At the End of the Passage': 91)

> Tom Sponson, at fifty-three, was a thoroughly successful man. He had worked up a first-class business, married a charming wife, and built himself a good house in the London suburbs that was neither so modern as to be pretentious nor so conventional as to be dull.
>
> (Cary, 'The Breakout': 233)

Dialogue such as we have in the first extract generally indicates 'scene', meaning that this section of the narrative is being presented in an expanded way. The third extract, on the other hand, gives a rapid summing up of Tom Sponson's situation which is offered directly by the narrator. The Kipling story seems to use both scene and summary: the direct speech gives us a sample of what is going on at the dinner table and what happened during the rest of the evening is indicated by means of the following paragraph in the voice of the narrator. From this we can see that 'summary' exhibits the control of the narrator while 'scene' is dominated by the characters. As with the variations in speech presentation discussed earlier, it is the movement from one to the other, the shifting between the voices of narrator and characters, that creates much of the interest in a text.

Two stories that merit comparison in this context are those by Maugham and Kipling that are quoted from above. They are also, incidentally, interesting to compare as examples of colonial and gendered narratives. 'The Force of Circumstance' begins in what was Malaya (it is set in the 1920s), a few months after the marriage of Doris and Guy, and ends six months later with Doris leaving her husband to return permanently to England. It contains Doris' memories, brief flashbacks in the form of scenes that are contained within the memories, and a long scene giving verbatim in direct speech (that is, with no summary by the narrator) an account of past events from Guy. But if we were to give a chronological account of all the important events of the story, we would have to start with what Guy tells Doris in that long speech, the story of his early years in Malaya, his co-habiting with the Malay woman, the birth of his children, and his marriage in England to Doris before getting to the point at which the text as we have it actually starts. Past events are crucial in this story. In many ways it has the structure of the early plays of Arthur Miller (cf. *All My Sons*, discussed in Chapter 7), where the action presented is all in the present but what happens is forcefully shaped by events in the past. Kipling's story 'At the End of the Passage', on the other hand, tells of two successive meetings a week apart between four men, representative figures of the British Raj in late nineteenth-century India. They work far apart from one another during the week but make great efforts to meet regularly on Sundays, not because they are especially friendly but because this is the way they keep their sanity. At the first meeting the doctor is concerned about the health, physical and psychological, of Hummil, their host. The following week he and the other two find Hummil dead. In this story there is little reference to earlier events (only a brief explanation of why Hummil has not gone to the hills for the hot weather) and the focus is almost exclusively on what is happening to the characters now.

Questions that might be asked about the experience of reading these two texts are, first of all, do we experience them differently? And if so, where does the difference lie? What is the effect produced when the Maugham story draws so much on the past by way of memory, analepsis and summary? Why is the crucial revelation presented in direct speech? And in the Kipling story, what is the effect of the concentration on the present, with its focus on scene rather than summary?

One possible response might be that we read the texts differently because of this difference in the presentation of time. (Though, curiously enough, the titles could almost be interchangeable.) Maugham seems to be concerned with the way in which the past reaches into the present and the emphasis on past events which are woven into the present narrative by means of analepsis and similar devices seems to embody this concern in the text. Kipling appears, on the other hand, to be interested in presenting a sense of the claustrophobia which is a major cause of Hummil's suicide and he achieves this in terms of structure by focusing almost entirely on the limited present, with a large proportion of the text consisting either of dialogue or of direct description of a scene and remarkably little reference to the past of any of the characters, whether by memory or analepsis. Indeed, almost the only references to the past are contained in brief conversational references.

## 5.7 CONCLUSION

It is important to reiterate at the end of this chapter what was said at the start of it: that the stories quoted here should not be read as examples of this or that narratological concept; however, when organising a course or sequence of stories, it may be worth keeping these concepts in mind, as they can provide a developmental sequence, a rationale, by means of which one can encourage both language development and valuable intertextual referencing as the stories are successively related to one another. The examination of elements of structure performed in this chapter is intended to be supportive of other methods of using short stories in the classroom rather than an attempt to provide an alternative methodology.

The following diagram can act as a checklist for features of narrative that might be taken into account when planning work on any story.

Cultural context

Textual structure 1:                                                                          Characterisation 1:
narrator–reader                                                                                        focalisation
relationship

'Story'
(i.e. what happens: the plot)

'Discourse'
(i.e. how it is presented)

Textual structure 2:                                                                          Characterisation 2:
ordering of the                                                                                   action and events
narrative

Intertextuality

*Fig. 2*   A model of narrative

# Chapter 6

# Teaching the novel

Some books are to be tasted, others to be swallowed, and some few to be chewed and digested: that is, some books are to be read only in parts; others to be read, but not curiously; and some few to be read wholly, and with diligence and attention.

(Bacon 1625/1890: 342)

## 6.1 INTRODUCTION

Novels present particular challenges for both the teacher and the student. This is often the experience of first-year undergraduates in a British university, and some of these problems are magnified in the foreign language context. Probably few language teachers would make a novel their first choice of a literary text for language teaching. Teachers of literature courses, however, have little choice in that novels will almost certainly be on the syllabus they are required to teach; and some language-based syllabuses have a strong literature input, for example, in Bulgarian English language schools the tenth-year syllabus is almost entirely devoted to literature, including long extracts from novels. For those of us who are wary of using novels in our class-rooms, some encouragement may be offered by a report of research in Turkish senior high schools, which included an investigation into the response of students to text selection (Akyel and Yalcin 1990). The results indicated that students felt 'that the most effective literary form for helping them develop their linguistic skills and cultural awareness is the novel' (ibid: 175).

Even with this encouragement, two very general questions present themselves at this point: first, how are teachers to help students become enjoyably engaged (and thereby fruitfully engaged) on what may initially appear to be alarmingly long and forbidding texts? Second, how are teachers to be enabled to find ways of reading that are stimulating and appropriate for themselves as continuing students of literature? It is not easy year after year to maintain one's enthusiasm for, say, *Lord of the Flies* or *Catcher in the Rye*, two of the titles on the Turkish Lise II [second-year high school] English syllabus mentioned by Akyel and Yalcin (180), excellent novels though they may be. Those teachers whose main concern is with language and who are not required to follow a literature syllabus have greater freedom to choose, use, discard and choose afresh a variety of texts that may be appropriate in a variety of ways to their primary concern of language. But all teachers need the opportunity to develop new insights into the texts they teach, whether chosen by themselves or set by a syllabus, to integrate their own thinking, both theoretical and applied, into their classroom work.

*Perhaps you could consider at this point what you yourself think might be some of the advantages in using longer texts, and in particular, novels (for either the literature or the language classroom).*
*What might be some of the problems?*
*What strategies have you developed in your own teaching of novels?*

In this chapter, though we will necessarily refer to a range of texts, we will focus on three novels in particular (see the second part of the references for publication details). It does not seem particularly useful to talk about teaching novels in a general way, but obviously much of what is suggested in the following pages as appropriate for a particular text could be generalised to others.

The first novel, Joseph Conrad's *Heart of Darkness*, has been selected because it is one of the central texts of modernism and appears on English literature syllabuses all over the world. Side by side with this, we will consider a novel by a contemporary Nigerian woman writer: *Second-Class Citizen* by Buchi Emecheta. The third is the novel *Cal* by Bernard MacLaverty, an Irish writer, which sets a love story against the background of communal troubles in Belfast. These novels have all been chosen because they raise significant cultural issues which are appropriate for discussion in both literature and language focused contexts.

*If you were asked to choose three novels to use as examples in a discussion of teaching methods, which three would you choose? What would be your criteria for selection?*
*Here are some suggestions:*
    *canonical status*
    *period*
    *is the novel a 'good read'?*
    *cultural similarity or cultural difference*
    *contrast and variety in the novels chosen*
    *variety/varieties of language e.g. novels written in 'standard' English or alternatively novels which draw on 'non-standard' varieties such as Caribbean English, Malaysian English, Scots, and so on*
*How would you rank these criteria in order of importance?*
*Would you wish to add any others?*

The approach exemplified here contrasts with that of the preceding chapter in that, while with the short story we attempted to develop particular instruments of analysis (primarily narratological), drawing on a wide range of short stories to illustrate the uses of these analytic tools, here we focus on three exemplary texts, the discussion of which will, we hope, suggest ways of reading and teaching which may be applied to other novels. In both chapters, whatever the particular texts discussed, the main object is the development of reading strategies that can be learned and then applied in a variety of situations.

The study of literature raises a wide range of questions, some text based, others of a more theoretical nature. Several of these considerations have already been referred to in Chapter 1 and they are particularly relevant in relation to novels. For example, how important is our knowledge of the author's life to our reading of his or her work? Does it make any difference if we know that Conrad himself made a voyage similar to that made by Marlow in *Heart of Darkness*? Or that Buchi Emecheta herself (and not just her heroine Adah) wrote a book entitled *The Bride Price*? Or that Bernard MacLaverty is a Catholic from Northern Ireland? Some purists contend that in theory this sort of information is (or at least ought to be) irrelevant to how we read; others argue that however unimportant such knowledge might be in theoretical terms, it is pedagogically valuable, indeed that information about the author (such as the fact that Conrad was Polish by origin and that English was not his first language, or that Kipling spent some years as a journalist in India) may help bring a text to life for the student.

A more problematic area is that of authorial intention. Students often ask 'What does the author mean by this?' implying that if they could get the answer to this question, all would become clear; in fact, this question is often another way of saying 'I don't understand this and I want an authoritative interpretation.' Even in those comparatively few cases where the author has given us some idea of what he or she meant at the time of writing it is important to remember that this is only one meaning out of many possible meanings. We may indeed find the views of other readers more insightful or illuminating than those of the author, even on the fairly infrequent occasions when the latter are available to us. The author's expressed view may well hold some particular interest for us but it is not the ultimate authority.

A third area of concern in dealing with the novels chosen for discussion in this chapter is the problem of universality. It has often been argued that one of the reasons for teaching literature is that it deals with universal human questions and experience. It might be argued, for example, that the issues raised in *Cal* about the tensions between different communities living in close juxtaposition are of universal interest and significance. On the other hand, the claims that have been made by many (not only Western) critics about the 'universal values' expressed through literature have been radically questioned by exponents of post-colonial and feminist theories, who argue that what has traditionally been propounded as 'universal' is largely the generalised experience of white males.

These issues are not necessarily confronted directly in the discussion that follows but they may be kept in mind and raised where relevant with students.

## 6.2 A PROPOSED FRAMEWORK FOR READING NOVELS

Information processing can be divided into five distinct phases: transformation, reduction, classification, storage and retrieval. I maintain that even in the case of literary reading, the text is mentally processed in basically the same way; although the more literary the reading the more complex will be the intellectual processes which take place within each phase.

(Isenberg 1990: 181)

Isenberg applies this five-phased process specifically to the reading of poetry, but it is possible to explore its application to other genres as a broad framework for developing reading and study strategies, which in turn will play their part in the development of literary competence.

## Transformation

The first phase is transformation, or the process by which students initially come to grips with the text, make it their own. What is the teacher's role at this stage? How can the teacher facilitate this process without dictating its development or foreclosing possible options? A common practice in literature courses is the introductory lecture or information sheet with, for example, basic biographical information about the writer, and notes on the historical setting and on the circumstances of the writing and publishing of the book. This provides a set of schemata and also a series of mental hooks to which the reader may attach references in the text. It has the merit of being a relatively painless and convenient way of kicking off the reading process and can be very useful. If, however, the same introductory format is used for every new text, it becomes increasingly predictable and thereby decreasingly effective, and unless carried out very tactfully, may actually impede the transformation process of personal engagement with the text.

One way of encouraging personal engagement is to start your work on the novel by giving students a section of the text (one of the key passages that you have already chosen) to read either at home or in class and to get them to formulate specific questions that they want to ask related to it. These questions may be addressed to the text itself, to the people that appear in it, the narrator, the author (theoretical discussions about intentionality can be dealt with later, if necessary), the historical circumstances, even to themselves as readers, questioning their own responses. The use of a specific addressee in this exercise is not just a gimmick; it is a way of helping the student to focus the question and give it a personal slant. To use a cliché of current criticism, by doing this they are learning to interrogate the text while at the same time bringing to the surface their own cultural and personal assumptions. In this exercise, the students are not necessarily expected to take up a co-operative attitude to the text, and this should be made clear to them at the outset. One way of doing this is for the teacher to perform her or his own 'interrogation of the text' in front of the class, perhaps even before they have read the passage in question. Take, for example, that paragraph in *Heart of Darkness* describing Marlow's first meeting with the accountant at the company station just as he has emerged from the valley of the dying slaves: if you imagine yourself as a first-time reader of this passage, what sort of questions would you ask? The students have the text in front of them and are asked to read silently the preceding scene (pp. 24–5). The teacher then reads aloud the following paragraph, breaking off at intervals to interpolate her own questions. This is a suggestion of how one might go about it:

> He had come out for a moment, he said, 'to get a breath of fresh air.' (*'fresh air' – that's an extraordinary expression to use – it sounds so out-of-place in that horrifying setting – and I see Marlow also thinks it's peculiar.*) The expression sounded wonderfully odd, with its suggestion of sedentary desk-life. I wouldn't have mentioned the fellow to you at all, (*'to you', that's the other men in the boat on the Thames, I suppose – he never actually addresses the reader directly, does he?*) only it was from his lips that I first heard the name of the man who is so indissolubly connected with the memories of that time. (*Yes, you keep hinting at this person – who is he?*) Moreover, I respected the fellow. (*'respected him' ? Why? the description makes him seem absurd*) Yes; I respected his collars, his vast cuffs, (*I like that 'vast'*) his brushed hair. His appearance was certainly that of a hairdresser's dummy; but in the great demoralization of the land, he kept up his appearance. That's backbone. His starched collars and got-up shirt-fronts were achievements of character. (*Are you being ironical here, Marlow? What's your tone of voice in making such a statement?*) He had been out nearly three years; and later I could not help asking how he managed to sport such linen. He had just the faintest blush, and said modestly, (*Why is he blushing? and why 'modestly'? He doesn't sound a particularly modest man – he must be embarrassed at being asked.*) 'I've been teaching one of the native women about the station. It was difficult. She had a distaste for the work.' (*I see – the woman washes your dirty clothes but you also use her sexually. Are you going to comment on this, Marlow?*) Thus this man had verily accomplished something. (*That's an extraordinary way of putting it – what exactly are you referring to here? So often you don't state your criticism clearly but leave us to guess at it. Do you really approve of this man?*) And he was devoted to his books, which were in apple-pie order. (*'apple-pie' – that's like 'getting a breath of fresh air' – it belongs to a totally incongruous register*).

(p. 26)

This approach, incidentally, is often useful for opening paragraphs of short stories (see also the first two paragraphs of *Cal*), where the object is to catch the reader's interest by raising questions about identity, situation or relationship. It is a way of using the techniques of think-aloud protocols (which are discussed more fully in Chapter 9) to bring to awareness and also to develop the strategies employed in text processing.

Whether prepared as homework or in class, there is some value in asking for the questions to be produced in written form (rather than in what might often tend to be rather vague oral formulations). There should be an opportunity for students to discuss them, probably initially in groups (where they might pool their questions and attempt to group them in broad categories before starting on the discussion). In feedback from the groups, these categories are likely to be illuminating in that they probably will link up with the third and fourth phases of information processing mentioned above, namely classification and storage. We mean by this that they will probably include clusters of questions related to: Joseph Conrad (his life but also his political views and his purposes in writing); the historical setting of the novel; the way it is written (style and also questions of narrative voice and point of view); the argument or theme; tropes and particular linguistic features (for example, the choice of lexis); the response roused in the reader (moral outrage, anger, boredom or whatever – and the reasons for these located within the reader as well as in the text). The establishment of such categories through this process of personal engagement with the passage rather than as given by the teacher or by secondary criticism can contribute to the development of reading strategies which may later be applied to other literary texts.

The teacher, meanwhile, can collect the written questions to use as the basis for preparing information sheets and follow-up tasks to be given out later; this means that the students are getting answers to questions they have actually asked.

## Reduction

The second phase of information processing is that of reduction, by which the information is made manageable. Some of this has already occurred in the process of questioning and discussing the text, but it can be carried further by a focus at this stage on content rather than form, on the 'what' rather than the 'how'. Isenberg (1990) suggests a number of techniques to explore the what happens? to whom? and why? of the storyline, for example predicting, ordering information, organising events and establishing relationships between events or characters. These techniques are not particularly novel in themselves but they can be planned and balanced systematically to help students with the task of personal processing of the text. For example, simple ways of doing this as the reading of the text progresses are by work on plot summaries, discussion of characters, and making flowcharts or diagrammatic representations of relationships between characters or events. Different individuals, pairs or groups may be assigned different tasks and the results of their work displayed visually by means of posters, OHTs and so on, rather than simply reported orally.

## Categorisation and storage

These are the third and fourth phases. Learning to create relevant and usable categories of analysis is an area of key importance in the development of literary competence. Linguistic and structuralist approaches to literature have been valuable in establishing new categories (such as structures of narrative) and in bringing greater precision to the discussion of those that are traditional (for example, plot and character). The emphasis in this chapter, however, is inductive rather than deductive; in other words, we are concerned with how students may be enabled to formulate their own categories of analysis.

We suggest that the initial question-asking exercise can provide the basis for much of the subsequent work on this text. If students are encouraged in their early discussions to form their own category groupings, this is an important step, and later when the teacher gives feedback on the questions that have been handed in, this issue can be foregrounded for class discussion. For example, someone may have asked the question of *Heart of Darkness*: 'Does Marlow express Conrad's own views?' Or of *Cal*: 'Is the novel fair to the Protestant characters?' These could provide the opportunity for a wider discussion of the issues of intentionality and the relation of biographical information to critical reading, a discussion which suggests analytic categories for dealing with other novels. Such a question would also open up, in the case of *Heart of Darkness*, the issues of the structure of the novel and the significance of the frame-work narrative, which is set on the River Thames, with its implied comment on Marlow's story. Or in relation to the question on *Cal*, one could ask what it is that we expect from a novel, in other words is 'giving a balanced view' an important issue? When work begins on another novel, the teacher can remind students of the categories that have already been established.

*Some of the categories that might emerge have already been mentioned (see above). At this point you may wish to add others.*

If you are working on a canonical text that has an established body of criticism attached to it, it is at this stage (that is, once the students have established their own confident relationship with the text) that, in our experience at least, there is great value for both language and literature students in turning to other critics. An enormous amount has been written, of course, about *Heart of Darkness*, and it is not difficult to select contrasting quotations from critics for discussion in class and as a basis for homework tasks. If the book is being studied as a set text at an advanced level, students will probably be expected to read more detailed background material and criticism, but even for such students, this kind of discussion will serve as an introduction to more advanced work. With a work such as *Heart of Darkness*, it should rapidly become apparent that there is no single authoritative critical voice. This is probably more of an issue where the novel is a prescribed canonical text in an examined course and where students are anxious to be assured of the 'correct' way of interpreting a novel for exam purposes. But to become aware of the variety of critically justifiable readings is in itself an advance in literary sophistication. The question has to be considered of whether these interpretations are mutually exclusive or whether they can they be understood as a series of transformations of the text, which may be more or less convincing.

### Retrieval

This will come into play in subsequent discussions of the novel and perhaps most importantly in essay or project writing. This, after all, is the main point (the main pedagogical as opposed to institutional point, at any rate) of getting students to write essays in the context of studying literature: it gives them the opportunity to make use of the conceptual structures that they have developed. The ability to retrieve relevant information will also in turn provide schemata for reading new texts.

**Follow-up activities**

These are some examples of possible follow-up activities:

- The whole class devises a chart showing who speaks (and possibly also what they say), and who is silent in *Heart of Darkness*;
- Students (individually or in pairs) write an official report of a violent incident described in the novel, for example a report by the social worker in *Second-Class Citizen* or a police report of Cal's arrest;
- One group prepares and role-plays a television interview with the author of *Cal*; and another group writes a review of the interview for a TV critic's column.

Such activities lead directly to engagement with some of the larger issues raised by criticism, such as the construction of the canon, the feminist notion of 'resisting readings', the use of other cultures to explore European concerns, the concept of 'otherness', expressed in relations of power, both interculturally and intraculturally, and the silencing of the marginalised. At an advanced level of language learning, or in a cultural studies context, these may be developed further.

These tasks and activities in our experience may be employed appropriately for both literature and language learners and from this common base either more specifically literary or more language-focused work can be developed.

## 6.3 THREE NOVELS

For the rest of this chapter, we will turn to the three novels already mentioned. In each case, we shall focus on a particular approach which we have found fruitful for that particular novel but which should then be generalisable to a range of other texts.

### 6.3.1 *Heart of Darkness* by Joseph Conrad

*Heart of Darkness* figures prominently in many literature syllabuses, whether simply as one set text among others in a general literature syllabus (for example, an American liberal studies course on 'Great Novels of the World'), as a central text of modernism or as an influential instance of colonialist writing. If it possible to read it in conjunction with another novel (or even extracts from another novel), that may be more illuminating than reading it on its own. An obvious choice is Chinua Achebe's *Things Fall Apart* (or one of the others from his *African Trilogy*) but there is a wide variety to choose from in African or other post-colonial literature, including novels by black writers in Britain. Or you might prefer to use Conrad's diaries or his short story 'An Outpost of Progress' as further (or pre-) reading. An illuminating exercise to try out on the short story (which can be found in the *Penguin Book of English Short Stories*) is to examine how Conrad uses the word 'civilisation' and its related forms by studying the instances in the text. These provide a lexical thread that runs through the story, and a close look at the collocation of such occurrences gives an insight into Conrad's ironic method while serving to introduce some of the key questions raised by *Heart of Darkness* about the nature of Western civilisation and the problematic use of the colonial experience to explore specifically Western European obsessions.

The question of the literary canon has already been discussed in Chapter 1. Here we consider it again in relation to the study of this particular widely taught and much written about novel, as this offers an opportunity to raise these issues more concretely.

For our students, we would suggest that it is important to problematise the text in the sense of encouraging them to ask questions about the significance of its canonical status. It appears on the syllabus – why? What are the implications? That it is a particularly 'good' novel? That it represents enduring values? That it is of 'universal' significance? What is the process by which this particular novel and this particular author has achieved or been granted inclusion in the canon?

For many readers, *Heart of Darkness* is the quintessential Conrad novel. It seems peculiarly representative in its combination of Conradian subjects: the use of 'exotic' settings; ships and navigation; colonialism; the discontents of European civilisation. And the narrative and stylistic features, too, are characteristic of much of his work: the displacement of the narrator; the use of symbolism; the complexity of construction; the use of polysyllabic adjectives. In many respects, it is the canonical work of a canonical author.

So how has Conrad come to be so firmly ensconced? His establishment has followed a very different trajectory from that of his contemporary Kipling, who was, in the last years of Queen Victoria's reign, immensely popular, but was only much later, and only after a period of explicit critical rejection, admitted to the canon of writers to be taken seriously. Popular success and the approval of the academic literary establishment do not necessarily go hand-in-hand. Conrad, indeed, did not become a popular writer until the publication of *Chance* in 1914. Yet by 1902 – a year after Queen Victoria's death – when *Heart of Darkness* was published in book form (the initial publication was in serial form in *Blackwood's Magazine* in 1899), Conrad was recognised by the literary journalism establishment as an important writer, worthy of review in serious literary magazines. By the time of his death in 1924, he was widely acclaimed as one of the grand masters of the modern British novel.

His place in the academic canon was assured by F. R. Leavis' inclusion of him in the great tradition of the English novel, that apostolic succession from Austen through Eliot and James to Conrad. Since Leavis' explicit canonisation of Conrad, his novels have spawned an extraordinary quantity of criticism. His work is susceptible to a wide variety of critical readings, which in turn ensures its continuing appearance on school and university syllabuses. In this sense, the canon can be seen to be self-perpetuating.

Chinua Achebe, writing in 1987 (an article based on a lecture given in 1975), acknowledges the secure canonical status of the novel he is attacking:

> Whatever Conrad's problems were, you might say he is safely dead ... Unfortunately, his heart of darkness plagues us still. Which is why an offensive and

deplorable book can be described by a serious scholar as 'among the half-dozen greatest short stories in the English language'. And why it is today perhaps the most commonly prescribed novel in twentieth century courses in English Departments in American universities.

In the history of Conrad's establishment, it is apparent that extrinsic as well as intrinsic factors are at work. For example, if we consider the conditions of production, it was possible for him to publish in serial form in a literary magazine. Serious literary journalism had become a minor industry and what was published in one journal would be reviewed in others, so his work was noticed if not always warmly approved. In terms of political history, his work appeared at what might now be perceived as the cusp of Empire, at a moment when British colonialism was at its height while at the same time beginning to come under profound criticism from within the colonising society. In terms of literary movements, he appears early in the development of what came to be called modernism; and modernism lends itself peculiarly to academic critical analysis. In short, a variety of factors work together to position Conrad optimally for insertion by Leavis into the great tradition of the English novel. And Achebe's attack has, it seems, ironically served to ensure continuing academic debate on this novel in particular.

You may find it an interesting exercise to consider with learners the question of the establishment of a canon in their own literary culture. If there is an established canon, are the elements in its construction similar to those outlined above? Or if a canon is in the process of construction, what are the forces operating to produce it?

A second broad question (among the many raised by this novel), and one related to the question of canonicity, is that of text to context: how important is contextual information? There is a theoretical approach that would argue that contextual information is not significant, that the text must stand on its own. This was the argument presented by exponents of New Criticism, most sharply by Wellek and Warren in their *Theory of Literature* (1949), where they distinguish between extrinsic and intrinsic approaches, arguing that an excessive reliance on the study of extrinsic information had produced 'the astonishing helplessness of most scholars when confronted with the task of actually analysing and evaluating a work of art' (139). This argument for a close reading of the text rather than an elaboration of the context was particularly forceful and effective in the reading of short poems, but was only rarely applied to longer productions such as novels – though not because it was considered theoretically inapplicable.

However, more recent critical voices have argued the importance of recognising and analysing circumstances of the production and reception of texts, and the significance of intertextuality, in both literary and more broadly social and historical terms. New Historicist critics have argued that literary discourse of any period should be read alongside others, such as scientific, religious or medical discourses; literature should not be specially privileged as some kind of unique or transcendent object but should be recognised as part of the complex discursive activity of particular societies. This argument for contextual study has obvious links with issues raised by post-colonialist and feminist criticism – both of which would be relevant to any discussion of *Heart of Darkness*.

Contextual information could be taken from the following sources (Spittles 1992 in the Macmillan series *Writers in their Time* is a useful reference book for this kind of activity):

- Textual history, or in other words writing (including revisions), publishing, critical reception of the novel;
- Conrad's other work, including diaries and letters;
- Conrad's life;
- Other literary writing of the colonial period (such as Kipling, Haggard, Cunninghame Graham);
- Other texts (speeches by public figures, newspapers of the period);
- Later histories of colonialism.

*Heart of Darkness* is a short but nonetheless extremely demanding novel. The students whom we teach, who include British undergraduates, complain of the difficulty it presents and the sheer dogged effort they have to put in to get it read in the time allotted. It is in this similar to many modernist texts, but the particular experience of reading demanded by this novel is significant and should be discussed at some stage in its study. The reading is itself a difficult task which seems to mimic the journey of exploration, the struggle against the stream which it describes. Moreover, the centre of the novel is in a sense a black hole – it is obscure, and student readers may need some reassurance that it is not just their inadequate command of the language that makes them feel they have missed the point but that this hiddenness at the centre is part of the meaning of the novel (see Marley (1995) for a discussion of the 'missing link'). Like other modernist novels, too, *Heart of Darkness* ideally requires rereading. In the limited time and with the limited linguistic competence of many learners, this may be an unrealisable goal, but it is possible to provide an approximation to rereading by working on a number of key sections first so that intratextual references and structural ironies become clearer. As McRae (1996) rightly points out, one should not confront students with difficulties at the start. 'The focus should be on what strikes them, what they find memorable or identifiable' (25). We suggest four possible passages below; other teachers might, of course, wish to choose different ones.

pp. 9–11   'Mind,' he began again ... And I got tired of that game, too.'
*Marlow in the boat on the River Thames with his companions.*

pp. 8–21   I left in a French steamer ... hints for nightmares.
*Marlow's voyage along the West African coast.*

pp. 26–8   Everything else in the station ... for a two hundred mile tramp.
*Marlow at the trading station prepares for his departure to the interior. For the first time he hears the name of Kurtz.*

pp. 106–7   The dusk was falling ... light of belief and love.
*Marlow takes Kurtz's packet of letters to his Intended.*

One possible way of using these passages is to ask students to read all four sections as preparation, and then in pairs or groups work on tasks such as the following:

- Supply their own suggestions for a linking narrative;
- Develop some way (perhaps by a diagram) of representing the character of Marlow as they see it emerging through these extracts
- Discuss the tone of the novel as they perceive it (for example, the ironies; attitudes to race and colonialism);
- The presentation of Kurtz's Intended; what does this suggest about the role of women in the novel?

This approach could then be used to provide the basis for a fuller reading.

### 6.3.2  *Second-Class Citizen* by Buchi Emecheta

Buchi Emecheta's novel does not advertise itself as a revisioning counter-narrative to *Heart of Darkness* in the way that, for example, Jean Rhys' *Wide Sargasso Sea* does to Bronte's *Jane Eyre*. It does, however, provide an illuminating contrast in a number of ways and can provoke a lively response from students, in both multi-cultural and mono-cultural groups. Though we shall be considering it in relation to *Heart of Darkness*, it can also be read as an enjoyable novel in its own right. If time is short, it is a novel that would lend itself to the treatment by which everyone in the class reads the beginning and end, but different sections of text are allotted to different groups or individuals to read and summarise for the rest of the class. This approach would work well here, as it is a straightforward linear narrative.

The novel tells the story of Adah, a young Nigerian woman, who follows her husband to England, to support him while he continues his studies. She triumphs over painfully adverse circumstances, which include repeated unplanned pregnancies and her husband's violent behaviour; the novel ends with her leaving him to establish her own life with her young children. It was published in 1974 but is set in the England of a decade earlier. The narrative is very straightforward: it is presented chronologically without either flashback, prolepsis or frame-narrative. The narration is third person and the point of view is Adah's throughout. There is little use of extended 'scene': the story is to a large extent told directly by the narrator with some passages of dialogue (that is, it is diegetic rather than mimetic).

This is a novel that can be usefully approached by those well-established language-teaching routes that start with external features and which, if consistently employed, can develop in students an awareness of the cultural semiotics of text presentation: the cover design, the photograph of the author on the back cover, the paragraph providing further information on the fly-leaf, and so on. In employing these methods, the teacher should be aiming not merely to introduce this particular novel, but to train students both to make the most of all such information that may be provided by the publisher and also to read it critically. (In all that follows, we refer to the 1994 edition, although the same questions can be asked about any version.) For example, *Second-Class Citizen* is published in Heinemann's African Writers series, a fact which is proclaimed on the front cover. How does this prominently displayed information position the book for its readers? Is it simply informative in a neutral way? Or does it imply that this is in some sense a marginal text, belonging to a non-mainstream genre, a kind of 'special interest' novel? In this edition we also find on the back-cover quotes from approving reviews in the broadsheet press (*The Guardian* and *The Sunday Times*). What effect are they intended to have on the way readers approach the novel? Do your students recognise the cultural connotations of these quotes from these particular newspapers? The cover design is bold and colourful, drawing attention to the theme of a racially divided society: how do your students interpret it? This introductory session may provide an opportunity to compare the appearance both of different novels (for instance, is a recent edition of a classic such as *Heart of Darkness* differentiated in appearance in any way from a contemporary novel such as *Second-Class Citizen*?) and of different text types (such as a novel, a biography and a history textbook), and also to establish a systematic approach to any text: noting author, title, date of writing, date of particular edition, publisher and ISBN. This kind of bibliographic training is particularly valuable for students entering higher education.

If a teacher decided to read *Second-Class Citizen* in conjunction with *Heart of Darkness*, how might it be done? Some possibilities are:

- Learners could be asked to draw up a double column of similarities and differences between the two novels. For example, on the simply descriptive level, they might find the following:

| *Heart of Darkness* | *Second-Class Citizen* |
|---|---|
| **The narrative structure** | |
| a framing narrative: the companions in the boat on the Thames; | no framing narrative |
| Marlow tells his story in first person | third person narrative |
| **The narrator** | |
| a male narrator; | a female narrator; |
| a European in Africa in the colonial period; | an African in mid-twentieth century Britain; |
| the narrator (white, male, professional) belongs to a powerful social group | the narrator (being both female and black) belongs to a group lacking power in society |
| **Stylistic differences** | |
| formal (Latinate) vocabulary complex syntax | fairly colloquial vocabulary simple syntax |

- Students might also be asked to make a comparison of their own responses to the two texts, for example, do they identify with any of the characters? What positive and what negative points would they make about each book? In talking about their own responses, can they relate them to the similarities and differences that emerged during the descriptive exercise?

- Students could be asked individually to choose what they consider key or characteristic short passages from the two novels for points of comparison of similarity or contrast. Keywords might be used for focus to indicate what these points are.
- Examination of the stylistic differences could be sharpened by the use of cloze techniques (see the exercises for an example).

### 6.3.3 *Cal* by Bernard MacLaverty

This novel (a contemporary version of the Romeo and Juliet theme) is very widely read in EFL classrooms – indeed the author has said (in an unpublished lecture) that *Cal* is more widely read by German teenagers than it is by British. It is certainly very popular with many German teachers of English, who argue that its subject matter of a divided community is of special relevance to the recent experience of Germany. For the language teacher in particular it has clear advantages for classroom use: it is not a 'difficult read', either in language or in plot construction, in the way that *Heart of Darkness* so obviously is; the characters are young and probably easy to identify with; the historical and political background may be complex but the central situation is clear-cut and simple. For the teacher who is concerned with cultural issues as well as language learning, it provides many opportunities for cross-cultural comparisons and, for those who teach English in the context of cultural studies such as German *Landeskunde* courses, it offers an opportunity for a fuller exploration of the social and political situation in Northern Ireland. The fact that there is a film version of the novel is a further advantage. And if there is a need to justify the choice of text to a syllabus-setting authority in terms of 'good' writing, MacLaverty is a well-known and respected contemporary British novelist. In 1997, his novel *Gracenotes* was short-listed for the Booker Prize.

The information processing framework set out at the beginning of the chapter, and the five steps of transformation, reduction, categorisation, storage and retrieval, are as relevant here as they are to *Heart of Darkness,* and even though we do not necessarily refer to the various elements in the process directly, it will be apparent that this framework underpins the approaches suggested.

In the discussion of this novel, we focus on the use of film and video in support of teaching literary texts. It has become commonplace for teachers working in the language tradition to use video in short snippets for particular activities. Teachers in the literature tradition may, however, wish to use video rather differently. In particular, some experienced and methodologically sophisticated teachers have reported that their students are sick of the 'snippets' approach when it comes to films based on literary texts, and it may be that in such cases it is more productive to work on the text initially and then provide students with the opportunity to watch the whole film right through, undistracted by pedagogic interruptions, if they so wish. The film of

*Cal* can be used in either way but, if small sections are to be used, it may be most productive to take sections that are close to the written text yet differ from it in interesting ways, particularly in the presentation of the central character.

The exercise of comparing film with book can be carried out either while reading the novel or after it has been finished. It is likely that one of the issues for discussion in the novel will be that of the character of Cal. There are various well-tried ways in which this can be done, such as suggesting or choosing terms in which to describe Cal (for example passive; courageous; a victim; indecisive); making a spider diagram of his network of relationships in the novel; writing short paragraphs about him from the points of view of other characters; and in addition, of course, discussion in groups or with the whole class. If you also ask learners to pick a scene from the novel which they feel particularly expresses Cal's character, it is likely that they will choose some of those that are represented in the film but with interesting differences: for example, where Cal waits for Marcella outside the library and carries her box of groceries (pp. 25–6); when Cal goes home to his father after being attacked (pp. 46–8); Cal and Shamie chopping wood together (p. 42); the conversation between Cal, Skeffington and Crilly (pp. 146–50); possibly the ending of the book.

Any one of these scenes provides interesting issues for comparison. Here we will consider Cal's arrival at his home after the attack by the Protestant youths. What impression do your students get of Cal and Shamie and their relationship from this scene as it is presented in the novel? How does Cal cope with his frightening experience? Is he in control of himself? Is he presented as a victim? Who is more active in this scene, Cal or his father? To support their impressions by a closer reading of the text, you might ask students to mark and look carefully at the apportionment of verbs to the two characters, and the kinds of verbs that these are (doing, feeling, thinking, seeing/hearing, speaking) and whether these actions have any effect on another person or on an object. Is there much difference between the two or are they equally active? (You are asking your students to examine what are known as the transitivity options.) This kind of analysis will show that in this scene Cal is given more verbs of action, perception and speech than Shamie.

If we compare this scene with the film version, there are considerable differences.

From inside the house Cal is shown opening the door.
He stands still.
The camera, positioned behind Cal's left shoulder, moves to Shamie, reading in the chair.
Pause while Cal waits for his father to notice him. The camera is on Shamie but what we hear is Cal's shaky breathing.
After a long moment Shamie looks up and sees Cal.
Shot of Cal, bleeding and pathetic, as seen by Shamie.
Shamie gets up and comes to him. Camera to side of Cal, both of them in the frame.
Shamie lifts Cal's chin.
Shot of both.

Shot of Cal (from Shamie's point of view).

Camera to the side again.

Long shot showing Shamie sitting Cal down on sofa and bringing him a drink.

Shot of Cal, hands shaking and teeth chattering as he lifts the glass to his lips.

Does this scene give the viewer the same impression of Cal as the corresponding scene in the novel? Our own feeling is that the emphasis has shifted from the novel's presentation of Cal as frightened but reasonably in control (he is even able to make a private joke about his reflection in the bathroom mirror) to a view of Cal as a suffering and passive, even self-pitying victim. This is brought out particularly in the long moment where he waits for his father to look up and pay attention to him. And once Shamie does notice him, Cal doesn't do anything for himself but is *done to*; he doesn't even wash off his own blood, as he does in the book. His active capacity is minimised and he becomes increasingly passive, presented as a victim, the one to whom things happen, and this seems to be a persistent feature of the film's interpretation of the character. Why should this be so?

A second area of comparison between book and film is in the contextualisation of the action in the political situation of Northern Ireland. In the book, the underlying violence is hinted at in the first pages by means of the images of the abattoir, the blood and knives, and the preacher's message, and only gradually do we become aware of Cal's own participation in this violence. In the film, the opening shots show the murder of Marcella's policeman husband and at intervals thereafter the initial image of the film recurs, that is, the windscreen wipers of the stolen car as seen from the driver's seat by Cal. The first meeting of Cal and Marcella is shown in the film, though not in the book, in the context of barricades and a military checkpoint. The ending is altered in the film to include a car chase and Skeffington's death. These areas of difference and students' responses to them can be explored, and together with this there can be a consideration of the different ways in which the two media present point of view and subjectivity.

## 6.4 CONCLUSION

Each of the novels discussed above is in some way representative: *Heart of Darkness* of the large number of canonical texts which certainly present a linguistic challenge, but also, perhaps, more interestingly, offer the opportunity for developing 'resisting readings' of various kinds. Buchi Emecheta is one of a large number of British novelists, poets and playwrights of African, Caribbean or Asian origin, who write in some cases about life in Britain (for example, Hanif Kureishi and Jackie Kay) and in others about their countries of origin (for example, Salman Rushdie and Emecheta herself in her novel *The Bride Price*). *Cal* is an example of a novel that focuses a specific historical moment through the lens of an individual's experience and is centrally concerned with social and political issues. Each in different ways can offer both literature and language learners opportunities for enjoyment, personal engagement and the development of a wide range of reading skills and strategies.

# Chapter 7

# Teaching drama

Drama is not made of words alone, but of sights and sounds, stillness and motion, noise and silence, relationships and responses.

(Styan 1975)

## 7.1 DRAMA ACTIVITIES AND PERFORMING A LITERARY WORK

In this section we are concerned mainly with drama, the one major genre which is usually written to be performed. Many of the suggestions below also apply to poetry – very much so to writers such as John Hegley and Liz Lochhead, rather less so to, say, Wordsworth. Prose is not usually suitable for performance as it stands, though adapting and then performing passages of a novel or story may be a valuable exercise.

David Birch (1991) suggests that the text of any play is in fact at least two texts: a text of literature and a text for performance. The formerly well-established practice of a school or class group 'putting on a play' at the end of term is now increasingly rare – which in many ways is a loss in terms of developing an understanding of drama. In place of such extended efforts, there has developed, particularly in the language-learning context, a greatly increased emphasis on mini-drama activities in the classroom such as improvisation and role play, which may or may not be linked to study of a text. In this chapter, both text-as-literature and text-for-performance will be considered. We could, however, go further and regard the printed play as a whole bundle of potential texts. For example, a number of recent studies have treated dramatic texts as samples of speech, albeit of a special kind, applying the concepts of discourse analysis to dramatic texts so as to illuminate both the similarities and the differences between speech in drama and naturally occurring spoken discourse. Among such studies are those by Burton (1980; 1982), who bases her analysis of Pinter on the exchange-act model of the Birmingham School; Short (1996) and Gautam and Sharma (1986) are concerned with speech acts and implicature; Lakoff and Tannen (1984) discuss politeness strategies; and the recent full-scale study by Herman (1995) applies a wide range of discourse analysis models to dramatic texts. While for the language teacher these studies offer insight into how speech works in drama and how it may be related to ordinary speech patterns and functions, for most learners, unless they have a particular interest in sociolinguistics or discourse analysis, it is the product mediated by the teacher rather than the process of analysis that will be of value. Additionally, the language teacher may look to the dramatic text for further pedagogic possibilities. A play could be regarded primarily referentially as a vehicle for ideas, and so a source of topics for discussion; as a means of improving spoken language through the use of scripted dialogue or by situation-related improvisations and role play; or as an interactional text, encoding relationships in language.

Reading plays is for most people a difficult and unfamiliar task. Even university students of literature often need help in learning how to read a dramatic text and it is worth spending some time initially on developing the required skills and attention to detail. For beginners, a play presents a text that is frequently boring and occasionally baffling. Unpractised readers of drama often skip over the stage directions, ignoring even the italicised or bracketed instructions on how a speech is to be uttered; they fail to pick up clues of who is addressing whom; they find it difficult to visualise what the set might look like, or what is actually happening on the stage. These issues can all be addressed in the language classroom in ways that encourage language awareness and language use.

There seems to be little value in simply having students read aloud unprepared texts in class – though reading in class as a performance activity is something different altogether. In its most minimal form, it means reading dialogue aloud, as if one were broadcasting a radio play, and using pauses, tone of voice (and sound effects) to put across one's own interpretation of what is happening. At its fullest, it means invited audiences, casting, rehearsal, costumes, props, choreography, directors and a great deal of hard work from all concerned. It is the opposite of an easy way out and almost always gives rise to intense emotions, both positive and negative.

Such fully-fledged performance of drama is beyond the scope of this book – many good books are available – but we suggest that classes studying a play should regularly engage in mini-performances of selected scenes, asking many of the questions which real producers and actors would have to ask. Many of these are considered in greater detail in the second part of this chapter in relation to the particular plays discussed. One problem that inexperienced readers of plays have is in visualising the stage and what is going on there. They can be helped to see the play by exercises such as sketching out a set, discussing costumes and lighting, and plotting characters' moves on the stage, either on paper or where possible by actually moving each other around in the classroom. And they can be helped to hear it by experimenting with passages of dialogue.

- What kind of stage should be used? Photographs, drawings and diagrams of different kinds of stage space can be shown and the consequences for performance discussed.
- What general style should be attempted: for example, naturalistic, melodramatic, Brechtian or TV soap opera?
- What costumes are appropriate? Does one strive for accuracy or is it enough just

to suggest the costume of a Roman senator, a Victorian lady, a soldier, a prostitute? Issues of realism versus Brechtian *Verfremdungseffekt* (alienation effect) can be discussed. What is gained or lost by setting Shakespeare's *Julius Caesar* in Roman, Elizabethan or modern dress, or perhaps in a specific period such as the 1930s in Italy? What historical analogies might illuminate the play?

- Props, scenery and music could be discussed in similar terms.
- Movement, positioning and use of voice can be discussed, practised and guided. How do the position and movement of the characters, particularly their eye movements, reflect and reinforce not only the spoken dialogue but also the subtext of the scene?
- Pacing and timing of action and speech are vital. Most inexperienced actors speak too quickly. It's important to experiment to get the variety of pace that is needed in a dialogue or a long speech. And pauses are vital – but very difficult to manage.
- Loudness must be under conscious control. There is a great variation in loudness even in informal native-speaker talk – on a bus, one half of a conversation may be heard from one end of the bus to the other, while the other is too soft even for the addressee. Drama is a good way of helping both the naturally quiet and the naturally loud to widen their repertoire and thus gain control and confidence.
- A whole range of phonological devices can be used. At the simplest level this can be done talking about and practising made-up exchanges such as the following, with some discussion of the italicised directions:

ANNE    (*Hesitantly*) Won't you – maybe – just try to get in touch with him?
SARA    (*Incisively*) I don't wish to discuss the matter any further.
ANNE  OK. It's your business.
       (*Pause*)
       I just think you're crazy.

Or students may be encouraged to be experimental, trying out a particular word or line in as many different ways as possible, perhaps also suggesting contexts for their own and others' performances and finding descriptive adverbials: gently, apologetically, regretfully, threateningly, and so on.

Really.
Really?
Really!

I'm so sorry.

Haven't we met before somewhere?

The concept of rehearsal is of special relevance in the teaching of foreign language, especially in teaching speaking. We usually think of the ultimate objective of language learning as spontaneous performance (though even this may be an oversimplification), but less fluent learners benefit enormously from time to rehearse, even in non-drama àctivities: going to live in a foreign country means days of silently planning the simplest utterances. For many, the greatest language benefit of drama is that it legitimises the extensive rehearsal – formal, informal and purely mental – which many need but might not otherwise get, due to embarrassment, lack of time or lack of focus. The process of debating what to do, of considering alternatives, also brings in a great deal of language – vocabulary and grammar, functions and notions, skills and strategies – which will be useful elsewhere.

Teachers should be – and no doubt are – aware of the fact that not everyone responds happily to drama and dramatic activities. Even learners who like drama may rebel at some of the physical activities suggested in books for foreign-language teachers. For example, though Maley and Duff's *Drama Techniques in Language Learning* (1982) is full of good ideas, not every student (or teacher) is going to feel comfortable with, for instance, lying on the floor doing 'directed relaxation'. On the other hand, it is worth giving some of their suggestions a try even where you may feel doubtful, for the response is sometimes unexpectedly positive, enough to convince even the most sceptical. But it is not important enough to make an issue out of it.

With less accepting learners, our recommendation is not to give up drama activities entirely but to negotiate what will be acceptable. It should be possible to convince a class studying a play that some kind of performance, however limited – standing up, moving a few chairs around – can contribute to understanding and general language improvement. Next time, the boundaries can be pushed a little further. No student should be required to do anything with which he or she feels uncomfortable, or which he or she feels is a waste of time.

## 7.2  PLAYS AS LITERATURE AND PLAYS AS PERFORMANCE

Most of what follows in this chapter will, like that on novels, be based on selected texts: Shakespeare's *The Tempest*; *All My Sons* by Arthur Miller; and Liz Lochhead's *Mary Queen of Scots Got Her Head Chopped Off*. They have been chosen at least in part because they are very different from one another: they represent different dramatic genres, different cultural matrices and they lend themselves to a variety of pedagogical approaches. They are also – an important consideration – easily available (see bibliography, second part, for publication details).

A fourth writer, Harold Pinter, will be mentioned briefly at several points in this chapter. Space precludes a separate section on Pinter, but we recommend a study of his short plays, *The Lover* and *The Dumb Waiter*, to exemplify some of the points discussed below and to provide a wider sample of the language of drama.

## 7.3  WAYS OF READING PLAYS: LINGUISTIC PARADIGMS

This chapter will be organised around plays rather than linguistic paradigms, but nevertheless it may be helpful initially to consider whether any particular approaches to the analysis of spoken discourse among those mentioned above offer insights into dramatic texts for classroom reading. The process is that outlined by McCarthy

(1996) as the reconstruction and deconstruction of texts, where what he describes as performance activities lead to a deeper understanding of how the language works in the text. Four possible approaches which in our experience have been illuminating in the classroom context are drawn on in the discussion of the plays that follows: Hymes' work on the ethnography of speech events; ethnomethodology; Gricean pragmatics; and the notion of speech acts. Pragmatics and speech acts have already been considered in section 3.7, but the next few sections (7.3.1–7.3.4) provide more detail on certain concepts and analytical approaches. The application of these to the teaching of particular texts follows later, and you may wish at this point to skip this more theoretical section and move straight to the discussion of the plays.

### 7.3.1　The ethnography of speech events

The text of a play is a potential rather than an actual speech event and, as we have already said, requires a considerable exercise of the imagination to make it come alive. An ethnographic approach, therefore, is probably most valuable where students have the opportunity to see a live production or a film of the play, where it is actually experienced as a speech event rather than a mute text on the page (though see the application of this method later in this chapter to *All My Sons*, where we deal directly with the text). The value of the ethnographic framework is that it requires the observers to pay attention to a range of features in the event, including their own reactions as a participant – even if a marginal one – in the scene, where they perceive, in the words of the epigraph to this chapter, that 'drama is not made of words alone, but of sights and sounds, stillness and motion, noise and silence, relationships and responses.'

The approach described here is that of the sociolinguist and ethnographer Dell Hymes. His taxonomy of speaking, first published in 1972, is offered as a tool, as a step in the progress towards possible models of sociolinguistic description, not as a theory in itself, and it is as an analytic and descriptive tool that we shall employ it in the consideration of drama texts.

Hymes developed his framework around the mnemonic SPEAKING, which, though at points somewhat strained, does what it is intended to do, that is, it helps one remember the key points of his approach.

Ways of reading a speech event

| | |
|---|---|
| S | Settings |
| P | Participants |
| E | Ends |
| A | Act sequences |
| K | Keys |
| I | Instrumentalities |
| N | Norms |
| G | Genres |

(adapted from Hymes 1972)

**Setting:** This can be subdivided into the actual physical setting of an event (for example, courtroom, kitchen, mosque, street or restaurant) and the scene, which signifies the conventional or psychological orientations of the setting.

**Participants:** These may be broadly divided into those who at any point are the speaker/reader/addresser and those who at any point are the hearer/receiver/ addressee. Questions of private person and public function also arise: how do these elements interact at any moment? How close or distant or overlapping are, for example, the persona of the politician and the same person in private life? How does Liam Neeson's fame as a film actor affect the audience's perception of his stage appearance as Oscar Wilde in a West End production? The roles of apparent non-participants (including that of the observer) and their relationship to and effect on the situation may also be significant.

**Ends** (or purposes): What are the goals of any event or interaction, in other words, what do participants hope or expect from what is going on (these may be conventional in the sense that they are shaped by the particular kind of event, such as a university degree ceremony)? In some events, different participants may have different goals, as in a legal case. And secondly what are the outcomes of any event, that is, what actually results from whatever is going on?

**Acts** (act sequence): This may be subdivided into the form of the message and the content of the message (cf. Jakobson). In a British general election, for example, the announcement of constituency results by the returning officer will follow a strictly prescribed form, but will vary in content.

**Key:** Key refers to the tone or attitudinal and emotional aspects of an event. It corresponds to modality among grammatical categories. Is the event a celebration? Is it wholly serious or can ironic or subversive elements be perceived? What kind of relationships are expressed between participants; do they change at any point; are they expressed verbally or by other means?

**Instrumentalities:** This applies to the forms of speech that are used, for example a particular register or dialect. Hymes, however, recognises that any speech event includes more than just speech. What additional channels are employed (such as gesture, mime, positioning of groups)?

**Norms:** What are the ordinary ways of conducting these interactions? And, by implication, how may these norms be disturbed or violated? Second, what are the norms of interpretation? Silence, for example, may be interpreted differently in different cultural settings.

**Genres:** In some cases, an event clearly falls into a particular genre, such as a televised snooker match, a pub-quiz programme, a traditional wedding reception. Genres appear briefly out of their usual context, often for comic effect – for example, in conversation where a speaker may parodically quote a genre such as political interview or sports journalism. In a play, genre references may function as a type of intertextuality: the play-within-a-play in *Mary Queen of Scots Got Her Head Chopped Off* has echoes of the similar scene in *Hamlet*.

### 7.3.2 Ethnomethodology

This approach broadly comprises considerations of turn-taking, adjacency pairs, openings and closings, holding the floor and silence. Its value for the study of dramatic texts is that it describes the taken-for-granted and largely unnoticed norms of ordinary interaction.

Most of us never reflect on how we 'manage' conversation; how we seem to pick up instinctively when we can start speaking without interrupting the other person; how we work changes of topic – and, very significantly, how we know when someone breaks the 'rules'. The most influential early work on the description of conversation in English is probably that by Sacks et al. (1974). We focus here on the main points that they make about turn-taking, which is particularly relevant to an understanding of Pinter's plays.

Where a conversation takes place between two people, they suggest that the 'rules' operate as follows:

1. For a conversation to happen at all, speaker change has to occur.
2. Almost always, only one person talks at a time.
3. Overlaps occur quite frequently but are generally very brief.
4. The majority of transitions from one speaker to the other occur without a gap or overlap, or with a very short gap or overlap.
5. Length of turn may vary considerably.
6. Length of conversation is variable, not fixed in advance.
7. Topic can change in the course of conversation.

Where more than two speakers are involved, turn-taking becomes considerably more complicated. For example, the order of turns varies (not just A-B-C-D-A-B-C-D, and so on); if A speaks first, anyone may follow and the order is quite unpredictable. So how is chaos avoided? What are known as 'turn-allocation' rules (or techniques) provide for orderly progression: the current speaker may by word or look or gesture select the next speaker, or a speaker may self-select by starting to speak at a suitable point, where he or she is not interrupting the previous speaker (a 'transition-relevance-place'). Where two people start talking at once, repair mechanisms are available; usually one will stop prematurely, or apologise. Overlap (which can generally be distinguished from interruption) quite often occurs in a supportive fashion. Pauses may also occur, inadvertently or deliberately, and may cause more or less discomfort, depending on the context of situation. Pauses may also be quite definitely manipulated in certain kinds of structured talk, such as counselling or group therapy, where a pause may be held deliberately, indicating, for example: 'I'm waiting for you to say something more'. The use and manipulation of both pauses and interruptions are related to the expression of power relations in certain kinds of interactions.

One approach to dialogue or group-talk in play texts that students may find interesting is to compare recordings (or even transcriptions) of ordinary conversation, full of untidiness and overlapping, with the tidied up quality of even the most apparently naturalistic drama script.

### 7.3.3  Pragmatics: the co-operative principle

The philosopher H. P. Grice was, like Sacks et al., interested in conversation, but approached it from a different angle. His concern was not to describe the mechanics of conversation but to get at the underlying principles that make conversation possible at all. The result was the formulation of four maxims that provided the basis for what he calls the co-operative principle (Grice: 1975).

Quantity: say just as much as you need to say, neither too much nor too little;
Quality: be truthful;
Relation: be relevant;
Manner: avoid obscurity.

To these Leech (1983) added a fifth, which is: be polite.

Any accidental failure to observe these maxims is regarded as a 'violation' of the co-operative principle; an intentional resistance is classed as 'flouting' it.

Clearly if this is taken as prescriptive, it is unrealistic. Much work on pragmatics (Brown and Yule 1983, for example) shows how, if we judge by the surface form of many of our everyday interactions (which may be quite amicable and even polite), one or other maxim is constantly being violated. We function socially, at least in informal situations, by filling in the gaps in one another's utterances. The oft-quoted example of:

Isn't that the phone?

I'm in the bath.

illustrates how a single utterance may in one breath superficially violate the maxims of quantity, relation and manner. Of course, it can then be argued that if we make sense of this exchange, we are implicitly operating by Gricean maxims because we assume that the answer 'I'm in the bath' can be understood as being sufficient, relevant and without obscurity and we interpret it accordingly as 'Well, I'm afraid I can't answer it as I'm in the bath. Can you take the call?'

A more serious criticism of Grice is that the maxims of the co-operative principle are culture bound: in effect, that it is based on the conversational patterns of the white Western middle class of the mid-twentieth century. Whatever the validity of this criticism, it can still be argued that Grice provides a very useful framework for examining our verbal communications, our expectations and norms and the ways in which these may be violated or flouted. Moreover, he helps us see more clearly how and why and to what purpose an interaction may be perceived to be *un*co-operative. These floutings are standard material for many comic routines, and also in absurdist drama: again you will find many examples in Pinter.

### 7.3.4  Speech acts

A further useful paradigm for the analysis of dramatic dialogue is that of communicative acts. The framework that we use here is a slightly expanded version of the development by Bach and Harnish (1979) of Searle's (1969) taxonomy. At the simplest level, this requires a distinction to be made between *declaratives*, *directives* and *commissives* (for example promises or offers), and *acknowledgements* (apologies or congratulations), to which might be added *interrogatives* as a separate category. Two further types comprise *effectives* and *verdictives*: these subdivide Austin's category of performative speech acts (speech acts which bring about some sort of change in the institutional state of affairs) into those that bring about a change by the act of utterance (such as naming a ship or firing an employee), and those that pronounce some kind of judgement (a legal verdict pronounced by a judge or the public declaration of the winner of a race).

Interrogatives in particular, in drama as in life, may be employed to produce a variety of communicative effects, and Pinter is again a rich source of examples.

## 7.4 TEACHING THE TEXTS

We now turn to particular plays. In each case we have suggested approaches which we have found particularly useful for that play, but there is no suggestion that what is described comes near to exhausting the potential of the text, or that the approaches suggested for one play should not be adapted and developed for another. Film, video and live productions can all be extremely useful, but the teacher who does not have access to any of these should not feel that they are essential; what *is* essential – whether the focus of the class is on drama for language or on drama as literature – is enabling students to enter into the text imaginatively.

### 7.4.1 *All My Sons* by Arthur Miller

Why this play? Simply because in our experience it is one of the most satisfactory of dramatic texts for classroom use and is widely applicable and adaptable. The central dilemma of private versus public morality, the tension between loyalty to the family and a wider social ethic, always seems to find a contemporary correlative in the experience of students, wherever they come from and whatever their experience may be. It is, therefore, constantly relevant. Because it is in theatrical terms a very traditional – even, some might say, old-fashioned – play (a well-made social drama-according-to-Ibsen), it has certain advantages: a small cast of fairly highly developed yet representative characters, a clear structure with strong climaxes to each Act, and a tight plot. Apart from the leisurely exposition of Act I, the pace is fast and there is an increasing build-up of tension – and unless the students are studying the whole play as a literary text, the slow introduction can simply be summarised and class time devoted to other sections.

The activities that follow are intended to develop an appreciation of the text for performance rather than as a literary object. If time is short, or if reading the whole play would be too demanding, it is perfectly possible to select key sections for close study in class and fill in the rest with plot summaries.

1. **Introducing the play** (developing skills for reading dramatic texts).

   Students are given a handout with the date of the play, the names of the characters, the brief descriptions of them that are provided in the play and one or two of their speeches. (This does not mean that the teacher should write his or her own summary version of the characters' features; there is plenty of information both provided explicitly and implied in the text.) On the basis of these, students discuss the characters and establish certain expectations. They also study the very detailed description of the set, possibly even sketching it out and then discussing its implications (the economic status of the family, relations with neighbours, significance of the toppled tree, and so on). If a video is available, a clip can be shown at this point: for example, the Mother's first entrance and the next part of the scene to the end of the account of her dream, followed by a discussion of the interpretation of the characters and the setting. Before showing the clip, different individuals (or pairs or small groups) could be given responsibility for observation and comment on specific features: the set, costumes, casting, characterisation or the tempo of the scene. Discussion then follows: is it what they had expected? Where were their own interpretations different? Have the implications of the set description (even if not the exact details) been realised in the film? Are the relationships between characters as they had imagined? Have they learnt anything more (for example, about the fallen tree, about the family's past history)?

   Keller, Chris and Kate are all introduced in this short scene, and the same method may be followed for later sections where Annie and George appear. If a video is not available, these scenes may be read – we would suggest, at this stage, silently – followed by group or pair discussion of particular features.

2. **Scene as speech event:** that is, developing the capacity to imagine a play through close analysis of a key scene.

   One of the most significant dramatic features of this play is the way in which the emotional tone of a scene varies, sometimes almost moment to moment. The middle section of Act II is a case in point, where the conflict between George and Chris reaches crisis point, only to be deflected by the Mother's entrance, which in turn is followed by the unease generated by Keller's apparent openness in contrast to George's wavering hostility. This is where an approach based on Hymes' framework can be illuminating. There is no need to follow his outline slavishly but it serves as a useful checklist for observation. In the brief suggestions that follow, we have drawn on the features that seem relevant.

   Is the *setting* important, either in terms of the physical space or its psychological resonances? The whole play is set in the backyard of the Kellers' home, where the neighbours come and go, therefore it is a space that belongs to the family yet is not entirely private; the psychological meanings show up George as the interloper.

   Who at any moment are the *participants*? Who speaks and to whom, who is significantly silent? Do some people have longer turns? (Consider the length of Keller's turns in particular – and Annie's long silences.)

What are the various *intentions* of the participants, expressed and unexpressed? Is the Mother putting emotional pressure on George by recalling shared memories? Are Keller's speeches a kind of concealed blackmail? Do George's intentions shift during the scene?

What are the *keys*, or emotional tones, at what moments do they change and how are those changes accomplished? For example, what effect does the Mother's entrance have? What range of emotions does she manipulate during the exchanges following her entrance – warmth, regret, nostalgia, shared experiences, and so on?

What *instrumentalities* are drawn on? What 'channels' are employed other than verbal, for instance gesture: the symbolic actions of hospitality as the Mother pours out grape juice for George.

What are the *norms* of interaction? Are they being observed or are they disrupted in some way? For example, the Mother's tactic is to pretend that the norm is that of a happy family reunion.

Neither *act sequence* nor *genre* seem so immediately relevant to this scene, although there are many other contexts where they are significant. For example, in *Mary Queen of Scots Got Her Head Chopped Off* (see section 7.4.3), the murder of Darnley is presented as part of a mummers' performance (a play within a play); the issues of message form in relation to message content can be explored here and the question of genre has obvious relevance.

Even where a video is available, we would suggest that students work initially from the text and establish through pair or groupwork their own understanding of the scene before watching the filmed version. Having thus established their ownership of the text, they may well want to disagree with the filmed interpretation – which is a far more fruitful way of using video than passively allowing it to dictate their reading of the play.

In preparation for this session students could be asked to read the scene, with different members of the group focusing on particular characters: what does Mother/George/Keller/Anne/Chris say? What do they feel at each point? How do they look? Who (if anyone) are they looking at? What are their particular tensions and in relation to whom? This can produce a much more lively and committed discussion than a rather general reading of the scene.

3. **Practising a key scene** (developing understanding of the structure and development of a scene). For this exercise, a fairly short but emotionally intense scene should be chosen. We have found the final section of Act II very effective; another possibility would be the confrontation between George and Chris earlier in the same act. Whichever scene you choose, it should be one with plenty of potential for variation of pace and dynamics.

The class should be divided into small groups, each consisting ideally of the number of characters in the scene, plus one. They are then asked to work on the scene as if for performance. They read it silently first, then try it out with different readers for the various parts, switching as they go through rather than reading the whole scene several times over. They then talk about the characters, their feelings and how these are expressed – by emphasis, by whispering or shouting, by movement (some guidance is given in the stage directions). Next they decide who will be the readers and who will be the director – a key role, this, and not to be given to the shyest or most retiring member of the group: whoever it is will have to be able to interrupt, to suggest alternative readings and to hold the group together. They decide together how to break up the scene into short rehearsable sections and work on them, gradually building up intensity, dramatic contrasts and gestures, together with effective use of both interruptions and pauses. The teacher moves from group to group, listening in, occasionally commenting or suggesting (preferably demonstrating) alternatives. To be effective, this activity must be allowed plenty of time. Depending on the numbers involved, the groups may present their own performances. And of course, at the end the video can be shown – which in our experience generally leads to lively discussion and disagreement and the defence of alternative interpretations.

4. **Predicting outcomes.** Prediction activities are familiar friends for the language teacher and it is true that they can be overworked. However, with any of Miller's plays, and this one in particular, prediction is an authentic activity in the sense the text positively cries out for it. If students carry out the previous activity of developing a key section of the text dramatically – particularly if it is the last part of Act II – they are generally emotionally engaged and full of ideas about what is going to happen. Indeed, the activity can be a continuation of the work they have been doing in their small groups.

If the teacher does intend to do some work on prediction, it is important that students do not take their texts home before this point; certainly all the work suggested above can be carried out in class and students may then take the books home after the session on prediction to read the (very short) final act to see how it really does work out – or they may watch part of it on video in the class. This would also be a suitable moment to introduce the question of the play's title, *All My Sons*, and to speculate on its meaning. Students could then be asked to discover the answer for themselves by reading the play at home or while viewing the last act.

### 7.4.2  *The Tempest* by William Shakespeare

This part of the chapter is perhaps inevitably addressed to Type A more than Type B teachers, though we hope that both groups will find useful ideas in it.

*Why* The Tempest?

In probably the majority of cases where a Shakespeare play is taught, it is in an institutional context where the teacher has little influence on the selection of texts: the play is simply part of the literature syllabus. In such cases, the choice is likely to fall on one of a small number of regularly recurring plays: *Romeo and Juliet*, *Macbeth*, maybe *Hamlet* or *Julius Caesar*. If, however, a teacher is in the fortunate position of being able to make his or her own choice, he or she will probably want to consider one that has not been done to death already. When this freedom is available, it would be worth considering one of the later plays – *The Winter's Tale* or *The Tempest* – for the simple reason that very few students will have read them; or a film might provide the inspiration, such as Kenneth Branagh's *Much Ado about Nothing* or *Henry V*, Ian McKellen's *Richard II*, *Shakespeare's Romeo and Juliet*, *Shakespeare in Love*, or Peter Greenaway's *Prospero's Books*. Alternatively, there may be the more localised factor of a performance in a nearby theatre.

In the rest of this section we shall be using *The Tempest* illustratively, exploring approaches to the text that can be adapted to other plays.

*Space and visualising*

With Shakespeare, one of the most important pre-reading considerations is theatrical space; this does not imply a mini-lecture on the Shakespearean theatre (though that may indeed at some point be of interest) but rather, exploring the question: what kinds of space best serve what kinds of play? The differences between the plays discussed in this chapter are expressed partly by means of different uses of theatrical space: for *Mary Queen of Scots*, a space that allows both for direct communication with the audience and flexibility of grouping of scenes on stage; a fixed set for *All My Sons*; and an open and adaptable space for imaginative representation for *The Tempest*. Students may be shown illustrations from any encyclopaedia of theatre, or, possibly more usefully, the teacher may draw diagrams of different kinds of stage and audience seating and thereby guide students to think about the variety of effects that may be produced by such differences. If feasible, they can move desks and chairs to simulate those spaces and act out mini-scenes to check their ideas. In multi-cultural groups, students may have a variety of experience to offer, for example, from the traditions of Kabuki and Noh from Japan or the open-air Ramlila presentations from North India. The possibilities of film techniques can also be explored, including the computer graphics of Greenaway's *Prospero's Books* and the cartoons of the *Animated Shakespeare* series. Useful vocabulary can be introduced during this pre-reading work: set, lighting, props, upstage, downstage, backstage, proscenium arch, theatre in the round, front-of-house, box office, and so on.

Paying attention to this preparatory work and making it as interesting and vivid as possible can help with the process of visualising scenes while reading, particularly in terms of relationship with audience.

*One play – many interpretations*

Two contrasting performances of Prospero's renunciation speech illustrate the range of possible interpretations: Sir John Gielgud (recorded on *Ages of Man*: CBS Classics 61830) and Heathcote Williams in Derek Jarman's film (PVC 2027A). Gielgud's is the flowering of a particular tradition of classical English verse speaking: rhetorical and full of dramatic contrast, it is very much a public performance. Williams, in contrast, speaks in a whisper, with little variation of tone or pace, and the effect is of a private introspective process. The director has also cut the last part of the speech so that the actual renunciation is omitted.

In a fascinating and superbly usable study, David Hirst (1984) compares four productions of *The Tempest*, chosen from among many possible contenders for their development of key themes and variety of staging and interpretation, and illustrates them with photographs and stills. We will not elaborate on his work here, but will instead in a similar spirit compare the interpretation of the figures of Caliban and Ariel in Greenaway's film with a stage production by Peter Brook.

Briefly then, Greenaway, in a film which sets out to be transgressive of established conventions, nevertheless presents what is in many ways a very traditional contrast between Ariel, who appears initially as a small delicate figure swinging on a trapeze while he sings strange ethereal music, and a Caliban (played by the dancer Michael Clark) who is a lithe, powerful and repulsively reptilian representation of male sexuality. Prospero in the film is played by an aged John Gielgud whose elegant classical diction floats above the characteristically violent yet beautiful visual imagery of a Greenaway film. Brook, on the other hand, produced an inversion of the usual characterisation: his Prospero was black, and the part of Ariel was taken by Bakary Sangare, a big and physically powerful black Malian actor – who, however, spoke with a consistently high, almost giggly tone and was extraordinarily light on his feet – while Caliban was acted by a white German actor, a tiny furious figure who lived in a cardboard box, which he carried round with him and which he retreated into at moments of fear or dudgeon or erupted from in bursts of rage. This was an explicit reversal of Jonathan Miller's anti-colonialist interpretation (described in Hirst), where Prospero and Ariel are presented as the powerful European incomers with the exploited Caliban as the black aboriginal inhabitant of the island; Brook's production focused on a different set of questions relating to power and control within the play. The unpredictability of this angry and fearful child Caliban provided an intriguing contrast to the imposing physical presence of Ariel, an embodiment of harmony and control and benign humour. To one member of the audience at least, the representation of these two key figures emphasised that the struggle between control and demonic rage in this play was not a concern limited to the magician Prospero but a recognisable aspect of common human experience. It also affected the gender issues raised by the play: how might it change the audience's response to Caliban's sexuality, for example, in the references to his attempt to rape Miranda?

A manifestly non-realistic work such as *The Tempest* offers considerable space for variety of interpretation, and one of the pleasures of this text is the potential play and contrast of different ways of exploring these themes visually. The play could be read initially fairly sketchily, paying closer attention to a few key scenes so as to focus on certain significant themes: colonisation and exploitation; nature versus nurture; power, its exercise and renunciation; conflict within the human psyche; questions of identity. In passing, it should be acknowledged that this can come close to the 'selected highlights' approach of TV sports programmes, where we are shown only the exciting moves and goals while the boring connective passages get cut out (Drakakis 1997). As language teachers we may have no problems with this; literature teachers, however, may feel under pressure to persuade their students to read the text in its entirety. The justification for this method is the same for both groups: that in most cases it brings success by enabling students to enjoy the selected scenes that they read, and this success may possibly persuade them eventually to tackle the whole play. After the initial reading, the teacher might introduce a range of different ways of expressing these themes in performance, with, if possible, examples from films (including films such as the cartoon *Animated Shakespeare* series already mentioned), audio recordings, photographs, descriptions, or critics' reviews of productions; students could follow this up by exploring their own ideas about the visual representation of these ideas. If students already have some knowledge of theatre, they could be invited to explore their own possible interpretations before considering those of others, but if they have very little previous experience, they may benefit from the imaginative stimulus of other interpretations.

In a long and difficult play such as this, it can be useful to focus attention on one or two key speeches, reading and analysing them in some detail, and wherever possible watching an actor speaking them on film or listening to an audio recording. An example of how one might set about preparing this approach is given in Appendix 1.

### 7.4.3 *Mary Queen of Scots Got Her Head Chopped Off* by Liz Lochhead

This play offers a wide range of possibilities for a group of advanced learners. At the time of writing, it appears on the Scottish Cultural Studies syllabus in at least one university in Hungary where British Cultural Studies is an option. It is an obvious candidate for inclusion in such contexts, particularly where cultural studies has a linguistic focus in terms of language, nation and identity.

In a recent article entitled 'Dedefining Scotland' (1997) Robert Crawford, a poet and Scottish academic, writes that the plural 'Scotlands' is finding increasing favour in the discussion of Scottish culture. It is a term that 'lays emphasis on the plural identity of the nation' (93). This is precisely what Liz Lochhead does in her representation of the figure of Mary Queen of Scots. The audience is offered not so much a version of events surrounding the historical woman as a revision of the myths that popular culture has built up around her. As Lochhead herself has said (1992), 'the story *must* still be alive for Scots today when a male, Irish-Catholic city Scot [Gerry Mulgrew, who directed the first production of the play] and a female, Proddy, rural Lanarkshire Scot [me] had been taught such different versions.' In the final scene of the play, the execution of Mary is enacted in the context of a series of contemporary children's games and quarrels which mimic the sectarian tensions of the adult world. The title of this scene of divisiveness is 'Jock Thamson's Bairns' – an ironic reference to the common Scottish saying 'We're all Jock Thamson's bairns', meaning that we are all essentially members of the same family and share the same universal values and behaviours.

In the following section, we consider some of the possibilities offered by the opening speech of the play by La Corbie (The Crow), who performs the roles of chorus and omniscient commentator in the play.

LA CORBIE: Country: Scotland. Whit like is it?
It's a peatbog, it's a daurk forest.
It's a cauldron o' lye, a saltpan or a coal mine.
If you're gey lucky it's a bricht bere meadow or a park o' kye.
Or mibbe … it's a field o' stanes.
It's a tenement or a merchant's ha'.
It's a hure hoose or a humble cot. Princes Street or Paddy's Merkit.
It's a fistfu' o' fish or a pickle o' oatmeal.
It's a queen's banquet o' roast meats and junketts.

It depends. It depends … Ah dinna ken whit like your Scotland is.
Here's mines.
National flower: the thistle.
National pastime: nostalgia.
National weather: smirr, haar, drizzle, snow.
National bird: the crow, the corbie, *le corbeau, moi!*
How me? Eh? Eh? Eh? Voice like a choked laugh. Ragbag o' a burd ma black duds, a' angles and elbows and broken oxter feathers, black beady een in ma executioner's hood. No braw, but Ah think Ah ha'e sort of black glamour.
Do I no put ye in mind of a skating minister, or, on the other fit, the parish priest, the dirty beast?
My nest's a rickle o' sticks.
I live on lamb's eyes and road accidents.
Oh, see, after the battle, man, it's a pure feast – ma eyes are ower big even for *my* belly, in lean years o' peace, my belly thinks my throat's been cut.

The first question most teachers are likely to ask is: how am I going to deal with all this unfamiliar vocabulary? The language of any text in Scots may appear to some readers (including British readers who are not familiar with Scots) to be a major obstacle to understanding. We would suggest that it should be recognised as a genuine but not disabling problem; in fact, though teachers may manifest anxiety, many students seem actually to enjoy the extra linguistic dimension. One way of dealing with this might be to ask students to read the first part of the speech silently, then discuss it with a partner, including (and this is important) reading the text aloud to each other, and only then mark the words (a) which they feel are a real obstacle to understanding; and (b) which they may not recognise but which do not prevent them grasping the general meaning of the speech. Some of these will be variant spellings of familiar words found in standard English (*daurk, o', ma*) and others actually will be Scots words (*gey, ken, smirr, corbie*). This exercise helps readers realise that in fact they can grasp a great deal of the meaning of the text in spite of some unfamiliar words. (In Appendix 1, you will find more detailed suggestions of how this might be done in class.) A development from this exercise could be a group discussion of the questions: 'What is meant by a dialect?'; and leading on from that, 'When is a dialect a language?' Many students will be familiar with these questions from their own national and linguistic contexts.

In the second place, the opening speech by La Corbie suggests a number of points for further development: for example, the comic anachronisms indicate that the play is less concerned with historical facts than with the representation of the interaction of historical events and personages as 'a metaphor for Scotland today' (Lochhead in *Time Out*, September 1987: 16–23), something which is developed further in, for example, the presentation of the Reformation leader John Knox as an Orange-man (that is, a member of a present-day Northern Irish Protestant group). The ambiguously androgynous figure of La Corbie herself highlights the issues of both gender and tradition which are explored in the play. And in her address to the audience, she draws attention to the variety of cultural groupings within the country, as Crawford puts it, the many different 'Scotlands':

> Country: Scotland. Whit like is it? …
> It depends. It depends … Ah dinna ken whit like *your* Scotland is.
> Here's mines.

Then, in the second part of the speech, as she introduces the two queens of the two countries, Mary of Scotland and Elizabeth of England, La Corbie presents a traditional (if ironically nuanced) version of the story which the theatrical forms of the presentation of the drama will set out to question and deconstruct.

> LA CORBIE: *(With both Queens by the hand, parading them)* Once upon a time there were *twa queens* on the wan green island, and the wan green island was split inty twa kingdoms. But no equal kingdoms, naebody in their richt mind would insist on that. For the northern kingdom was cauld and sma'. And the people were low-statured and ignorant and feart o' their lords and poor! They were starvin'. And their queen was beautiful and tall and fair and … Frenchified. The other kingdom in the island was large, and prosperous, with wheat and barley and fat kye in the fields o' her mouth o' her greatest river, a great port, a glistening city that sucked all wealth to its centre which was a palace and a court of a queen. She was a cousin, a clever cousin a wee bit aulder, and mibbe no sae braw as the other queen, but a queen nevertheless. Queen o' a country wi' an army, an' a navy and dominion over many lands.

*(Burst of dance from DANCER, a sad or ironic jig.)*
Twa queens. Wan green island. And ambassadors and courtiers came from many
lands to seek their hauns ...

In the scenes that follow, the two queens Mary and Elizabeth are presented both in
relation and opposition, though they never meet; this is achieved by doubling parts
so that the two characters of Mary and Marian (Elizabeth's maid) are played by a
single actress, and similarly with the characters of Elizabeth and Bessie (Mary's
maid). The doubling is an economical device for providing implicit commentary on
the parallelism and differences of the two queens' situations. In another theatrical
device, the murder of Mary's husband Darnley is enacted as a play within a play,
when the killers disguised as mummers (traditional folk-play actors) come to entertain Mary in her private apartments. The intertextual references to *Hamlet* and the
ritual character of the mummers' actions and speech all contribute to Lochhead's
purpose of 'revisioning' the national myth of Mary, the tragic queen.

The play or parts of it ('selected highlights') may be read if that is appropriate in
the particular linguistic and cultural context of a group of students. On the other
hand, the introductory speech quoted above can on its own provide plenty of
material for discussion and language activities.

As the use of the Scots language can raise questions of language and cultural
identity, so also the use in this play of particular theatrical forms can introduce
comparisons and contrasts with the use and significance of local cultural styles, and
in turn both can lead on to a consideration of how national and regional under-
standings of history are revisioned in the home culture.

## 7.5 CONCLUSION

In this chapter we have attempted to present a variety of linguistically oriented ways
of reading dramatic texts with language learners, which aim to lead beyond the
language on the page to a developing understanding and enjoyment of them as texts
designed for performance. The range of dramatic genres represented also provides a
chance to make contrasts and comparisons; learners should be encouraged to read
the selected plays intertextually, with cross-referencing to other texts, both in English
and within their own culture, wherever the opportunity presents itself.

# Chapter 8

# Assessment and evaluation in literature lessons and courses

## 8.1 THE CASE FOR *NOT* ASSESSING

Nearly all of this chapter will be devoted to the 'what' and 'how' of assessment in literature lessons. The first question, though, must be: should we assess at all? Or rather, as assessment is compulsory or obviously demanded in some classes, we can formulate the question as: should we assess all our literature classes?

Our answer to this is a definite no. It is important to be definite, because social and political trends (in Britain at least) are now leading to demands for assessment where none has existed. One manifestation of this is national curriculum tests for young schoolchildren, while another, more relevant here, is the introduction of certification and credit schemes in adult education, an area in which most non-vocational classes were previously taken largely for enjoyment, personal satisfaction and perhaps, in the case of language teaching, as preparation for a holiday abroad.

We are not against more assessment in principle, or in all cases. In schools, for example, the extension of certificated assessment at sixteen-plus has undoubtedly done some good to some children. In adult education, though, at least some of the recent assessment initiatives seem to have been extraordinarily counter-productive: perceived as a way of creating jobs for new 'managers', they have alienated teachers and learners, who in some cases have abandoned 'official' classes and set up alternative classes in private houses. The lesson to be learned from this – and it can apply with children too – is that many people learn, and even teach, for pleasure, especially in a subject such as literature, and attempts to impose formal assessment structures will be resented.

Rejection of formal assessment does not preclude some informal kind. A term sometimes used is 'non-invasive assessment' (by analogy with non-invasive surgery) which means collecting information without the learners perceiving it as a test. Of course we would want teachers to collect information informally on how their learners are coping – are they understanding the texts, for example? We would even advocate teacher training in this area, and observations by colleagues or heads of department (see Chapter 9) in teaching situations where formal tests are inadvisable but specific attainment is important. In many other situations, though, especially with adults enrolled for pleasure, not even this is necessary: the normal human mechanisms of feedback and sensitivity to others should be enough, and insistence on systematic assessment would almost certainly damage the classroom ambience.

## 8.2  TYPES OF ASSESSMENT FOR LEARNERS, TEACHERS AND THE CURRICULUM

Any assessment or evaluation may give us information about any one or two, or all three, of the following:

- Learners: 'Mary has a French vocabulary of about 5000 words'; 'John can write good essays in English on Russian novels';
- Teachers, possibly including the assessor: 'I've not succeeded in explaining narratology to this class'; 'Mary's students perform better in grammar tests than Peter's'; 'Mary's students write about literature in Leavisite terms, Peter's have a more linguistic approach';
- Curriculum, including textbooks and classroom methods: 'I'm getting better results with this book'; 'It's not working, making them write essays so early in the course'.

**Note:** There is no universally agreed distinction between assessment and evaluation, but the latter term is certainly more general: we suggest that you consider assessment as data collection, plus numerical analysis (scoring) where appropriate, while evaluation is assessment plus interpretation, making inferences and decisions or recommendations for future activity.

Each kind of assessment can be used for several purposes. Learner assessment can be used, *inter alia*, for placement ('which class should she go into?'), diagnosis ('what specific teaching, revision, etc., does she need?') and certification ('should he be awarded a pass in the examination?'). Teacher assessment can also be for certification, but is often for consciousness raising and professional development. Curriculum assessment can be formative, for instance when a coursebook is being piloted in draft form prior to revision, or summative, as when a school decides whether or not to buy a commercially available coursebook.

Much fuller discussion of these concepts can be found in specialist books. Our reason for mentioning them here is to stress the need for clear thinking about what kind of assessment one is doing; in particular, avoiding the temptation to assess only the learners, and in particular to blame all 'failures' on learner inadequacies. There are two things wrong with this:

1. In most cases, except perhaps when we are testing students new to our course, results can also tell us something about our teaching (or that of other teachers, where applicable).
2. Often neither learner nor teacher is to 'blame': the concept of blame is simply inapplicable if we accept that responses and outcomes are individual and unpredictable (see Chapter 1).

This does not mean that we should be complacent about negative results, but that we should sometimes cast our net more widely. If they have not learned what I expected, have they learned other things? Are they interested, motivated, confident? How would *they* feel about a change of direction in the teaching?

The results of assessment should never lead automatically to a change of curriculum, but should be an input to periodic reflection and, where possible, discussion with the learners.

Most of the ideas in this chapter are potentially equally applicable to diagnostic assessment within a course and to certification at the end of a course. In our view, the same general kinds of assessment should be used for both purposes, though one can sometimes justify being slightly less rigorous and 'kinder' in diagnostic tests, where a major purpose is encouragement, slightly more rigorous and 'tougher' in certification, where one is in fact vouchsafing to a third party, for example an employer or university, that the students can do certain things.

This chapter does not deal directly with preparing students for external examinations, such as the Cambridge Proficiency or GCSE English Literature. We would strongly advise, however, that assessment on such courses should not, at least in the early stages, closely follow the target examination format. We have seen courses which are little more than a series of mock examinations, with preparation and feedback, but these do not seem effective, especially for the weaker students, who receive repeated evidence of failure but are given no structure within which to improve. It is far better to start from where the students are, to teach and test what interests them and what they want and need to know, and to establish good learning habits. Later, one can determine whether a particular external examination is really a desirable and realistic target and, if so, move slowly towards the content and the exercise types which it demands.

## 8.3 TYPOLOGY OF POTENTIALLY ASSESSABLE OUTCOMES

The following subsections (8.3.1–8.3.5) consider in turn the kinds of thing that can be assessed. Fuller consideration of some of the practicalities of assessment (though not all – this is not a book on assessment) will be found in 8.4, and sample tests or test items in 8.5.

One more definition before we proceed. Just as evaluation is a more general and inclusive term than assessment, so assessment is more general than testing, including (1) a wider range of methods, but also (2) a wider range of things to be measured. Under (1), we are thinking mainly of non-invasive assessment (see 8.1) and even impressionistic mental note-taking on learner performance in general classwork. Under (2), the biggest difference is that assessment can include getting information on how learners feel, and this is the subject of the next subsection.

### 8.3.1 Affective outcomes

Educationalists use the term affective to mean something close to emotional: it concerns what we (learn to) want, fear, love or hate. In many situations, especially for young children, affective learning may be more important than the learning of facts and intellectual skills. In particular, it has been argued that a school language teacher's first job is to 'make' the children like the language!

The affective domain includes, perhaps as its most important area, self-confidence and self-image. If a child does well in early schooling, this normally leads to a desire for further success, and to positive attitudes to school and society in general, while early failure may cause children to turn against school, and sometimes even lead to crime and other psychological problems. Thus doing well at a language, as at other subjects, may be good for the psyche, even if the language is never 'needed'.

In this context too, literature learning can be seen as, to some extent, just another area to which the same principles, and in particular the need for a successful learning experience, apply. And yet it is different too, because literature is inherently affective in a way which perhaps applies to no other subject. One can experience strong and complex feelings about mathematics or geography, but feelings are central to literature; one may argue about whether all novels, plays or poems depend for their effect (partly) on emotional response, but certainly the large majority do – this is the author's intention, and this is why people buy them, read them (outside the school) or see them in the theatre. Sometimes the emotional 'package' provided by literature may be of a limited, transient kind, such as the 'cheap' thrill of a routine adventure story or erotic novel, but good literature may go beyond this to an 'education of the sensibilities', an enhanced awareness and understanding of one's own emotional life.

How do the two kinds of affective learning go together? We are very unsure about this, and suspect that there is no universally valid answer. Sometimes the two can clash: we know one person who learned German to a very high level, largely through literature, but now hates most German literature and claims to be a complete philistine. More usually, we think the two can reinforce each other, producing a person whose pleasure in a foreign literature is reinforced by self-assurance in his or her own factual knowledge, aesthetic understanding and linguistic mastery of it.

Assessment of affective response should mainly be by something other than 'tests'. It can be by questionnaires or interviews, and these are discussed briefly in section 9.4. It can be part of regular guidance meetings, for individuals or small groups, with tutors or advisers, either outside lesson time or more informally when the class is doing groupwork. Most of all, it should be a normal part of talking about texts in class (see section 2.4.5).

Affective elements can also be included in 'test' questions, but this must be done with extreme care. First, learners have to believe – and this is very difficult in some cultures – that they are not being tested on the rightness of their tastes, or whether they like what they should like. Second, are the questions suitably phrased, and the texts suitably chosen, so that even those who disliked everything will have enough to say? One practical tip is to let students discuss something they dislike by comparing it to something they liked better:

Is Kleist's *Der Zerbrochene Krug* effective for you as a comedy? Which features are present, and which absent, which you consider important to genuine comedy?

Include in your answer comparisons with the kind of comedy you most enjoy, in any genre (books, film, theatre, or TV).

### 8.3.2 Learning how to learn

Writers about education, especially that of children, have in recent decades given increasing importance to the idea of 'learning how to learn'. The argument begins by asserting that much of what we learn in schools is, of itself, probably useless: we may never need to know the details of Hannibal's wars, or the species of buttercup, or Euclid's proofs; even the foreign languages we learn, though probably more useful for more people, cannot be guaranteed extensive real-life use. Our learning of these things, though, has not been a waste of time, because in learning them we have acquired some general set of skills and attitudes which will enable us to cope with some different tasks in the real world. Sometimes there is a similarity – we learn French at school, and are thus better able to cope with learning Japanese ten years later for our job, while sometimes the difference is almost total – we learn about polysemy in literature, and this (allegedly) fosters general qualities which make us better at running a drapery business!

This is a very ancient idea, found for example in the old saying that education is what remains when one has forgotten all one ever learned. It underlies the teaching of classical languages, and even sport, in old-fashioned private schools. People of a certain social class really did seem to believe that the Battle of Waterloo was won on the playing fields of Eton.

Despite this dubious pedigree, the general idea is certainly valid, and has re-emerged under more scientific labels such as 'transfer of training'. Learning to do many kinds of things does undoubtedly help us to do many other kinds of things: some reasons for this are affective – see the previous section – others appear to involve skills of logic, planning and so on. Readers are referred to books on educational psychology for further details.

### 8.3.3 Literature-related knowledge and skills

We now turn from the possible general benefits of literature in foreign-language teaching to those which are more direct, in other words more obviously related to literature or language. First, we consider the area of literature, under three subheadings.

#### 8.3.3.1 Factual knowledge

This is perhaps the most basic kind of learning. Students can learn the names of Shakespeare's plays, or the dates of Villon's birth and death, or the historical, social and physical circumstances in which Walther von der Vogelweide wrote and performed his verses, or the real people to whom the characters in Woolf's *Orlando* correspond. The category might perhaps be extended to learning sections of text by heart, and to (verbatim?) knowledge of critics' opinions.

Before commenting on the usefulness of this kind of knowledge, we should note that it is rather rare in its pure form, and that most apparently factual knowledge involves some interpretation or at least selection. Even a crude test of 'what happened in Chapter 3' – the German *Inhaltsangabe*, for example – requires more processing, prioritising and mental reworking than is obvious at first sight. When the (primary or secondary) text is in a foreign language, there are additional processes to be gone through, such as guessing or checking unknown words, or deciding whether to 'parrot', rework or omit incompletely understood material, which a native or advanced speaker of the target language may easily forget or underestimate. Nevertheless, more or less 'pure' factual knowledge can be taught, learned and tested. How useful is it? Most writers on teaching would probably give low priority to this kind of learning, and prefer the types discussed below. We agree, on the whole, but with the obvious reservation that you need some facts before you can do anything else of value. In particular, you need a good knowledge of the relevant primary text(s) – to talk or write well about a novel, you should have read it thoroughly, preferably several times. It is harder to generalise about the need for secondary knowledge – for a *roman à clef* such as *Orlando*, the extratextual knowledge mentioned above is obviously very important, but we believe that some works can be studied by some learners in some situations very profitably without bothering too much about who the author was, when and where they wrote, what 'ism' they espoused, and so on. If teaching is successful, learners may later want to find these things out for themselves, and may learn much more in doing so.

### 8.3.3.2 'Delicate sensibility'?

As we saw earlier, literature teaching has been much influenced by F. R. Leavis and his claim that literature study

> trains, in a way no other discipline can, intelligence and sensibility together, cultivating sensitiveness and precision of response and a delicate integrity of intelligence.

> (Leavis 1943)

Can these qualities be assessed? We suspect that many traditional kinds of literature-in-FL assessment, notably final examinations and course essays in French, German, and other languages in British universities, are trying to do roughly that: writers of such assessment instruments are usually inexplicit about their objectives, but those few we have managed to corner have tended to argue in Leavisite terms.

Our opinions about this are mixed, but mostly negative; the issues have already been rehearsed. At its best, Leavisite teaching, and consequently testing, moves the learner away from mere acquisition of factual knowledge to genuine and detailed engagement with literary texts, and ability to explain his or her own response. At its more common worst, the learner/testee has to read the mind of a privileged élite and to acquire or pretend to acquire their values, to (pretend to) feel what a gentleman (sic) would feel. At its best, Leavisite response merges imperceptibly into the kind we favour; at its worst, one is reminded again of Molière's (ironic) claim quoted earlier, written nearly 300 years before Leavis:

> Les gens de qualité savent tout sans avoir jamais rien appris.
> [Persons of quality know everything without ever having learned anything.]

### 8.3.3.3 The skills of literary criticism

For Type A courses at least, the skills of literary criticism are probably the most important domains for testing. The brevity of this section should not indicate otherwise: we can be brief here, because to spell out what is assessable would be to repeat much of Chapters 3–7.

It is now almost a platitude that teaching skills is more important than teaching facts, and few readers will not have heard some version of the Confucian proverb 'Give someone a fish and you feed them for a day; teach them to catch fish and you feed them for life'.

This principle has long been accepted in foreign *language* teaching, even in the Latin and Greek teaching of the medieval and early modern period: set books were studied, and much rote learning required, but the ultimate tests were recognised as the 'unseen', that is, translation of an unknown passage from (say) Latin to English, and the 'composition' – translation into (say) Latin (prose and verse). Even today, the language component of courses in French, German, and other languages at British (and many other) universities often follows a similar pattern. The literature component, by contrast, often seems more skewed towards factual knowledge, with exam questions and essay topics such as 'Is the *Nibelungenlied* essentially Christian or pagan?'

Though we see a place for such questions, we believe that, at least for the more 'academic' kind of literature in a foreign language, the ultimate test would be something more analogous to the language unseen.

In our Advanced Certificate in English Studies examination at Edinburgh, for example, one of the poetry questions typically takes the form:

> Write a critical analysis of the attached poem [TITLE]. Your answer should include discussion of paraphrasable meaning, deviance and regularity, but can also deal with other topics. You should include some reference to your own personal reactions to the poem and an attempt to account for these.

In other words, students are being tested on the range of concepts covered in Chapter 4, and their ability to apply these to a new text. Questions on novels, stories and drama could likewise test application of the concepts in Chapters 5–7, with modifications due to constraints of time – students cannot read a complete novel in the examination room.

Although we have illustrated this point with an examination question, it is essentially a point about objectives. Even in an uncertificated course without formal assessment, we would, given similar objectives, aim to provide practice in and informal feedback on a similar range of skills.

### 8.3.4 Language competencies

#### 8.3.4.1 General and miscellaneous

Any kind of successful foreign language study must, almost by definition, involve learning some of the core elements of that language: certainly vocabulary, almost certainly grammar, very probably some orthographical patterns, maybe some (but often not much) phonology. Foreign language study through literature involves all these kinds of learning, and sometimes (see Chapter 2) it is the main or only kind of learning – or at least of intended learning.

There are, however, certain kinds of knowledge about a target language, or perhaps rather skills or even areas of awareness, which language-through-literature may in favourable circumstances promote more effectively than would 'general' language teaching. For example:

1. Recognising the norm and the deviant. Learners may become skilled at iden-tifying what is normal, neutral English and what is not, and in some cases finding reasons for the use of non-neutral forms and/or understanding the effects.
2. Recognising polysemy. That is, understanding that a piece of text has two (or more) meanings, recognising when this is intentional, and again under-standing reasons and/or effects.
3. Recognising cohesion, especially lexical cohesion. Literary texts often have patterns in their vocabulary, over and above those necessary for simply telling the story, and a good learner may be able to spot such patterns ('There are lots of religious words in Chapter 18, though it's not overtly about religion'), thereby demonstrating and at the same time probably extending (by checking unknown words and secondary meanings) his or her vocabulary knowledge.

These three points echo areas covered in Chapter 4, and the list could be extended to echo the rest of Chapters 3–7. We are not, however, simply repeating the ideas in these chapters: our point is that, in developing awareness of and ability to find for oneself certain features in a *text*, one also becomes aware of these features in a *language*, especially a foreign language. With good teaching, this awareness/ability can transfer to other areas of language performance, including speaking and writing, and to the reading of non-literary texts.

#### 8.3.4.2 The skills of reading

Most foreign-language teachers now recognise that reading is a skill, which can in some contexts usefully be taught separately from grammar, vocabulary and other 'system' areas of language. They are also aware of subskills such as skimming (reading a text quickly for general meaning), scanning (reading for specific information), and recognising cohesive devices, which range from conjunctions to pronouns which refer back to previously mentioned people and things (see Halliday and Hasan 1976).

Some of the reading skills taught for coping with non-literary texts may sometimes be questionable for literature: it is not always wise, for example, to read a short story quickly for 'general meaning'. Nonetheless, a wide variety of reading skill questions are possible and worth considering. Crabbe (1993) provides a particularly wide variety of question types, some of which require the testee to locate paragraphs in a simplified reader and to process them in a way which is intended to test extensive reading skills. Crabbe especially emphasises the understanding of cohesive links as part of global text understanding, and perhaps also using knowledge of the world, though the rubric is sometimes not totally clear about the expected direction of reasoning ('What would you expect to happen in a violent explosion after studying the details in the paragraph?').

### 8.3.4.3  The skills of interactive speaking/listening

In its narrowest sense, literature study seems to involve only the receptive skills – mainly reading, but sometimes also listening (films, plays, poetry recitals). As already discussed (especially in Chapter 2), however, it not only can be connected with, but is now very frequently used as an integral part of, speaking or fluency activities, mainly because (*inter alia*) language teachers feel that its intrinsic interest fosters the genuine exchange of ideas, while avoiding the potential embarrassment of learners talking directly about their own emotional lives.

The objectives of 'speaking about literature' are likely to be, on a general level, similar to those of FL speaking or fluency classes in general. They are not restricted to a knowledge of language system – lexis, grammar, phonology and so on – though they may pre-suppose certain minimum levels in these areas, but are likely to be expressed more in terms of 'skills'. Some of these are ends in themselves – what an individual needs to be a good speaker of language X – others are (also) learning devices which may enable the learner to improve by means of speaking and listening. As in earlier sections, our list is not meant to be exhaustive nor our definitions complete; see Ur (1981), Lynch (1996a, b; 1997) and Pica and Doughty (1985) for more in this area.

Our partial list is as follows:

1. Initiation: being able to start a discussion, or introduce a new topic, for example. Many writers have pointed out that in traditional classrooms almost all learner turns are answers, but in real-life FL use people mostly need to ask questions, and start conversations.
2. Turn-taking and turn-giving. Often in pairwork or groupwork one student is dominant, the other(s) say(s) very little. Both sides need to learn (and receive help!) in modifying such patterns: in many real-life situations, both social and

business talk is more successful when turns are shared more equally. Changing behaviour can involve many kinds of learning, from set routines such as 'Can I just …' or 'Sorry I'm monopolising …') to intonation, pause behaviour, body language, eye contact and many other features.

3. Negotiation of meaning. Among other things, this can include confirmation checks ('Have you understood me?'), comprehension checks ('Have I understood you?'), self-repetition, other-repetition and reformulation; see Pica and Doughty (1985). Even in our native language, we may not do enough of this, and misunderstandings may result. Non-native speakers often need to do even more, and can often use these strategies to compensate for weaknesses in core linguistic areas, especially in pronunciation.

### 8.3.4.4 Increasing functional range

This is not, from a logical point of view, entirely separate from the previous section. While that was concerned mainly with the interpersonal, this section is concerned more with the intellectual, though there is inevitable overlap. Examples of functions which learner utterances might perform include the following (based loosely on the 'Embryonic' coding system; see Long *et al.* 1976: 144–5).

| | |
|---|---|
| *Qualifying* | ('She uses verbs – or mostly verbs …') |
| *Reformulating* | ('It's very crafty – I mean, the words are carefully chosen …') |
| *Expressing reservations* | ('I don't entirely agree.') |
| *Providing examples* | ('For instance in line 2 …') |
| *Deducing* | ('It must be addressed to a former lover.') |
| *Inducing* | ('Perhaps the basic pattern is a pentameter?') |
| *Defining* | ('A Shakespearian sonnet is …') |

The extent to which students and teachers use the categories in these or similar lists can be explored by systematic coding – see section 9.3.2.

Just as learners' classroom language is often limited in 'interactional' terms, it can be limited in these 'intellectual' terms too, and in many classrooms it seems that learners do little more than answer, and occasionally ask, factual questions. This can be a problem area in first-language classrooms (see Brown *et al.* 1994), but is more serious in a foreign language. British learners, for example, may have studied French or German for ten years or more and yet have hardly ever had to, for example, 'express reservations'. One of the main justifications for pairwork and groupwork is that they can provide opportunities for a wider range of functions, but this will not happen automatically: learners also usually need (1) suitably challenging tasks; (2) careful initial guidance, including but not limited to possible phrases for some of the above functions; and (3) examples of native speakers or more advanced learners performing these functions – minimally just the teacher, ideally videotaped discussions too.

## 8.4 THE PRACTICALITIES OF ASSESSMENT

As assessment is often constrained by institutional rules, and strongly influenced by students' past experience and expectations, it would be inappropriate to prescribe in detail. In the following guidelines, we take as read qualifications such as 'where appropriate' and 'other things being equal'.

1. Assessments should be short and frequent rather than long and 'special occasions'. Labels such as 'examination' should be avoided, and the test should be seen as a non-threatening activity: a part of learning. Numerical marks may not be necessary, and if given should not be read aloud or displayed.

2. Assessment should not be comparative between students: all students should be compared with outside criteria (can they do X? Do they know Y?). Rank ordering should not be necessary.

3. Marking should be 'positive', emphasising what students can do rather than trying to catch them out. If, however, something important has not been learned, the marking should make this clear.

4. There should be a mixture of in-class work with time limits, like traditional examinations, and out-of-class assignments. (In Britain at least, since the 1970s, received opinion has moved away from examinations, which are supposed to be too stressful for some students. But assignments too can be stressful, and can be unfair when some students have better-educated friends and relatives or can pay for help. We favour a compromise.)

5. There should be a mixture (over a period, not usually in the same test) of questions about 'set books' or other texts already studied in class, and questions which require the application of ideas to new texts. Such new texts should be reasonably short, and there should be plenty of time for reading them: in a timed test, such reading time should be separate from writing time.

6. All outcomes considered important should be tested (over a period – certainly not all in the same test!). These can include both language and literature, together with a carefully chosen subset of the outcome types mentioned earlier in this chapter. Some types will almost certainly not be appropriate, and students should be told in advance, in terms suited to their linguistic and conceptual level, what types of outcome will be tested.

7. Again over a period of time, there should be tests of reading, writing and speaking (perhaps of listening too, but we will not comment further on this as it may not be a priority in all circumstances). In the early stages these should be, or should include, single-skill tests, such as tests of reading which involve little or no writing – see the example below. The justification for this is that such tests can provide more precise diagnostic information; we can see more precisely what problem a learner has in (for instance) reading, without the uncertainty added by problems of (again for instance) written expression. Single-skill tests can also be more motivating – see next point.

8. Integrated tests, which involve reading and writing, or reading and speaking, or possibly all three, have greater authenticity and real-world validity than single-skill tests. They can, however, be demotivating, as they provide more ways to go wrong, and can work against the interests of weaker students. We favour a gentle introduction, and gradual expansion when (and if) final certification approaches.

9. Because response to literature is very personal, it is important to offer choices in assessment tasks. These choices can be on various levels:

- which texts are discussed;
- what aspects of them are discussed;
- in some cases even the form of the answer, for example oral presentation, written essay or a piece of creative writing.

The learners should also have a choice in how personal or impersonal their answers should be – as mentioned elsewhere, they should never be forced to 'bare their souls' or to manufacture approved aesthetic or emotional reactions.

All these choices must, like other choices in life, be balanced with an awareness of future realities, and learners who do face outside examinations should, over a period, be guided ever closer towards playing the examination game, but this should not preclude some real learning and self-expression first.

10. A balance is needed between assessing students' learning of 'facts', including other people's opinions, and their ability to produce their own ideas: neither is satisfactory by itself.

11. Assessment can be fun – see example 10 in the table below. This is only possible, though, when students can relax: if outside pressures make this impossible, it is better to be serious.

## 8.5 SAMPLE TESTS OR TEST ITEMS

All the examples below may constitute either a complete test, or one item or section in a longer test, depending on circumstances. We give these examples in the form of a table, indicating for each one the main kind(s) of outcome tested, and, separately, which one or more of the four skills of reading, listening, writing and speaking are mainly involved. (Reading before the course is not included – feel free to insert it if you wish.)

| Test no. | Description | Area tested | L, R, W, S? |
|---|---|---|---|
| 1. | Underline sentences in a story which show the type of narrator, and use a letter key (supplied) to show which type. | Skills of literary criticism. | R |

| Test no. | Description | Area tested | L, R, W, S? |
|---|---|---|---|
| 2. | List the words or short phrases in a poem which are not 'standard' English, or are used in non-standard ways. Give more standard alternatives where possible. Comment on literary effect (*written answer*). | Skills of literary criticism. Language knowledge (vocabulary). | R and W |
| 3. | Choose any text you have read in the last six months – inside or outside class – and which you have enjoyed. Describe the text, and explain why you enjoyed it (*written answer*). | Affective reactions. Language skills (writing) including summary, giving reasons, etc. | W |
| 4. | Name some poets described as 'Romantic'. What do they have in common? Can one be a 'Romantic' today? How is the use of the word similar to or different from other uses – with upper-case or lower-case 'r'? (*Essay*). | Factual knowledge. Own literary judgements. Language knowledge. | W |
| 5. | Read the first pages of four (previously unknown) stories (supplied). How would you expect each story to continue? Which of the stories would you like to read and why (*written answer*)? | (Depending on stories chosen.) Knowledge of literary genre. Knowledge of culture (e.g. British). General language competence. | R and W |
| 6. | Read six passages, source not given. Which are literature, which are journalism, which could be either? Give reasons. | Knowledge of genre. General language competence. | R (and W) |
| 7. | Talk in pairs, each telling the other about the last book he/she has read. You should ask each other searching questions, trying to find out from the specific examples about your partner's general tastes in literature, knowledge, attitudes, and way of reading. After pairwork, report orally to whole class on what your partner said. | Skills of oral interaction, including justifying, exemplifying, clarifying, challenging, cross-examining, etc. Some literary knowledge. | S (and L) |
| 8. | Watch a short film, or film extract, and rewrite it as (part of) a short story. (Work in groups, discussing each other's ideas.) | General language skills. Knowledge of genre. Creative writing. Negotiating skills. | L, (S, R), W |
| 9. | Read a short story or part of a story, and rewrite it as a film script. | As 8. | R, (S, L), W |

| Test no. | Description | Area tested | L, R, W, S? |
|---|---|---|---|
| 10. | The characters in a novel you have just read were put through a computer spelling checker. Here are the results. Identify the originals. | Factual knowledge. | R, W (spelling) |

# Chapter 9

# Research and development

This chapter looks at various kinds of activity in which teachers and learners can engage with the aim of understanding more about their teaching and learning, of widening their repertoires, and of developing new material in a principled way.

## 9.1 RESEARCH INTO READER RESPONSE

Reader response has been a recurrent theme in this book. In the first chapter we suggested that it provides a valuable theoretical framework for the use of literary texts in a language-teaching context, a view which is exemplified both explicitly and implicitly in those sections concerned with approaches to teaching the various genres. As we have indicated, our focus in this chapter is primarily practical. This is not to say that the wider issues of reader-response research are uninteresting or irrelevant to the practising teacher; rather, that since they have been thoroughly reported and discussed elsewhere (see, for example, O'Malley and Chamot (1990) on language acquisition, Short and Van Peer (1989) and Van Peer (1986) on literature), our intention is to suggest ways in which some of the principles and experience of that research may be adapted for application in the classroom.

Classroom-based reading research can be conducted at three levels: first, that of the broad-based, ongoing, regular evaluation by the teacher of learner response to reading materials, such as that which is frequently employed in library or extensive reading schemes, and which involves every student in the class; second, what is sometimes – perhaps rather misleadingly – described as 'ethnographic' research, on responses to a particular text or texts (which could be a group project for students); and finally, introspective research on the individual reading process.

### 9.1.1 Ongoing monitoring and evaluation

Where library periods are included in the timetable, or where a teacher is fortunate enough to have a class library actually in the classroom, some system of monitoring and evaluation can – even, perhaps, should – be built into the reading programme. The simplest way of achieving this is by a reading diary. Students may keep their own diaries, or, if preferred, a large wall-diary can be used where readers enter (with dates and names) their comments on books as they read them. The latter system works well with younger age groups and where there is a limited number of titles so that several students have the chance to read and comment on each one. It also has the advantage of saving the hard-pressed teacher the task of checking individual reading diaries.

On the other hand, the individual reading diary is not merely an indicator of reader response; it can become a valuable educational tool in that students are trained in the habits of recording important details about a book: in the early years, they may note simply title and author, but gradually other information can be added such as date and publisher/publisher's series (for example, Oxford University Press Bookworms), even perhaps place of publication and ISBN. This, incidentally, provides valuable training in learning how to deal with books for more academic work later on. Diaries may also vary widely in range, detail of recording and in terms of the addressee; some are simply notes under headings, others may be more like book reviews in being primarily recommendations or discouragements to their peers; some may be addressed to particular fellow reader(s) (where the diary-writing programme has been set up specifically for pairs or small reading groups) or the diary may be directly addressed to the teacher. (But note the caveat later in this chapter in section 9.4 on the use of learner diaries as a research instrument.)

Whichever method is used, it should be regarded as more than just a monitoring device to check that reading is happening. It is in fact an important source of information: by means of it, the teacher learns which titles are popular or unpopular; who reads and enjoys what sort of books; and, perhaps, from some of the comments, the reasons for like or dislike. It becomes in effect a mini-reading research project, providing an ongoing evaluation of library titles and leading, where institutionally feasible, to a revision and updating of the library. The Edinburgh Project on Extensive Reading (EPER) (see also section 2.4.1), which has carried out considerable research in this area, provides a valuable resource for teachers or institutions who are interested in developing both reading and research into reading. EPER maintains an extensive database of simplified readers in English together with accounts of their employment in reading schemes in various countries and suggestions as to how to set up such schemes.

### 9.1.2 'Ethnographic' projects

A second approach to reader response is by means of a so-called 'ethnographic' project. This can be conducted on a small scale after reading any text, whether a poem or novel or indeed a simple/simplified text (see Alderson and Urquhart (1984) on simplification). Like any research project, it will raise broader research issues: identifying the research question; deciding the population to be researched and selecting the appropriate sample; questionnaire design; the use of interviews; validity and generalisability of data. Even at quite an elementary level, some of these issues will be need to be raised and discussed. This kind of research has a particularly valuable role in a cultural studies programme, where issues of similarity and difference between the home and target cultures will be of special interest.

The simplest kind of project would take a single short text, such as a lyric poem, and be directed towards finding out readers' response to it, both as a whole and in particular lines or images, and their reflections on it in relation to their own life experience. These responses could then be linked to factors such as the reader's gender, age or national and cultural background.

We will consider here a rather longer text, the popular romance *My Hero* by Debbie Macomber (for a full-scale ethnographic project on the readers of romances, see Radway 1984). The scenario is this: after reading the novel – which for our present purposes we will assume has met with a mixed reception in the class – a small group decide to undertake a research project to find out who reads such novels, who does not read them, and the reasons for their choice; they are not concerned so much with this particular text as with a type of text. They will need to decide on the sample to be researched: are they concerned with members of their own school class only, or do they want a larger representation of that particular age group? Or are they perhaps interested in finding out the differences between their contemporaries and readers of a previous generation? Discussion about who it is they want to find out about will also help them clarify their central research questions. Which language(s) will they include; is it only novels in English that they are interested in, or will they ask their subjects about romance novels available in whatever is the language of the social context outside the English classroom? How will they phrase their questions: closed, open, with a choice of alternative responses? Will they follow up some of the questions with further questions or prompts? Do they want written responses to their questionnaire or will they carry out interviews orally? How much demographic information will they need? Once they have got their information, how will they collate it? How cautious should they be about attempting to generalise from their findings? (The answer is almost certainly: very cautious!) And finally, what will be the most interesting way of presenting the results?

Engaging with this kind of project work can hold the attraction of taking literature out of its usual restricted classroom setting and relating it to ordinary life and experience, as well, of course, as offering opportunity for wider language practice and the development of presentation skills. If students decide to carry out their project outside the classroom, some care needs to be taken over the choice of texts to be researched so that they are reasonably accessible to the non-specialist reader.

### 9.1.3 Introspection

A third variety of reading research is concerned less with the product than with the process of reading. What are known as 'think-aloud' studies (or 'think-aloud protocols', sometimes familiarly referred to as TAPs) have been around for a long time as a research method in cognitive psychology; they have been adapted for studies of ESL reading, and in a more recent development in attempts to explore the reading of literature, both in the mother tongue and in a second or other language. The method has been described as the disclosure of thought processes by means of stream-of-consciousness commentary while information is being attended to. Readers are given a chunk of text and, as they read, asked to verbalise their processes and responses (in other words, to think aloud); sometimes the researcher may mark the text at certain points at which readers are asked to pause in their reading and verbalise. Now anyone who has sat an advanced driving test and been required to comment on their driving while they drive will know how difficult this can be, and the same sorts of difficulties attend the attempt to be explicit about thought processes while reading. So why do people go on employing it as a research method and more specifically, why are we concerned with it here?

It must be acknowledged that all forms of introspective research, including TAPs, are open to criticism, and not only from a traditional empiricist viewpoint. Self-reports on linguistic behaviour have frequently been shown to be unreliable. Moreover, though introspective methods aim to uncover process, the possibility of this happening has also been questioned: are such levels of processing recoverable? To what extent can the researcher be sure that self-reports actually describe the processes rather than the product? How much (no doubt largely unconscious) guesswork is going on in the reporting? However, despite the acknowledged force of some of these criticisms, research within this paradigm continues: the contention is that as TAPs have proved to be a useful research tool in the domain of problem solving and in uncovering second-language learning strategies, so they may also be relevant in the field of reading research, both in the area of second language reading, generally of non-literary texts, and more recently with the development of an interest in the processes of reading literary texts (Short and Van Peer 1989). Here we are concerned less to justify introspection as a research method in itself as to consider how such methodologies may be serviceable in a pedagogic context and in particular how they may be employed by both teachers and learners as tools for developing strategies for reading literary texts. The use of TAPs described below is based on work (using poems and short stories) with a variety of readers in Britain and elsewhere; they include language learners in schools and universities as well as language teachers.

We offer as an example the following English translation of an anonymous Chinese poem (in Stallworthy 1973).

> Green rushes with red shoots,
> Long leaves bending to the wind -
> You and I in the same boat
> Plucking rushes at the Five Lakes.
>
> We started at dawn from the orchid-island:
> We rested under elms till noon.
> You and I plucking rushes
> Had not plucked a handful when night came!

This poem, though simple, requires 'reading between the lines' to be understood. Van Peer (1988) argues that 'the experienced reader' will realise almost immediately that the point of the poem lies in the last two lines and interpret it in the light of those lines. While we may or may not agree with his pre-suppositions (depending on where we position ourselves theoretically on the reader-response continuum), we may nonetheless be interested to explore at a deeper level how, in terms of process, people might read this poem. One way would be to adapt the method employed by Short and Van Peer (1988) in their systematic line-by-line comparison of their own processes in reading the poem 'Inversnaid' by Gerard Manley Hopkins. In this particular experiment, each of the researchers read the poem separately, pausing at the end of each line in order to verbalise their thinking process (this can be done by written notes, or more satisfactorily, as they did, by speaking into a recorder); finally, they compared the records of their reading. This approach tries to get at the first-time reading process and is concerned with immediate response, prediction, inferencing and evaluation. But of course we do not read poetry simply line by line and you may be more interested in getting at what happens after the first rapid skimming through. In that case, ask your readers to read the poem once right through, quite rapidly and without comment; to pause at the end and comment; and then go back to reread it slowly, interpreting and commenting as they go.

Whichever method you use, you may wish to give your readers some guidance before they start with written or spoken instructions and perhaps even a brief prac-tice with another poem to give them confidence. Here are some examples of the kind of instructions you might offer:

- You may find yourself asking questions: what does this mean? Who is speaking? etc. Then say so.
- You may feel certain emotions in reponse to what you read; you may like or dislike it. Then say so.
- You may notice patterns or contrasts of words or images or sounds. Then say so.
- You may be reminded of things in your own life. Then say so.
- You may find yourself imagining quite vividly (for example, visualising or hearing) certain things in the poem. Then say so.
- You may not be sure of the meaning of certain words and may make a guess. If this is the case, then say so.
- As you reread, you may find yourself going backwards and forwards in the poem, reinterpreting it. If this is so, then say so.

Here is a possible start to the first-time line-by-line reading with comment:

*Green rushes with red shoots* – two things, I suppose, green and red, contrasting colours, maybe this will have some significance; and it's to do with nature and things that are alive and growing. Setting the scene.
*Long leaves bending to the wind* – similar nature images; very peaceful.
*You and I in the same boat* – you and I presumably male and female – direct address, like a love poem. Does *in the same boat* have any symbolic meaning?
*Plucking rushes at the Five Lakes* – are they working or playing? are they alone or are there lots of other rush-pluckers? The Five Lakes somewhere well known in

the world of the poem e.g. is it somewhere everyone goes to pluck rushes? For me it produces a far-away faintly exotic feel, dreamy and rather idyllic. Also 'plucking' has a faintly archaic quality.

*We started at dawn from the orchid-island* – yes, it's filling up with romantic nature imagery, dawn, the orchids – *we* presumably means just the you and I – or are others involved?

*We rested under elms till noon* – in the boat? no, on land, surely? and rested, so not much work done.

*You and I plucking rushes* – the repetition of you and I – what is it? a bit ironic now? and plucking rushes, when we've just been told they rested till noon – implication: we were supposed to be plucking rushes.

*Had not plucked a handful when night came!* – ah yes, very nice. It's not telling us straight out, just leaving us to draw conclusions. You and I falling in love instead of doing the work we had been sent out to do.

Yes, I like that poem. Why do I like it? I suppose because it's neat, it's understated, and I like the way it all comes together at the end with those last two lines.

In our experience, the value of such exercises lies less in any formal 'research' findings than in the discoveries made by readers themselves as they carry out the exercise and compare notes with other readers. With the help of the teacher, they begin to learn more about ways of reading, and to become aware of possible strategies that they can call on – as well as learning to link evaluation closely with the moment-by-moment experience of the text. And, importantly, if the procedure is set up in a non-threatening manner, the think-aloud exercise in itself becomes an enjoyable and empowering exploration of the reading process.

## 9.2 SYLLABUS DEVELOPMENT

Few teachers in whatever discipline are fortunate enough – or, on the other hand, would perhaps even wish – to have the opportunity to develop their own syllabus from scratch. Most are realistically quite grateful to be provided with the framework of a given syllabus within which to work, so long as it is not too constricting. There is, however, a broad range of syllabus types, differing both in organisational principles and in terms of the degree of detail that is specified. Language syllabuses tend to be precise and directive, while literature and cultural studies syllabuses may be very much more open, depending on how far they are structured around particular texts. Cultural studies syllabuses, in particular, may be little more than a list of broad concepts around which are grouped a set of subtopics. In such a case, the syllabus is spelled out largely by means of carefully designed teaching materials. Whichever of these forms they take, however, the majority of syllabuses are fairly dry documents. What we attempt to do in this section is to consider ways in which the individual teacher can put some flesh on the skeleton of the particular syllabus within which he or she has to work.

Rather than dealing broadly with syllabus types – there are, after all, a large number of books specifically concerned with syllabus and curriculum development (for example, Clark 1987) – it seems more useful here to consider specific examples. We have chosen these from two teacher development programmes in which we have been personally involved, and from a research project in Cameroon (Abety 1991): these are the Bulgarian Cultural Studies Syllabus project, which includes literature as an aspect of the study of culture; the Literature in English syllabus designed for use in secondary schools in Malaysia; and an exploration of the 'notional syllabus'.

The Bulgarian syllabus (*Branching Out: a Cultural Studies Syllabus* 1998; see also Reid Thomas *et al.* 1997) is untypical of most syllabuses in its format. It is in two parts: a fairly detailed introduction including an account of the project together with a rationale and guide to the theory and practice of teaching cultural studies, followed by a set of illustrative teaching materials. Perhaps the most interesting feature of this syllabus is its history, the way it actually evolved. It represents one aspect of a much wider programme for the development of language teachers who are broadening their language work to include cultural studies. The programme includes in-service training and an all-country information exchange network (co-ordinated by the British Council), through which teachers share their experience by means of lesson plans ('diary sheets') with their own comments on the lessons, and a network magazine *NetNews*. The syllabus development was remarkable in terms particularly of its process, which was closely linked with teacher development: it was, quite literally, planned and written over a period of a year and a half by fifty teachers, with contributions and criticism from their students, plus input from the project managers and consultants; it was trialled and commented on by other teachers, heads of schools and teacher trainers, and then revised in the light of these comments; and finally it is to be implemented over the period of an academic year by means of teacher-led seminars. It is a very unusual example of a 'bottom-up' teacher-generated initiative, a genuinely progressivist form of curriculum renewal (see Clark 1987 for a description of different models).

The second syllabus example (from which we take the extended quotation given below) is an official document distributed by the Malaysian Ministry of Education. It is a fairly typical example of a common variety, what might be described as a slot and filler syllabus: a developmentally constructed framework is provided for each literary genre (drama, prose fiction and poetry) in terms of aims, objectives and learning outcomes, but without specifying any particular texts. Within that framework the teacher has almost complete freedom to select appropriate texts.

The third example, from Cameroon, does not present a fully worked out or operational syllabus; rather, it suggests a set of literary 'notions' analogous to the language notions propounded by Wilkins (1976) in his pioneering work on the notional syllabus, which are then sequenced developmentally. This was based on research with experienced teachers of literature in twenty-four schools in Cameroon. We include it here because it makes explicit the thinking that lies behind many syllabus documents and encourages the teacher to think carefully about student readiness for particular concepts and the order in which each new concept is introduced. The segmentation of the syllabus implies that the processes involved in studying literature are both coherent and progressive. As an example, Abety (1991) takes the broad notion of meaning in poetry:

> [This] can only be acquired progressively so we segment it into five aspects. First, there is the 'situation' in the poem which could be that of one person addressing another … it could be a dialogue between two or more persons, a report by a narrator … and so on. Whatever is the case, there is always something happening. The situation must be understood first, so the notional syllabus places it at the first level. Secondly there is 'prose' (basic or surface) meaning which is simply the meaning of the poem as expressed by the words used in the poem. This too is set at level one. Then there is the 'implied' meaning or interpretation which must be linked logically to the surface meaning. This aspect is reserved for level three. The interpretation of a poem usually brings out its 'subject' matter (or 'theme' or 'message') which is a fourth aspect of meaning. The last aspect – 'tone' – which is the attitude of the poet towards the subject matter as well as towards the readers, is reserved for the fifth level. In covering the notional syllabus, the students are therefore involved in concrete and cumulative learning through recycling.
>
> (ibid: 102–3)

While none of these three examples may be precisely applicable to any one reader's situation, it could be useful to consider the types they represent in relation to your own experience.

- Is your syllabus based on language? In other words, are you drawing on literature 'as a resource', primarily for teaching language, fitting literary texts of your own choosing into a language syllabus expressed through a coursebook?
- Is your syllabus structured round the choice of particular literary texts? In that case, do you have to teach set books, or is the rubric more general, as in some school-leaving exams in Britain, where the text type is specified but the teacher decides which particular texts will be read, for example a Shakespeare play, five twentieth-century poems and a contemporary novel?
- Is your syllabus organised around concepts or topics (which may be literary notions or more broadly social themes)? In that case, are some literary texts specified, or do you have freedom to choose your own?
- Is your syllabus constructed around the learning of literary skills?
- And finally, does your syllabus assume (or specify) some kind of examinable product at the end of the course/semester/year?

There are numerous books available on syllabus types and development, and this is not the place to examine these questions in any detail, but the distinction between orientation towards product and orientation towards process may fruitfully be borne in mind. Does your syllabus assume that there will be some kind of assessment of students' work – and if so, is this summative or formative? In other words, is it geared towards product in the shape of an end-of-course exam and/or assessable essays and coursework? Or does it emphasise process, as, for example, certain courses in Continuing Education in British universities have traditionally done (though in fact these days such courses are increasingly certificated and therefore product-led). What are the advantages and/or disadvantages of each type, and how can you exploit them most fully in your own situation? The Bulgarian teachers already mentioned felt strongly that, while their cultural studies syllabus was primarily concerned with process, they needed to be able to exhibit some kind of publicly accessible product to reassure students, parents, heads, and, indeed, the teachers themselves that learning was going on in their classrooms and that students were progressing. In these circumstances, they decided that the most appropriate method of assessment would be for each student to put together a representative portfolio of their work over a semester or a year, which would be both a visible product and a reflection of process.

### 9.2.1 Working within a syllabus

Whether you work with a syllabus of prescribed texts or have freedom to choose your own, it can be a useful exercise to plan your own pathway through that syllabus in terms of concepts and skills. As an illustration, we shall consider a syllabus that specifies skills in terms of learning outcomes, which are clearly linked with the developmental progression of literary 'notions', but does not prescribe or even recommend specific texts. This is an extract from the Malaysian Ministry of Education's syllabus for secondary schools (*Kesusasteraan Dalam Bahasa Inggeris* 1990), dealing with prose:

A.  PROSE
Prose refers to continuous pieces of writing which comprise works of fiction and non-fiction. In this programme, the prescribed texts for prose are the novel and the short story.

   In prose, the writer seeks through the creative use of language to highlight and explore issues and concerns of human interest from which the reader may draw lessons by way of comparing and contrasting. This, in turn, leads to a further understanding of themselves and of the world around them.

| No. | Learning outcomes | Contents |
|---|---|---|
| 1 | To understand the contents of the text; | story/information |
| 2 | To recognise and discuss issues of life as presented in the text; | issues of universal concern. For example: love, service, sacrifice |
| 3 | To understand theme and message in the text; | explicit meaning<br>implicit meaning |
| 4 | To understand plot in the text; | main and subplots<br>sequence of plots<br>reasons for events<br>results of these events<br>relationship between events |

| | | |
|---|---|---|
| 5 | To describe characters and interpret their interactions and relationships with one another; | physical attributes<br>social position<br>attitudes and beliefs<br>personality<br>kinds of relationship<br>actions and reactions<br>interactions with one another<br>character development<br>roles and functions<br>in developing the story |
| 6 | To understand and interpret the contribution of setting (place and time) to the story; | nature of the setting<br>atmosphere and mood created<br>by the setting on:<br>    a. character<br>    b. story<br>    c. reader |
| 7 | To understand the author's point of view; | assuming omniscience |
| 8 | To identify common literary devices authors employ to achieve their effects; | for example: figures of speech |
| 9 | To communicate an informed personal response to the text; | reasons to support one's response to the text;<br>relating the story to one's own feelings and responses |
| 10 | To produce a piece of work (oral/visual) in response to the text studied. | for example: comic strips, radio scripts, painting |

How might you, as a practising teacher, develop this framework? One way would be to add a third column, focusing more precisely on the particular literary 'notion' involved, with further columns noting titles of suitable texts and particular examples from those texts. You might also want to consider an additional column with suggestions for forms of assessment. We give an example of how item (6) could be expanded in this way for the top classes in secondary school or first-year university or training college students (see page 164).

## 9.3 CLASSROOM OBSERVATION

### 9.3.1 General

Classroom observation requires great caution. Teachers who have collaborated happily for months or years on materials design, lesson plans, student questionnaires and interviews, and see each other as personal friends, can fall out quite dramatically

| Learning outcomes | Contents | Texts | Examples | Assessment |
|---|---|---|---|---|
| To understand and interpret the contribution of setting (place and time) to the story | nature of the setting<br><br>atmosphere and mood created by the setting on<br>a. character<br>b. story<br>c. reader | 'The Force of Circumstance' by Somerset Maugham (a short story set in Malaya under British rule) with K. S. Maniam's novel *The Return* (1981), which deals with the effects of British colonialism on post-colonial Malaysia by examining three generations of an Indian family settled in Malaysia. | First para. of description: effects of 'foreignness' of the scene on the British woman Doris – also what expectations are raised in the reader.<br><br>Choose one of the many passages which indicate the significance of the time in which the novel is set. | *Note:* Keep a neat looseleaf copy of work for student portfolio.<br><br>Follow-up work (after discussion in class, groups or pairs) e.g.: essay/composition on how novel has affected your view of history; comment on similarities/differences between Maugham's and Maniam's presentation of their *Malay* characters. |
|  |  | Short stories by e.g. Shirley Geok-lin Lim with 'The Horse Dealer's Daughter' by D. H. Lawrence | Compare Lim's use in dialogue of SE Asian variety of English to create atmosphere of place (and social group) with DHL's use of English rural dialect.<br><br>Also compare the descriptions of people and places – are there significant differences in the use of description? and if so, what and why? | Rewrite speeches in standard English/turn a paragraph of narration into dialect – comment on the difference this makes. |

if a programme of mutual observation is introduced without careful planning. Observation as part of initial training is also fraught with potential for conflict and emotional crises. The following suggestions are very tentative, and should be adapted to your own situation.

It may be best if a group of teachers begin by observing a video recording, or reading a written summary, of a lesson by a stranger whom they will never meet. They can then discuss the lesson in groups. No opinions will be regarded as 'right' or 'wrong', but the supervisor or group leader, if any, should encourage open-mindedness: as we never know all the details of another teacher's situation, we should be extremely slow to condemn, for something which may seem to us boring or unjustified, for example, may have a hidden logic which we cannot guess. Instead of criticism, the group should be looking at alternatives – 'She could have done it like this …'. (In the realms of general language teaching – not specifically literature – Fanselow (1987) is a useful introduction to this idea of classroom research as 'generating and exploring alternatives'.)

We suggest that the examples offered for discussion should be a mixture of the (allegedly!) good, bad and intermediate. The first examples could be from videotaped sample lessons produced by organisations such as the British Council or Eurocentre: broadly speaking, these are intended as positive models, but no doubt some teachers will find plenty to criticise. This might be followed by a written summary of a fictional lesson, perhaps a rather chaotic and improbable one with some 'deliberate mistakes': this should be presented with a straight face, but learners will soon, one hopes, decide it is a sort of joke example illustrating many things that they would wish to avoid. This, however, can provide an opportunity for the tutor or group leader to stress the need to be positive – not 'what is wrong with this teacher?' but 'how can we help them?' After this, teachers can perhaps talk about incidents from their own lessons, first using memory alone, then audio, then video; then about short pieces of each other's lessons, first using the teachers' own self-report, then once again audio and video. If anyone feels that the atmosphere is becoming too negative or personal, or judgmental in other ways, this part of the research should be delayed or abandoned.

### 9.3.2 Coding systems

One technical question about classroom observation is whether it should use a coding system, and if so what system. A coding system is a way of assigning classroom events to specific pre-set categories. There are hundreds to choose from, including one, the Stirling system (Mitchell *et al.* 1981) co-written by one of us. This system contains five 'dimensions', each with up to eleven 'categories'. We give details of one dimension only, which is Dimension B: Language activities.

1. Interpretation: meanings of target language made explicit in native language, as in translation.
2. L1: use of native language.

3. Real FL: real messages transmitted in target language, e.g. instructions for moving furniture.
4. Transposition: focus on relationship between spoken and written word, e.g. reading aloud, dictation.
5. Presentation: focus on global comprehension, e.g. listening or reading text.
6. Imitation: students to imitate a model, e.g. repetition.
7. Drill/exercise: focus on form and/or appropriacy of utterance, e.g. structural drills, question and answer.
8. Compound: brief occurrences of more than one of the above in the same sequence.

Other coding systems, from various sources, are brought conveniently together in the appendices of Allwright and Bailey (1991). Despite our personal interest in coding systems, we do not especially recommend them to readers of this book, for two reasons: first, published systems are designed for general language lessons, not for literature teaching; second, to use a system properly entails mastering a number of technical conventions which may distract from the main purposes of collaborative/action research. If you do want to code lessons, we suggest that you devise a simple system of your own, designed to match the categories used in lesson plans and to give basic information on timings, on who speaks to whom about what, and so on. For those who want to pursue this, practical advice is found in Allwright and Bailey (1991) and ideas to explore in Malamah-Thomas (1987), though neither of these is about literature teaching.

### 9.3.3 Audio and video recording of lessons

Our advice on this is simple: if in doubt, don't! Recording, especially by video, can be very disruptive, and our experience is that teachers always feel more 'on trial' than they expect, even if the recording is done by friends and will not be made public. There may also be problems of equipment failure which interfere with the lesson. Good research can be done on the basis of written accounts, especially if it is small-scale and collaborative. Do not, therefore, introduce audio and video recording for research purposes if they are not already a normal part of your lives.

On the other hand, if you are really comfortable with recording, by all means try it; you can always stop it if it causes trouble. The following tips may be useful:

1. Try to record for several consecutive lessons, using the same procedure each time. The disruptive effects, if any, will be greatest in the first lesson, or at most the first two, so discard the first (two) tape(s) if you want representative data.
2. Even built-in microphones in small tape recorders will probably catch most of what the teacher says, but it is very hard to record student voices adequately. If you need high-quality student data, get specialist advice on radio-microphones or similar.
3. Ask teachers' permission to film or record, and do so only if permission is freely given.

4. Give the teacher the right to view or listen to the tape first, and to erase it if anything causes embarrassment.

5. Ask students' permission too, and give them erasure rights if they want them, though this is less likely to be an issue.

6. Give the teacher the opportunity, if desired, to explain his or her objectives, etc. to camera, or on audiotape, before or after the lesson, but do not insist on this.

7. Do not later show or play the tapes to outsiders in any contexts not agreed at the time of recording.

## 9.4 QUESTIONNAIRES, INTERVIEWS AND DIARIES

This is a much safer kind of research than classroom observation, though it too requires caution and mutual respect: nobody, teacher or student, should be forced to do anything outside their normal work, nor should they be exposed to criticism or other personal attack. Everything should be done by agreement, and there should, if possible, be 'rewards' for all involved: for example, if students write diaries to help you understand their learning strategies, you can ask them what feedback they want – correction of language errors, your own advice on strategies, or both, or neither? We will not list all the possibilities as to who can do research on whom with diaries, questionnaires and interviews: the short answer is that any aspect of teaching or learning can be studied, and the more collaboratively the better. Nor will we advise in detail on construction and use of instruments such as questionnaires and interview schedules, as these are subjects for entire books – Nunan (1992) or Allwright and Bailey (1991) are good starting points, whilst Bailey (1978) – a different K. Bailey, Kenneth not Kathleen! – is an old but very sound and thorough textbook. The following seven points are intended to supplement rather than replace the fuller guidance in these books.

1. Of the two main kinds of 'instruments' for collecting this kind of data, interviews and questionnaires, it is impossible to say which is 'better'. The answer will depend on the context, and the textbooks offer no consistent guidance. Our own rule of thumb, however, is that interviews seem to work better with teachers, and questionnaires with students, especially with adolescents.

   Teachers have sometimes told us that they have no time to complete a questionnaire, then spent hours telling us what they have no time to write! (We speculate that this may have to do with the personality types of teachers, and of course with their plentiful practice in speaking within their jobs.) At the other extreme, working with twelve-year-old children, we used to expect that they would be reluctant to write or find it difficult, but in fact their greatest problem is telling an adult face-to-face what they feel, while their writing, even that of the allegedly 'less able', is consistently informative. For younger children, though, interview may be only choice.

2. A group interview may sometimes be better than a one-to-one interview. Again this applies most clearly to adolescents, but a wide variety of learners, especially the less fluent or confident, may express themselves better when peers are present to provide support, confirmation and elaboration. The main drawback is that some individual, divergent opinions may be suppressed.

3. The main alternative to interviews and questionnaires is the learner or teacher diary. These can be useful, in language teaching generally, both as an 'activity' (learner training, or writing practice, for instance) and for research. Kathleen Bailey is the best-known researcher in this area – see again Allwright and Bailey for details.

   Our own attitude to diaries (especially learner diaries) is rather cautious. While the 'reading diaries' described earlier (section 9.1.1) are well tried and tested, certain other kinds may be problematic, even harmful. In Howell-Richardson and Parkinson (1988) some of the dangers are pointed out, especially those of uncertain purpose and audience – are the diaries private thoughts, appeals for help to the teacher or a vehicle for language development? – and that of playing at psychology in interpretation. By all means experiment with diaries if your students (or colleagues) agree, but there is a lot to be said for more direct methods of collecting data. If you do use diaries, you should consider stipulating in advance that they will remain private, but can be used to prepare questionnaire or interview answers.

4. Research is not just evaluation. This may seem obvious, but in our experience teachers and learners, however approached by researchers, or however encouraged to do their own research, always seem to start by assuming that the real question is 'Is the course OK?' This is understandable, as it addresses what is normally the greatest practical concern, and also the greatest source of emotional 'pluses' and 'minuses', for everyone within the group. There are, however, two problems:

   (a) Traditional 'course evaluation' by interview or (usually) questionnaire is not a particularly good way of finding out how a course is going or has gone, though it can highlight some kinds of detailed strengths and weaknesses, e.g. sessions especially liked or disliked. Some individuals, nationalities, social groups, and so on, tend to be over-critical, others not to criticise at all; and all sorts of distortions are possible. Careful question design (see again Kenneth Bailey) can reduce but not eliminate these.

   (b) Even if evaluation does yield a fairly clearly picture of 'how they liked it', in terms of 'marks out of ten' this is not an adequate guide to future practice. A picture of what they liked most or least, for instance, is better, but may still be misleading. Only by asking more general questions, as outlined in the next section, can teachers/researchers hope to get the kind of understanding which will help them with this particular class or course, and also inform their teaching in a more general way.

5. Rather than just asking about the course, good research will usually ask about other related matters, such as learners' needs, tastes in literature, past experi-

ence, preferred learning styles. And the fundamental question will not be 'how do you like it?' but 'how do you see it?' Another way of putting it is to say 'teach me' – don't just fill in the blanks in my questions, but give me a picture of your categories – do you distinguish between fluency and accuracy, between 'serious' and 'trivial' literature, between …? If you are a learner, what do you expect from a teacher, and what is inappropriate?

6. In any extended research, everyone, teachers and learners, should be invited to participate in a process of change. If opinions are sought, they should be acted on in some way, and then sought again. This 'action research' is now the kind favoured by many teachers, for instance in the research 'special interest groups' of the IATEFL (International Association of Teachers of EFL) – see Edge and Richards (eds 1993), especially the article by Bridget Somekh. This book is mainly about general language teaching, but is eminently applicable to literature lessons.

Change is the key concept, with several facets. You will probably think first of changing the teaching materials, the texts studied, or the methods. This should certainly be considered, but both learners and teachers should also be open to the idea of changing themselves, in small ways and sometimes in big ones. Perhaps we can learn to like authors we have so far rejected, or see virtues in a way of studying, or of teaching, which has so far been alien to us. At least we can try for a week or so! Education is quintessentially about change; the experience of reading or seeing great literature should also change us in some way: and using a foreign language well requires change on every level, from tongue positions to social behaviour. When all three come together, then, the importance of change, and openness to change, can hardly be overstated.

# Appendix 1

# Study questions and exercises

**Note:** Most of the questions have no specific right answers. For those that do, or may do, see the possible answers in Appendix 2.

## 1 INTRODUCTION

1. Does your teaching of literature in a foreign language fall neatly into one of the two general types described in section 1.1? If not, which features does it share with each of the two types?

   If you teach more than one very different type of class, choose just one class for the purposes of the question. If you are not (yet) a teacher of literature in a foreign language, base your answer on your experiences as a learner.

2. Which of the 'reasons or benefits' mentioned in section 1.5 are most relevant in your classes (or in the specific class you chose in question 1 above)? Are there any other reasons or benefits important to you?

   - cultural enrichment
   - rhetoric
   - mental training
   - separating 'sheep' and 'goats'
   - authenticity
   - memorable language
   - non-trivial texts
   - multiple interpretation (opinion gap)
   - convenience
   - other?

3. From your own experience as learner and teacher in literature classes, think of specific examples of the following potential problems mentioned in Section 1.6. (The problems may have arisen for you, for your classmates, or for students whom you were teaching.)

   - remoteness
   - difficult language

- deviant language
- lack of authenticity
- imbalance of skills
- imbalance of knowledge
- imbalance of power
- lack of staging posts
- other?

Briefly analyse the problem in each case. Was it a matter of the text chosen? The approach? Was it foreseeable? Was it solved? If not, could it have been solved?

## 2  WHAT CAN TEACHERS AND LEARNERS DO WITH LITERATURE?

4. Think of a prediction activity (see section 2.4.7), or a (short) list of prediction questions, relating to a work of literature which you know well. Sketch out exactly how you would use this in a lesson, and design one or more appropriate worksheets. How would you follow up or go back to the prediction activity? What would you expect to achieve?

5. Following the same procedure as in 4, devise and comment on examples of some of the 'games' mentioned in section 2.4.6 (guessing games, connections, interpreting pictures, detecting differences, choosing candidates).

    Which of these do you consider most useful for your own classes? What would they achieve?

## 3  THE LANGUAGE OF LITERATURE AND WAYS OF 'TEACHING' IT

6. Think of literary texts which contain a very distinctive variety of language, for example, dialect or technical language (see list in section 3.2), but which you would be willing to consider using in class. What problems does each of these texts pose for students? What opportunities does it offer? How would you cope with the problems and exploit the opportunities?

    Are there any texts whose language is so distinctive that you would not consider using them? Which ones, and why?

7. Do you have to, or choose to, teach texts which contain a lot of traditional 'literary' language, comparable to the Thomas Gray example (section 3.3)? If so, think of a short passage from such a text, or a complete text such as a poem, which you know fairly well but not by heart. From memory, describe the main features which are different from standard English, and estimate how frequent they are. Then look at the text – did you under-estimate or over-estimate? Discuss teaching implications as in question 6 above.

8. Underline anything in the poem below – 'Gather ye rose-buds' by Robert

Herrick (in Harrison 1937) – which you find distinctively 'literary', comparable to the Thomas Gray example (section 3.3). You may select vocabulary, syntactic patterns, or other features. Of the things which you have underlined, which would probably cause difficulty to your students, and which not? Why? How could you help the students?

> Gather ye rose-buds while ye may,
> Old Time is still a-flying:
> And this same flower that smiles today,
> To-morrow will be dying.
>
> The glorious Lamp of Heaven, the Sun,
> The higher he's a-getting
> The sooner will his race be run,
> And nearer he's to setting.
>
> That age is best which is the first,
> When youth and blood are warmer:
> But being spent, the worse, and worst
> Times, still succeed the former.
>
> Then, be not coy, but use your time;
> And while ye may, go marry:
> For having lost but once your prime,
> You may for ever tarry.

9.  Consider how intertextuality (see section 3.8) comes into play in understanding the following texts. As usual, you should consider the implications for teaching: even if you would not dream of teaching these particular texts, does your experience of coping with them as a reader give rise to any pedagogical thoughts?

**Text A:** 'Adonais' (in Harrison 1937; two extracts from a long poem)

> I weep for Adonais – he is dead!
> O, weep for Adonais! though our tears
> Thaw not the frost which binds so dear a head!
> And thou, sad Hour, selected from all years
> To mourn our loss, rouse thy obscure compeers,
> And teach them thine own sorrow! Say: 'With me
> Died Adonais; till the Future dares
> Forget the Past, his fate and fame shall be
> An echo and a light into eternity!'
>
> Where wert thou, mighty Mother, when he lay,
> When thy Son lay, pierced by the shaft which flies
> In darkness? where was lorn Urania
> When Adonais died? With veilèd eyes,
> 'Mid listening Echoes, in her Paradise

She sate, while one, with soft enamoured breath,
Rekindled all the fading melodies,
With which, like flowers that mock the corse beneath,
He had adorned and hid the coming bulk of death.

(*Several pages later*)

Grief made the young Spring wild, and she threw down
Her kindling buds, as if she Autumn were,
Or they dead leaves; since her delight is flown,
For whom should she have waked the sullen year?
To Phoebus was not Hyacinth so dear
Nor to himself Narcissus, as to both
Thou, Adonais: wan they stand and sere
Amid the faint companions of their youth,
With dew all turned to tears; odour to sighing ruth.

(Percy Bysshe Shelley)

**Text B:** 'The Conundrum of the Workshops' (in Kipling 1939; first half [approx.] of the poem)

When the flush of a new-born sun fell first on
    Eden's green and gold,
Our father Adam sat under the Tree and scratched
    with a stick in the mould;
And the first rude sketch that the world had seen
    was joy to his mighty heart,
Till the Devil whispered behind the leaves, 'It's
    pretty, but is it Art?'

Wherefore he called to his wife, and fled to fashion
    his work anew -
The first of his race who cared a fig for the first,
    most dread review;
And he left his lore to the use of his sons – and
    that was a glorious pain
When the Devil chuckled 'Is it Art?' in the ear
    of the branded Cain.
They builded a tower to shiver the sky and wrench
    the stars apart,
Till the Devil grunted behind the bricks: 'It's
    striking, but is it Art?'
The stone was dropped at the quarry-side and the
    idle derrick swung,
While each man talked of the aims of Art, and each
    in an alien tongue.

They fought and they talked in the North and the
     South; they talked and they fought in the
     West,
Till the waters rose on the pitiful land, and the
     poor Red Clay had rest -
Had rest till that dank blank-canvas dawn when
     the Dove was preened to start,
And the Devil bubbled below the keel: 'It's
     human, but is it Art?'

The tale is as old as the Eden Tree – and new as
     the new-cut tooth -
For each man knows ere his lip-thatch grows he
     is master of Art and Truth;

(Rudyard Kipling)

**Text C:** *The Stone Canal* (Macleod 1996; five short extracts from a novel)

(a)  Dee's heard about copyright, but it's one of those things she doesn't quite
     believe, a song of distant Earth.                              (p. 35)

(b)  'Yeah,' he grinned. 'Well, back to the Judean People's Front.'
     'What!?? Don't you mean the People's Front of Judea?'
     Reid smote his forehead. 'Of course. See ya mate.'
     He edged through the crush and vanished into the crowd.        (p. 82)

(c)  It's early afternoon and the watches are beeping fifteen.      (p. 125)

(d)  'Get back to your constituencies, and prepare for government,' I said.
     Nobody laughed.                                                (p. 210)

(e)  I remembered my first life-extension treatment, and my heart stopping. I
     had not known then what dry seas I would love Annette beside, what rocks
     would melt before we'd be immortal.                            (p. 308)
                                                                (Ken Macleod)

## 4  THE TEACHING OF POETRY

10. Pick a poem at random from an anthology, and look carefully for examples of
    alliteration, assonance, consonance, reverse rhyme, pararhyme and rhyme, and
    other kinds of phonological regularity (see section 4.3.1). How many of these
    are obvious on first hearing or reading, how many are more hidden? Comment
    on any patterns you find, and on the contribution of alliteration, rhyme, and so
    on, to your personal reaction to the poem.

    Repeat this process for several poems. Do some have no clear-cut sound
    patterning at all? Do some have much more than others? How does this affect
    your reaction? Are there any implications for teaching?

11. Repeat exercise 10 for lexical regularity (see section 4.3.2). For this exercise you should probably use fairly modern poems (later than 1870, perhaps) as all of us tend to miss some nuances of meaning (at least) in older poems.

12. Repeat exercise 10 for deviant language (see section 4.4). Again, choose fairly modern poems.

13. Repeat exercise 10 for ambiguity and polysemy (see section 4.5). Again, choose fairly modern poems.

14. Repeat exercise 10 for mimesis (see section 4.6). Again, choose fairly modern poems.

## 5  TEACHING SHORT STORIES

15. On focalisation: rewriting a passage.

This passage is from the opening section of *The Gourmet*, a film script by Kazuo Ishiguro, which was published in a collection of contemporary fiction (Ishiguro 1993).

1. A CHURCH IN A LONDON STREET. 1904. NIGHT.
   A large church set back from the street. A horse-drawn carriage stands outside.
   Close shot: a wooden plaque on church gate reading:

   *I was hungered and ye gave me meat*
   *I was thirsty and ye gave me drink*
   *I was a stranger and ye took me in.*

   Matthew 25:35

2. CHURCH CRYPT. NIGHT.
   *Point of view*: unseen protagonists as they search around the darkened crypt with a lantern. The lantern reveals ragged men heaped one on another, sleeping in whatever posture the conditions allow. A chorus of snores.

3. CHURCH. Night.
   Viewed from the pulpit. Shadows. We see the empty pews by the moon-light coming through the windows.
   Breathing is heard. At first barely discernible, it grows clearer: the sounds of two men in physical exertion. Their shapes emerge from the shadows, coming slowly towards us down a side aisle: two men dressed in cloaks and hats. They are carrying something between them.
   We hear whispering again, sinister, the words barely discernible.
   WHISPER 1: Perhaps over there. *(Heavy breath.)* Over towards that door.

> WHISPER 2: Yes, yes. *(Heavy breath.)* We'll take it through to the vestry.
>
> WHISPER 1: Just a little further now. As you say, the vestry.

(a) Read the passage and decide what might happen in the rest of the story.

(b) What is the point of view in this passage (in other words, who or what sees what is going on)?

(c) Re-present the scene by rewriting it from a different point of view while as far as possible retaining the atmosphere of the original: (1) in the first person, using one of the 'unseen protagonists' as the focaliser; (2) in the third person, employing the voices of a third person narrator and the 'unseen protagonist' focaliser.

(d) What kinds of changes did you make e.g. of information? sequencing? addition/deletion of words or phrases? Were the two versions very different? Was one easier to write than the other? Which of your two versions do you feel was more effective, and why?

(e) Read the brief summary of the story given below. What reasons do you think Ishiguro might give for choosing to write this story in the form of a film script?

> This first scene, set in 1904 in a London church, is a prelude to the main story which is set in London in the 1980s and concerns Manley, the gourmet of the title. A world-famous food guru, he craves more and more exotic gourmet experiences and is willing to go to any lengths to satisfy his craving, to the extent of becoming slightly mad in the process. At last he plans and carries out his ambition, the ultimate out-of-this-world taste experience, by capturing and cooking a ghost – the ghost of the pauper who was murdered in the London church of the first scene. Not surprisingly, it makes him very sick.

16. On the presentation of speech and thought.

**Text**

Conrad J. 'An Outpost of Progress,' *Penguin Book of English Short Stories*: 57.

This passage comes at the end of the long first paragraph of the story, setting the context for the action. Kayerts and Carlier are the two Europeans in charge of a trading outpost of the Great Trading Company. Their predecessor, the first agent, had died of fever before they arrived on the scene.

> 1. The director had the cross put up over the first agent's grave, and appointed Kayerts to the post. 2. Carlier was told off as second in charge. 3. The director was a man ruthless and efficient, who at times, but very imperceptibly, indulged in grim humour. 4. He made a speech to Kayerts

and Carlier, pointing out to them the promising aspect of their station. 5. The nearest trading-post was about three hundred miles away. 6. It was an exceptional opportunity for them to distinguish themselves and to earn percentages on the trade. 7. This appointment was a favour done to beginners. 8. Kayerts was moved almost to tears by his director's kindness. 9. He would, he said, by doing his best, try to justify the flattering confidence, etc., etc. 10. Kayerts had been in the Administration of the Telegraphs, and knew how to express himself correctly. 11. Carlier, an ex-non-commissioned officer of cavalry in an army guaranteed from harm by several European powers, was less impressed. 12. If there were commissions to get, so much the better; and, trailing a sulky glance over the river, the forests, the impenetrable bush that seemed to cut off the station from the rest of the world, he muttered between his teeth, 'We shall see, very soon.'

The purpose of this exercise is to examine the interaction of the voices of the narrator and the characters in the way that speech and thought are represented in the narrative.

(a) Divide the paragraph into sections that broadly belong to: the director, Kayerts and Carlier.

Of these, do some represent speech and some represent thought?

(b) Underline any words/phrases/sentences in any of these sections that you feel represent the voice of the narrator rather than that of the characters: for example, sentence 3 is a comment on the director and seems to be entirely the voice of the narrator.

(c) Speech and thought are presented in a number of different ways here, ranging from narrative report ('appointed Kayerts to the post') to direct speech ('We shall see, very soon').

Drawing on your reponse to question (b), comment on the ironic effects of this interweaving of the voices of narrator and characters in sentences 2, 4, 9, 10 and 12.

17.

**Text** (see page 178)

From *The Mirror* Wednesday April 7, 1999.

(a) Try to construct the 'implied reader' of this newspaper text.
    You could draw on evidence from the layout (e.g. headlines and captions); from the story (that is, the content); from the discourse (the way the story is presented).

(b) In this report, two stories are combined. Indicate them in the text in some way (you could use highlighting or underlining). How are they connected in the text? Which in your opinion is the main story?

# PRINCE'S ISLE OLD PIE FEUD

## Blind man sold out of date food

### By LOUISE HANCOCK

**IT'S known as a Royal's rural paradise, but tomorrow the island of Berneray will again play host to Prince Charles.**

But as the heir to the throne opens the new £6.7 million 920-metre causeway linking Berneray – his favourite Scots isle – with North Uist, villagers will be seething behind their smiles.

For the normally tranquil 130-strong Hebridean community is split – over a bad meat pie.

Blind piano tuner, Donald Morrison, claims greedy store-owners took advantage of his handicap by selling him out-of-date goods.

But after he complained to trading standards, Donald, 46, was banned from one of the isle's only two shops.

Last night he complained the pie was not fit to give to his dog.

#### Stupid

He said: 'Because of the stupid ban I now face a 45-minute walk to the other shop on the island instead of the 15-minute hike to Ardmaree.

'It's not my fault the pie was so old. I did not dare even give it to Angus, my guide dog.'

A council spokesman said: 'The shop's practice was totally unacceptable. They have been warned if this happens again further action will be taken.'

Shop boss Kate Mackillop was not available for comment yesterday.

But a female shop assistant said: 'It's a carry-on but I don't want to get involved.'

Kate's brother-in-law, Donald Mackillop secretly sheltered Prince Charles several times during a four day stay on the island in 1980.

During his stay – made into a TV film, A Prince Among the Islands – he planted potatoes, mended fences, dipped sheep and fished for prawns.

(c) Can you distinguish sections in the report that correspond to Labov's division of narratives into abstract, orientation, complication, evaluation, resolution and coda? Are all these divisions present? If any are missing, can you explain why this is so?

(d) Donald Morrison's speech is given in direct form in the second half of the report. In the first half, we are given the same utterances in the form of reported speech. Mark in your text three sections of reported speech from the first half. Rank them in order according to whether you feel the voice of the narrator or of the speaker is more apparent. What features in the text influenced your ranking?

(e)  Could you employ any of Propp's character functions to describe the people in the story (for example, hero/heroine/villain/donor)?

(f)  Do you recognise any features that belong specifically to the register of popular journalism? One example might be the dropping of articles in 'Blind man'.

## 6  TEACHING THE NOVEL

18.  This exercise is intended to help teachers design an introductory lesson for their own students to Buchi Emecheta's novel *Second-Class Citizen* (1994). The idea of this lesson is that it would constitute the first encounter with the novel and would therefore come before any discussion of the information provided by the cover of the kind suggested in Chapter 6.

The questions given below provide a range of options; it is not intended that all the questions should be used in a single lesson.

These are the opening paragraphs of the novel:

It had all begun like a dream. You know, that sort of dream which seems to have originated from nowhere, yet one was always aware of its existence. One could feel it, one could be directed by it; unconsciously at first, until it became a reality, a Presence.

Adah did not know for sure what gave birth to her dream, when it all started, but the earliest anchor she could pin down in this drift of nothingness was when she was about eight years old. She was not even quite sure that she was exactly eight, because, you see, she was a girl. She was a girl who had arrived when everyone was predicting a boy. So, since she was such a disappointment to her parents, to her immediate family, to her tribe, nobody thought of recording her birth. She was so insignificant. One thing was certain, though: she was born during the Second World War. She felt eight when she was being directed by her dream, for a younger child would not be capable of so many mischiefs. Thinking back on it all now that she was grown up, she was sorry for her parents. But it was their own fault; they should not have had her in the first place, and that would have saved a lot of people a lot of headaches.

Possible questions:

(a)  • Before reading, write down (or brainstorm) all the associations that the word 'dream' holds for you
     • Read the opening paragraphs of the novel
     • The word 'dream' occurs four times in these two short paragraphs; underline all the words or phrases in the text that seem to you to be associated with 'dream'
     • What do these underlined words and phrases suggest to you about Adah's dream? Are they like or unlike the associations that 'dream' holds for you?

- What sort of dream do you think Adah's will turn out to be?

(b) The first word of the novel is 'It'. Read the first paragraph carefully and think about what the 'It' might refer to.

(c) • What do you know about Adah after reading these paragraphs? (for example, she is a girl, and an unwanted girl; she has a dream; she was born during the Second World War; she belongs to a family and also to a tribe)
   • What have you inferred about her? (for example, life has not been easy either for her or her parents; she is angry with her society for preferring boys to girls; her dream is very important to her; she is strong willed and independent)

(d) At two points in these paragraphs the narrator addresses the reader directly. Mark these points. If these were both taken out, what difference would it make to you? Why do you think the writer uses direct address at this stage in the novel?

(e) • Read the last sentence of the second paragraph. How would you describe the 'tone' of it?
   • By the end of these two paragraphs, how do you feel about Adah? What kind of person is she? Does she interest you?
   • What kind of story do you expect from this beginning?

19. Using literary cloze for *Heart of Darkness*.
   This kind of cloze exercise is designed for students who have already read a good part of *Heart of Darkness*, as it assumes some familiarity with Conrad's style and is intended to stimulate a more careful consideration of what he is doing with his choice of particular words or phrases. It is an example of so-called 'controlled' cloze, or gap-filling, where the deleted words have been selected, rather than pure, 'objective' cloze where every *n*th word is removed. The reason for the deletion in each case is given in Appendix 2 alongside the answer. For some of the gaps, a choice of possible gap-fillers has been offered; in other cases, there is simply a blank for readers to fill in for themselves.

'We ... (1) ... slowly along the overhanging bushes in a whirl of broken twigs and flying leaves. The fusillade below stopped short, as I had foreseen it would when the squirts got empty. I threw my head back to a glinting whiz that ... (2) ... the pilot-house, in at one shutterhole and out at the other. Looking past that mad helmsman, who was shaking the empty rifle and yelling at the shore, I saw vague forms of men running bent double, leaping, ... (3) ..., distinct, ... (4) ..., evanescent. Something big appeared in the air before the shutter, the rifle went overboard, and the man stepped back swiftly, looked at me over his shoulder in an extraordinary, profound, ... (5) ... manner, and fell upon my feet. The side of his head hit the wheel, ... (6) ... and the end of what appeared a long cane clattered round and knocked over a little camp-stool. It looked as though after wrenching that ...

(7) … from somebody ashore he had lost his balance in the effort. The thin smoke had blown away, we were clear of the snag, and looking ahead I could see that in another hundred yards or so I would be free to sheer off, away from the bank; but my feet felt so very … (8) … that I had to look down. The man had rolled on his back and stared straight up at me; both his hands clutched that … (9) It was the … (10) … of a spear that, either thrown or lunged through the opening, had caught him in the side just below the ribs; the … (11) … had gone in out of sight, making a fearful gash; my shoes were … (12) …; a pool of blood lay very still, gleaming dark-red under the wheel; his eyes shone with an amazing lustre. The … (13) … burst out again. He looked at me … (14) …, gripping the spear like something … (15) …, with an air of being afraid I would take it away from him. I had to make an effort to free my eye from his gaze and attend to the steering. With one hand I felt above my head for the line of the steam whistle, and jerked out … (16) … hurriedly. The tumult of angry and warlike yells was checked instantly, and then from the depths of the woods went out such a tremulous and prolonged wail of … (17) … fear and utter … (18) … as may be imagined to follow the flight of the last hope from the earth. There was a great commotion in the bush; the shower of arrows stopped, a few dropping shots rang out sharply – the … (19) … in which the … (20) … beat of the stern-wheel came plainly to my ears. I put the helm hard … (21) … at the moment when the pilgrim in … (22) … pyjamas, very hot and agitated, appeared in the doorway. 'The manager sends me –' he began in an … (23) … tone, and stopped short. 'Good God!' he said, … (24) … at the wounded man.'

1. ?
2. passed/traversed/circled
3. bending/stumbling/gliding/twisting
4. distant/clear/incomplete
5. ?
6. sharply/hard/once/twice
7. ?
8. warm and wet/cold and wet
9. ?
10. ?
11. ?
12. bloody/full/soaked/wet
13. shooting/fusillade/attack/noise
14. piteously/anxiously/uncertainly/hopefully
15. ?
16. ? after ?
17. appalling/mournful/tragic
18. sorrow/terror/despair
19. ?

20. steady/quiet/languid
21. right/down/a-starboard
22. cotton/old-fashioned/pink/blue
23. loud/official/pompous
24. staring/glaring/gazing

Answers and comments are given in Appendix 2.

## 7  TEACHING DRAMA

20. *The Tempest* (William Shakespeare): developing reading strategies.

The question that confronts any novice reader of Shakespeare is 'How do I make sense of this?' Unless students are experienced (and indeed, even if they have read some Shakespeare or similar drama already), it is worth doing some introductory work on an important speech. Lazar (1993) gives in considerable detail an example of how a teacher might prepare a speech from *Julius Caesar*. Here our concern is less with contextualising the speech than with helping learners develop reading strategies at a fairly basic level, for example, sorting out the constituents of the sentence and recognising textual cohesion.

The example given here is what is sometimes called Prospero's renunciation speech, in which he announces his intention to give up the practice of magic. It should be noted that what follows is not intended to be a close reading, but it should be just enough to provide guidance for developing reading strategies and a teacher's checklist when preparing, for example, syntactic constituents; significance of tenses; use of inversions; alliteration.

1. Ye elves of hills, brooks, standing lake and groves;
2. And ye that on the sands with printless foot
3. Do chase the ebbing Neptune, and do fly him
4. When he comes back; you demi-puppets that
5. By moonshine do the green sour ringlets make
6. Whereof the ewe not bites; and you whose pasttime
7. Is to make midnight mushrooms, that rejoice
8. To hear the solemn curfew; by whose aid -
9. Weak masters though ye be – I have bedimm'd
10. The noontide sun, call'd forth the mutinous winds,
11. And 'twixt the green sea and the azur'd vault
12. Set roaring war. To the dread rattling thunder
13. Have I given fire, and rifted Jove's stout oak
14. With his own bolt; the strong-bas'd promontory
15. Have I made shake, and by the spurs pluck'd up
16. The pine and cedar. Graves at my command
17. Have wak'd their sleeper, op'd, and let them forth,
18. By my so potent art. But this rough magic

19. I here abjure; and when I have requir'd
20. Some heavenly music – which even now I do -
21. To work mine end upon their senses
22. That this airy charm is for, I'll break my staff,
23. Bury it certain fathoms in the earth,
24. And deeper than did ever plummet sound,
25. I'll drown my book. *[Solemn music]*

(a) • Read carefully through the speech and underline what you think is the key statement (the turning point) of this speech. Would you agree that it is 'this rough magic/ I here abjure'?
   • Why might you decide it was the key statement?
   • What tense is the verb?
   • Who is the subject?
   • If we say that 'abjure' is a 'performative verb', what does that mean?

(b) • In the lines following 'I here abjure', underline any important statements of intention. Are these clauses dependent or independent (subordinate or main clauses – depending on terminology)?
   • What time do they refer to?

(c) • The first part of this long speech (before the lines 'But this rough magic/ I here abjure') is partly addressed to the elves and partly concerned with what Prospero has achieved with their help. Mark the point where we see the shift of focus from the elves to Prospero.
   **Note:** Notice how odd the syntax is: the speech starts off with an invocation ('Ye elves'). This goes on until l.8, at which point we would expect a main clause, but instead we get 'by whose aid', so that in effect there is no grammatically independent clause in the first sentence. This kind of 'faulty' syntax is not uncommon in Shakespeare and it certainly does reflect the way in which people speak, in that often our speech may not be strictly grammatical but is nonetheless perfectly comprehensible.
   • Mark all the verbs that follow the subject 'I' in ll.9–18. How would you describe them in terms of tense and aspect? See Appendix 2 for answer.
   • Try changing them into simple past tense. Does this make a difference to the meaning in any way? Again see Appendix 2.

(d) • Instances of the use of subject–verb inversion: students might be asked to mark such OSV structures as 'This rough magic/ I here abjure' or the parallelism of inverted and non-inverted clauses in line 11.

   *To the dread rattling thunder*
   *Have I given fire,/* and rifted Jove's stout oak
   With his own bolt; //*the strong-bas'd promontory*
   *Have I made shake,* /and by the spurs plucked up
   The pine and cedar.

(e) • The semantic function of alliteration in emphasising meaning and relationship can be explored in the last lines (ll.22–5) where key words are given additional emphasis by alliterative highlighting:

> I'll *b*reak my *s*taff,
> *B*ury it *c*ertain fathom*s* in the earth,
> An*d d*eeper than *d*i*d* ever plummet *s*oun*d*,
> I'll *d*rown my *b*ook.

21. *Mary Queen of Scots Got Her Head Chopped Off* (Liz Lochhead)

This exercise explores more fully the suggestions for work on La Corbie's introductory speech. The text is given in Chapter 7.

(a) Read the speech through carefully, aloud if possible (this really does help).

(b) Underline all the words that are unfamiliar to you.

(c) Work out why you find the underlined words difficult to understand. Is it because of the pronunciation (related to accent) or is it because of lexical or grammatical differences from Standard English (related to dialect)?

(d) A glossary of the words that belong to Scots dialect is given below. (One or two, e.g. *duds,* are not specific to Scots but are also found in other dialects.)

| | | |
|---|---|---|
| gey | = | very |
| bere | = | shining |
| bricht | = | bright |
| kye | = | cattle |
| ken | = | know |
| smirr | = | haze, light rain |
| haar | = | sea-mist |
| corbie | = | crow |
| duds | = | clothes |
| oxter | = | armpit |
| een | = | eyes |
| braw | = | fine |
| rickle | = | mess |

Now that you know these Scots dialect words, reread the speech.

(e) A number of apparently unfamiliar words will remain, but these are Standard English words which are pronounced differently in Scots and therefore spelled differently to reflect the pronunciation e.g. sometimes a consonant is omitted, as in *ha'* for *hall*, *ha'e* for *have*, or a vowel sound changes e.g. *daurk* for *dark*, *stanes* for *stones*.

Read the speech once again, aloud. Can you make sense now of most of the words you underlined?

(f) In your own country, do you have a number of different geographical dialects? Do writers sometimes write in a particular dialect? If so, why do you think they make that choice?

Make a list of reasons why you think Liz Lochhead chose to write this play in Scots rather than in Standard English.

## 8  ASSESSMENT AND EVALUATION IN LITERATURE LESSONS AND COURSES

22. How important or relevant is it (you may wish to substitute other criteria), in your situation, to assess each of the main kinds of 'outcome' mentioned in Chapter 8? (If there are any other kinds, or subdivisions within these kinds, which you wish to add to the list, space is provided.)

| Type of outcome | Very important | Important | Fairly important | Not really important | Not at all important |
|---|---|---|---|---|---|
| Affective outcomes (e.g. enjoyment of literature) | | | | | |
| 'Learning how to learn' | | | | | |
| Factual knowledge | | | | | |
| 'Delicate sensibility' | | | | | |
| Skills of literary criticism | | | | | |
| Skills of reading | | | | | |
| Skills of interactive speaking/listening | | | | | |
| Functional range | | | | | |
| Other | | | | | |
| | | | | | |

If you have said that certain types are unimportant, explain why. For the other types, outline possible tests or items.

23. Rank the sample tests or test items (section 8.5) in terms of their relevance to your situation. (Consider the *type* of test or item, not necessarily the specific example.) For the three most useful types, devise a similar test (item) relevant to your learners and to specific texts which they (might) study.

## 9  RESEARCH AND DEVELOPMENT

24. Work with one or more colleagues. Ask all the group to read section 9.1. Then find a poem which is new to everybody; ask each member of the group, separately and in private, to read the poem and introspect, using a tape recorder. Report back and compare results.

25. Find an example of an official syllabus for the teaching of literature, and 'develop' a small part of it along the lines suggested in section 9.2.1. Again, this is best done in groups, comparing answers.

26. Ask a colleague to observe one of your lessons, and to let you observe one of his or hers. For the first half of the lesson, observers should just make informal notes, for the second half they should use a 'coding system' – try the one in section 9.3.2, or see Malamah-Thomas (1987) for alternatives. After both observations, have an informal meeting with your colleague, and discuss what you have learnt. In the light of this experience, how useful do you consider peer observation, with or without coding, for your own personal development?

# Appendix 2

# Some possible answers to selected study questions

This Appendix offers possible (or, in a few cases, definite) answers to some of the questions we ask, either in the main text or in the study questions section. Not all our questions are 'answered' in this way, as in many cases your answer will depend wholly or largely on personal opinion, professional context and/or other individual factors.

## SECTION 3.3, ASSIGNMENT 1

1. Father Thames, you have seen many generations of lively children playing and enjoying themselves on your green banks. Who is now enjoying themselves cutting (rowing) through your clear waters, and keeping birds in cages? Who are the latest set of lazy children, playing with hoops or knocking a ball about?
2. Both, but mainly content.
3. Most readers would probably be put off.
4. Nostalgia is still 'big business', and usually includes some 'old-fashioned' language, but not usually 'elevated' like this example.

## SECTION 3.3, ASSIGNMENT 2

1. The last sentence in each stanza is different – you could call these two sentences 'B', the rest 'A'. (But does the last *line* in each stanza revert to 'A'?)
2. A – instructions for using a gun.
   B – lyrical description of nature.
3. Differences of vocabulary are substantial and obvious. The grammar is more subtly different: 'A' has short sentences and apparently clumsy repetition, 'B' has slightly unusual features such as an adverbial phrase ('in the gardens') between verb and object.
4. It brings out differences on several levels – most obviously between ugly war and beautiful flowers, but also between the apparently uneducated military instructor and the 'sensitive' poet!

## SECTION 3.8

1. *The Great Escape* (film).
2. *Day of the Jackal* (novel).
3. 'Hail the new-born king' (from a hymn).
4. Title of a BBC radio programme (unchanged).
5. Henry the First (King).
6. 'On the wagon' is colloquial for 'not drinking alcohol'.
7. 'It's a sin to tell a lie' (song).
8. 'Out of sight, out of mind' (proverb).
9. 'Dog days', a very old idiom, originally meaning 'hottest days', now sometimes 'boring days'.
10. 'Pulling the plug' is a modern idiom for suddenly stopping an activity, as for example when a sponsor withdraws support.

## SECTION 4.4

(a) *Reaps a swathe* is normally used of a scythe, etc. in a field. A fairly typical metaphor – the double image makes the description more graphic.

(b) *Disenchanted* can usually only be applied to humans, and forces us to reinterpret the earlier 'enchanted' in an unlikely way. A standard humorous device, though with a serious point.

(c) *Half happy* is unusual: we normally say *fairly happy, half awake,* and so on. Perhaps used to indicate an unusual state, the precarious happiness of wartime.

(d) Line 2 is pragmatically deviant: *sleeping* equals *dead,* and one doesn't normally talk to dead people. But of course poets regularly address the alive and the dead, and animal, vegetable and mineral! The effect is to reassure the real addressees – patriotic Britons – that the national hero Drake will be resurrected when needed.

(e) *The light … lies dead* is deviant. When we get to line 6, we can interpret both *dead* and *shed* as near-synonyms for *remember'd not.* It is rhetorically effective to hold back the most explicit term until the end.

(f) Lines 3 and 4 are syntactically deviant: we would expect a passive or a human subject. But then we realise that the houses will not literally be rebuilt, and the names rewritten, but they will reappear when the sand blows away. The strange syntax suggests this eerie imitation of human action.

(g) '*Mistier*' is semantically deviant as it normally applies to things we see: '*less distinctly*' or '*less clearly*' would be prosaic alternatives. The last line may violate Grice's maxims of quality (exaggeration/hyperbole?) and quantity (too precise?).

(h) All four phrases are slang, a surprising register for poetry about death. The repetition violates the maxim of quantity, and the capital letters on '*Pops*' and '*Stops*' are typographically deviant.

(i) Suns usually rise and set, cities rise and fall (collocation).

(j) Most of the 'content words' (nouns, verbs, adjectives), are lexically deviant. A paraphrase, inadequate of course, might be: 'I shall not dishonour the human tragedy of death with a pompous platitude.'

(k) Very unusually, the referential meaning of these lines, though not of course the effect, is largely explained by the next two lines:

> The gale, it blows the saplings double
> And thick on Severn show the leaves.

Unlike lines 3 and 4, lines 1 and 2 make the wood seem animate, possibly human, a common device in nature poetry. (**Note:** 'in trouble' does not have the modern meaning, it is more like 'in travail', but still deviant as applied to trees.)

## SECTION 4.6

'Regentropfen', which means 'Raindrop'.

## QUESTION 8 (APPENDIX 1)

Vocabulary: *ye, spent, coy, tarry.*
Syntax: *gather ye, a-flying, go marry* (and so on).
  The poem should not be difficult for fairly advanced students; the problematic words 'coy' and 'tarry' are guessable. The message should be quite familiar, if not banal!

## QUESTION 9 (APPENDIX 1)

### Text A

The names and the general story are taken from classical mythology – see any encyclopaedia for details.
  For many students this text would be rather remote; those who can enjoy it tend to do so without needing the mythological details.

### Text B

The references are of course to events in the bible – Adam and Eve, Cain and Abel, the Tower of Babel, Noah's Ark. Students can enjoy working out these references as a sort of detective activity, and they often enjoy the poem more than their teachers do!

### Text C

(a) 'The Songs of Distant Earth', a science fiction story by Arthur C. Clarke.
(b Approximate quotation from *The Life of Brian*, a film by the Monty Python team, satirising political factionalism.
(c) An allusion to the opening of *Nineteen Eighty-Four*, a science fiction novel by George Orwell.
(d) A quotation from a speech by David Steel, a former leader of the Liberal Party in Britain, and a famous example of excessive optimism.

(e)    An allusion to Robert Burns' poem 'A Red Red Rose' (Burns 1990: 465–6):

> Till all the seas gang dry, my dear,
> And the rocks melt wi' the sun …

These are examples of the many intertextual elements in a typical, moderately 'literary' novel, of which the average native speaker reader probably retrieves fewer than half. All can be profitably explored if students wish, but none are necessary for enjoyment of the story.


## QUESTION 19 (APPENDIX 1)

1. *tore* 'tore slowly' is an apparent oxymoron that expresses the paradox of the whole journey, but as we read on we realise that it also describes the literal tearing down of overhanging twigs and leaves.
2. *traversed* The most precise of the possible verbs and appropriate in terms of register.
3. *gliding* and 4. *incomplete* Both words express the dreamlike shifting quality of the experience.
5. *familiar* The word is unpredictable and shocking in the context – on the previous page we have been given a description of the helmsman that distances him, defamiliarises him, almost presenting him as a member of a different species, yet here in the moment of death he looks at Marlow in a 'familiar' manner, as one of the human family.
6. *twice* It is the precision that makes the effect here – though *hard* could be argued for as alliterating with *head* and *hit*.
7. *thing* The object has not yet been clearly identified; the fact that we don't yet know what it is gives it a sinister quality.
8. *warm and wet* Alliterative but also slightly shocking in that the alteration from the more usual collocation *cold and wet* draws attention to the fact that the man's blood is still warm.
9. *cane* A repetition.
10. *shaft* and 11. *blade* The spear is seen in its parts.
12. *full* No doubt the shoes were also *bloody*, *soaked* and *crimson* but these adjectives all seem to collocate more normally with *shoes* than the adjective *full*, which has the effect of turning the shoes into containers – once again a kind of defamiliar-isation effect. We read in the next paragraph that Marlow was 'morbidly anxious to change my shoes and socks'.
13. *fusillade* The word was used at the beginning of the passage.
14. *anxiously* Perhaps again this emphasises the intimacy of the relation between Marlow and the dying helmsman, rather as *familiar* has done already.
15. *precious* The word makes us question what is happening; why is the spear 'precious'? is it another aspect of the dream/nightmare-like quality of the experience, where all normality has been turned upside down?

16. *screech after screech* A chance to consider the varying connotations of different sound words; what about *bellow after bellow*, *howl after howl*?

17. *mournful* Expresses the feelings of the one who makes the sound, whereas *appalling* would express those of the hearer and *tragic* would perhaps be a more impersonal adjective; much of the novel is about Marlow's own ambivalent attitude towards the Africans: does he perceive them as wholly 'other' or as people with emotions similar to his own?

18. *despair* The opposite of the *hope* that is in flight from the earth.

19. *silence* Probably quite easy to guess as a contrast to the *commotion* earlier in the sentence.

20. *languid* Not an obvious choice in terms of register – and therefore interesting to discuss why he uses it.

21. *a-starboard* The technical term, expected from this speaker; perhaps also emphasises his authority.

22. *pink* Alliteration – but also the slight absurdity of the colour in that context – what are the connotations of *pink*?

23. *official* It should be obvious as the only word offered that would follow *an* – but also emphasises the contrast between the man's behaviour in his role as messenger and the shocked human reaction that follows.

24. *glaring* Perhaps the least obvious of the three possibilities – what are the connotations of *glaring*, in comparison with *staring* and *gazing*? Does the choice of *glaring* bear any relation to themes that have already emerged in this passage?

## QUESTION 20 (APPENDIX 1)

(c) The answer to the second question is that they refer to past time but with perfective aspect.

In the third question, as it stands, the use of the present perfect indicates a necessary relationship with the present. A simple past would not imply any necessary relationship with the present moment whereas, as the speech stands, it is all organised around the key present performative 'abjure'.

# References

## SECTION A: CRITICAL, ACADEMIC AND PEDAGOGIC WORKS

Abety, P. A. (1991), 'The notional syllabus in literature', in C. Brumfit (ed.), *Assessment in Literature Teaching*, London: Macmillan.

Achebe, C. (1989), 'An image of Africa: racism in Conrad's *Heart of Darkness*', in *Hopes and Impediments: Selected Essays*, New York: Doubleday Anchor.

Akyel, A. and E. Yalcin (1990), 'Literature in the EFL class: a study of goal-achievement incongruence', in *ELT Journal* 44/3, 174–80.

Alderson, C. J. and A. H. Urquhart (1984), *Reading in a Foreign Language*, London: Longman.

Allwright, D. (1991), 'The death of the method', *Revue de Phonétique Appliquée*, 99/101: 79–87.

Allwright, D. and Kathleen Bailey (1991), *Focus on the Language Classroom: an Introduction to Classroom Research for Language Teachers*, Cambridge: Cambridge University Press.

Bach, K. and R. M. Harnish (1979), *Linguistic Communication and Speech Acts*, Cambridge MA: MIT Press.

Bailey, Kenneth (1978), *Methods of Social Research*, Chapter 6 ('Questionnaire construction'), 92–137, London: Collier Macmillan.

Baker, M. (1992), *In Other Words: A Coursebook on Translation*, London: Routledge.

Barthes, R. (1977), 'Introduction to the structural analysis of narrative' in *Image, Music, Text*, trans. Stephen Heath, New York: Hill and Wang (first published 1966).

Bassnett, S. (ed.) (1997), *Studying British Cultures*, London: Routledge.

Benson, C. (1993), 'Advanced Text Study and Translation – Course Materials: Varieties of English', mimeo, Institute for Applied Language Studies, University of Edinburgh.

Benton, M. (1992), *Secondary Worlds. Literature Teaching and the Visual Arts*, Milton Keynes: Open University Press.

Berthon, H. E. (1930), *Nine French Poets 1820–1880: with an Introduction on the Structure of French Verse and Explanatory Notes*, London: Macmillan.

Birch, D. (1989), *Language, Literature and Critical Practice*, London: Routledge.

Birch, D. (1991), *The Language of Drama*, London: Macmillan.

*Branching Out: a Cultural Studies Syllabus* (1998), Bulgaria: The British Council.

Bransford, J. D. and M. K. Johnson (1972), 'Conceptual pre-requisites for understanding: some investigations of comprehension and recall', *Journal of Verbal Learning and Verbal Behaviour*, 11: 717–26.

Brown, G. and G. Yule (1983), *Discourse Analysis*, Cambridge: Cambridge University Press.

Brown, G., A. Anderson, R. Shilcock and G. Yule (1994), *Teaching Talk*, Cambridge: Cambridge University Press.

Brown, G., K. Malmkjaer, A. Pollitt and J. Williams (eds) (1994), *Language and Understanding*, Oxford: Oxford University Press.

Brumfit, C. (ed.) (1991) *Assessment in Literature Teaching*, London: Macmillan.

Brumfit, C. (1994) 'Understanding, language, and educational processes', in G. Brown *et al.* (eds), *Language and Understanding* , Oxford: Oxford University Press.

Brumfit, C. J. and R. A. Carter (eds) (1986), *Literature and Language Teaching*, Oxford: Oxford University Press.

Burton, D. (1980), *Dialogue and Discourse: A Sociolinguistic Approach to Modern Drama Dialogue and Naturally Occurring Conversation*, London: Routledge and Kegan Paul.

Burton, D. (1982), 'Through a glass darkly: through dark glasses', in R. Carter (ed.), *Language and Literature: An Introductory Reader in Stylistics*, London: Allen and Unwin (reprinted Routledge 1991), 195–214.

Buttjes, D. and M. Byram (eds) (1990), *Culture and the Language Classroom*, London: Macmillan.

Bygate, M. (1987) *Speaking*, Oxford: Oxford University Press.

Carter R. and J. McRae (1996) *Language, Literature and the Learner: Creative Classroom Practice*, London: Longman.

Carter R. and W. Nash (1990), *Seeing Through Language*, Oxford: Blackwell.

Cherrington, R. and L. Davcheva (eds) (1998), *Teaching Towards Intercultural Competence*, Bulgaria: The British Council.

Clark, J. L. (1987), *Curriculum Renewal in School Foreign Language Learning*, Oxford: Oxford University Press.

Cluysenaar, A. (1976), *Introduction to Literary Stylistics*, London: Batsford.

Collie, J. and S. Slater (1987), *Literature in the Language Classroom*, Cambridge: Cambridge University Press.

Collie, J. and S. Slater (1993), *Short stories for Creative Language Classrooms*, Cambridge: Cambridge University Press.

Cook, G. (1994), *Discourse and Literature*, Oxford: Oxford University Press.

Corbett, J. (1997), *Language and Scottish Literature*, Edinburgh: Edinburgh University Press.

Crabbe, D. (ed.) (1993), *Guidelines 5, 1: Classroom Tests*, Singapore: RELC.

Crawford, R. (1997), 'Dedefining Scotland', in S. Bassnett (ed.), *Studying British Cultures,* London: Routledge.

Crystal, D. and D. Davy (1969), *Investigating English Style*, Harlow: Longman.

Cureton, R. D. (1993), 'The auditory imagination and the music of poetry', in P. Verdonk (ed.), *Twentieth-century Poetry: from Text to Context*, London: Routledge.

Danesi, M. and A. Mollica (1988), 'From right to left: a 'bimodal' perspective of language teaching', *Canadian Modern Language Review*, 45/1: 76–89.

Davies Roberts, P. (1986), *How Poetry Works*, London: Penguin.

Davis, C. (1995), 'Extensive reading: an expensive extravagance?', *ELT Journal*, 49/4: 329–30.

Drakakis, J. (1997), 'Shakespeare in quotations', in S. Bassnett (ed.), *Studying British Cultures,* London: Routledge.

Duff, A. and A. Maley (1978), *Drama Techniques in Language Learning*, Cambridge: Cambridge University Press.

Duff, A. and A. Maley (1990), *Literature*, Oxford: Oxford University Press.

Durant, A. and N. Fabb (1990), *Literary Studies in Action*, London: Routledge and Kegan Paul.

Eagleton, T. (1983), *Literary Theory: an Introduction*, Oxford: Blackwell.

Edge, J. and K. Richards (eds) (1993), *Teachers Develop Teachers Research*, Oxford: Heinemann.

Edwin, M. (1993), 'The teaching of literature in English in Malaysian secondary schools', in Brumfit and Benton (eds), *Teaching Literature: A World Perspective,* London: Macmillan.

Ellis, J. B. (1974), *The Theory of Literary Criticism: A Logical Analysis*, Berkeley.

Ellis, R. (1984), *Classroom Second Language Development*, Oxford: Pergamon.

Ellis, R. (1985), *Understanding Second Language Acquisition*, Oxford: Oxford University Press.

*ELT Journal* (1990), 44/3 [volume on using literature in language teaching].

Empson, W. (1930), *Seven Types of Ambiguity*, London: Penguin (first published 1961).

Fabb, N. (1997), *Linguistics and Literature*, Oxford: Blackwell.

Fanselow, J. (1987), *Breaking Rules: Generating and Exploring Alternatives in Language Teaching*, New York and London: Longman.

Fish, S. (1980), *Is There a Text In This Class? The Authority of Interpretive Communities*, Cambridge MA: Harvard University Press.

Flynn, L. and S. West (1989), *Cal: Heinemann Fiction Project: Teaching Strategies for Literature and Language*, London: Heinemann.

Gautam, K. and M. Sharma (1986), 'Dialogue in *Waiting for Gadot* and Grice's concept of implicature', *Modern Drama*, 29: 580–6.

Genette, G. (1980), *Narrative Discourse*, trans. J. Lewis, Ithaca: Cornell University Press.

Gilroy, M. and B. Parkinson (1996), 'State of the art article: teaching literature in a foreign language', *Language Teaching*, 29/4: 213–25.

Graddol, D., L. Thompson and M. Byram (eds) (1993), *Language and Culture* (BAAL Papers), Clevedon: Multilingual Matters.

Grice, H. P. (1969), 'Utterer's meaning and intentions', *Philosophical Review*, 78, 147–77.

Grice, H. P. (1975), 'Logic and conversation', in D. Steinberg and L. Jakobovits (eds), *Semantics: an Interdisciplinary Reader in Philosophy, Linguistics and Psychology*, Cambridge: Cambridge University Press: 53–9.

Gumperz, J. J. and D. Hymes (1972), *Directions in Sociolinguistics*, Oxford: Blackwell.

Halliday, M. A. K. and R. Hassan (1976), *Cohesion in English*, London: Longman.

Haynes, J. (1995), *Style*, London: Routledge.

Herman, V. (1998), *Dramatic Discourse*, London: Routledge.

Hill, D. A. (ed.) (1994), *Changing Contexts in English Language Teaching*, Milan: The British Council.

Hill, D. A. (ed.) (1996), *Papers on Teaching Literature from the British Council Conferences in Bologna 1994 and Milan 1995*, Milan: The British Council.

Hill, D. A. and S. Holden (eds) (1990), *Effective Teaching and Learning*, Oxford: Modern English Publications.

Hirsch, E. D. (1987), *Cultural Literacy: What Every American Needs to Know*, Boston: Houghton Mifflin.

Hirst, D. (1984), *The Tempest*, Basingstoke: Macmillan.

Hobsbaum, P. (1996), *Metre, Rhythm and Verse Form*, London: Routledge.

Howell-Richardson, C. and B. Parkinson (1988), 'Learner diaries: possibilities and pitfalls', in P. Grunwell (ed.), *British Studies in Applied Linguistics 3: Applied Linguistics in Society*, London: CILT, 74–9.

Hymes, D. (1972), 'Models of interaction and social life', in J. J. Gumperz and D. Hymes (eds), *Directions in Sociolinguistics,* Oxford: Blackwell.

Isenberg, N. (1990), 'Literary competence: the EFL reader and the role of the teacher', *English Language Teaching Journal,* 44/3.

Iser, W. (1974), *The Implied Reader*, Baltimore: John Hopkins University Press.

Iser, W. (1978), *The Act of Reading*, London: Routledge and Kegan Paul.

Kelly, L. G. (1969), *25 Centuries of Language Teaching*, Rowley, MA: Newbury House.

*Kesusasteraan Dalan Bahasa Inggeris* (1990), Malaysia: Ministry of Education.

Kerby, A. (1993), 'Hermeneutics', in Makaryk, I. R. (ed.), *Encyclopedia of Contemporary Literary Theory*, Toronto: University of Toronto Press, 90–3.

Krashen, S. (1985), *The Input Hypothesis: Issues and Implications*, London: Longman.

Labov, W. (1972), *Language in the Inner City*, Philadelphia: University of Pennsylvania Press.

Labov, W. and J. Waletzky (1967), 'Narrative analysis: oral versions of personal experience', in J. Helm (ed.), *Essays on the Verbal and Visual Arts*, Seattle: University of Washington Press.

Lakoff, G. (1987), *Women, Fire and Dangerous Things. What Categories Reveal About the Mind*, Chicago: University of Chicago Press.

Lakoff, R. and D. Tannen (1984), 'Conversational strategy and metastrategy in a pragmatic theory: the example of *Scenes from a marriage*', *Semiotica* 49 (3/4): 323–46.

Lakoff, R. (1975), *Language and Woman's Place*, New York: Harper Colophon.

Lawrence, D. H. (1920), Introduction to *New Poems*, New York: Huebsch.

Lazar, G. (1993), *Literature and Language Teaching*, Cambridge: Cambridge University Press.

Leavis, F. R. (1943), *Education and the University*, London: Chatto and Windus.

Leavis, F. R. (1984), *The Great Tradition: George Eliot, Henry James, Joseph Conrad*, London: Chatto and Windus.

Leech, G. N. (1969), *A Linguistic Guide to English Poetry*, London: Longman.

Leech, G. N. (1983), *Principles of Pragmatics*, London: Longman.

Leech, G. N. and M. H. Short (1981), *Style in Fiction: A Linguistic Introduction to English Fictional Prose*, London: Longman.

Lewis, C. S. (1961), *An Experiment in Criticism*, Oxford: Oxford University Press.

Lochhead, L. (1992), 'Rough Magic', Perth programme notes for *Mary Queen of Scots Got Her Head Chopped Off.*

Long, M., L. Adams, M. McLean and F. Castaños (1976), 'Doing things with words – verbal interaction in lockstep and small group classroom situations', in J. Fanselow and R. Crymes (eds) (1976), *On TESOL '76* Washington, DC: TESOL: 137–53.

Lynch, T. (1996a), *Communication in the Language Classroom*, Oxford: Oxford University Press.

Lynch, T. (1996b), 'Pausing for breadth', *IATEFL Newsletter*, 131: 20–1.

Lynch, T. (1997), 'Nudge, nudge: teacher interventions in task-based learner talk', *ELT Journal*, 51/5: 317–25.

McGrath, J. (1981), *A Good Night Out: Popular Theatre: Audience, Class and Form*, London: Eyre Methuen.

Makaryk, I. R. (1993), *Encyclopaedia of Contemporary Literary Theory*, Toronto: University of Toronto Press.

Malamah-Thomas, A. (1987), *Classroom Interaction*, Oxford: Oxford University Press.

Maley, A. (1989), 'Down from the pedestal: literature as resource', in R. Carter, R. Walker and C. J. Brumfit (eds), *Literature and the Learner: Methodological Approaches*, Basingstoke/London: Modern English Publications and The British Council, 10–24.

Maley, A. and A. Duff (1978), *Drama Techniques in Language Learning*, Cambridge: Cambridge University Press.

Maley, A. and S. Moulding (1985), *Poem into Poem*, Cambridge: Cambridge University Press.

Marley, C. (1995), 'A little light on the *Heart of Darkness*' in J. Payne (ed.), *Linguistic Approaches to Literature: Papers in Literary Stylistics*, Birmingham: English Language Research Centre, University of Birmingham.

Mey, J. L. (1993), *Pragmatics: an Introduction*, Oxford: Blackwell.

Mills, S. (1996), *Feminist Stylistics*, London: Routledge.

Mitchell, R., B. Parkinson and R. Johnstone (1981), *The Foreign Language Classroom: an Observational Study*. Stirling Educational Monographs No. 9, Stirling: Department of Education, University of Stirling.

Morris, C. W. (1938), *Foundations of the Theory of Signs*, Chicago: Chicago University Press.

Nash, W. (1990), *Language in Popular Fiction*, London: Routledge.

Nash, W. (1986), 'The possibilities of paraphrase in the teaching of literary idiom', in C. J. Brumfit and R. A. Carter (eds), *Literature and Language Teaching*, Oxford: Oxford University Press, 70–88.

Newton, K. (1990), *Interpreting the Text*, Hemel Hempstead: Harvester Wheatsheaf.

Nunan, D. (1992), *Research Methods in Language Learning*, Cambridge: Cambridge University Press.

Oller, J. W. Jr. (1995), 'Adding abstract to formal and content schemata: results of recent work in Peircean semiotics', *Applied Linguistics*, 16/3: 273–306.

O'Malley, M., J. Michael and A. U. Chamot (1990), *Learning Strategies in Second Language Acquisition*, Cambridge: Cambridge University Press.

Parkinson, B. (1990a), 'The teaching of poetry: dealing with deviance', in D. A. Hill and J. Holden (eds), *Effective Teaching and Learning*, Oxford: Modern English Publications, 115–19.

Parkinson, B. (1990b), 'What, if anything, is English for literary studies?', *Edinburgh Working Papers in Applied Linguistics*, 1, 25–34.

Parkinson, B. (1994), 'Missed metaphors', in D. A. Hill (ed.), *Changing Contexts in English Language Teaching*, Milan: The British Council, 107–12.

Parrott, M. (1993), *Tasks for Language Teachers. A Resource Book for Training and Development*, Cambridge: Cambridge University Press.

Payne, J. (ed.) (1995), *Linguistic Approaches to Literature: Papers in Literary Stylistics*, English Language Research Centre, University of Birmingham.

Pennycook, A. (1994), *The Cultural Politics of English as an International Language*, London: Longman.

Pica, T. (1994), 'Research on negotiation: what does it reveal about second-language learning conditions, processes and outcomes?', *Language Learning*, 44/3: 493–527.

Pica, T. and C. Doughty (1985), 'Input and interaction in the communicative language classroom: a comparison of teacher-fronted and group activities', in S. Gass and C. Madden (eds), *Input and Second Language Acquisition*, Rowley, MA: Newbury House, 115–32.

Pope, A. (1878), *Essay on Criticism*, (Aldine edition), London: Bell (first published 1711).

Pope, R. (1995), *Textual Intervention*, London: Routledge.

Propp, V. (1968), *Morphology of the Folktale*, Austin: University of Texas Press (first published in Russian in 1928).

Radford, J. (ed.) (1986), *The Progress of Romance: The Politics of Popular Fiction*, London: Routledge.

Radway, J. (1984; revised 1991), *Reading the Romance: Women, Patriarchy and Popular Literature*, Chapel Hill: University of North Carolina Press.

Reid Thomas, H., A. Pulverness and L. Davcheva (1998), 'Working towards a syllabus for Cultural Studies', in R. Cherrington *et al.* (eds), *Teaching Towards Intercultural Competence*, Bulgaria: The British Council.

Richards, I. A. (1929), *Practical Criticism: a Study of Literary Judgement*, London: Routledge and Kegan Paul (republished 1964).

Ricoeur, P. (1981), *Hermeneutics and the Human Sciences* (ed. and trans. J. B. Thompson), Cambridge: Cambridge University Press.

Rimmon-Kenan, S. (1983), *Narrative Fiction: Contemporary Poetics*, London: Methuen.

Sacks, H., E. Schegloff and G. Jefferson (1974), 'A simplest systematics for the organisation of turn-taking for conversation', *Language*, 50/4.

Said, E. W. (1993), *Culture and Imperialism*, London: Vintage.

Schmidt, R. (1990), 'The role of consciousness in second language learning', *Applied Linguistics* 11/2: 129–58.

Searle, J. R. (1969), *Speech Acts: an Essay in the Philosophy of Language*, Cambridge: Cambridge University Press.

Searle, J. R. (1983), *Intentionality*, Cambridge: Cambridge University Press.

Sell, R. D. (ed.) (1991), *Literary Pragmatics*, London/New York: Routledge.

Sell, R. D. (1995a), 'Why is literature central?', in Sell (1995b), 4–20.

Sell, R. D. (1995b), *Literature throughout Foreign Language Education: the Implications of*

*Pragmatics*. London: Phoenix ELT.

Short, M. (1988) (ed.), *Reading, Analysing and Teaching Literature*, London: Longman.

Short, M. (1994), 'Understanding texts: point of view', in G. Brown *et al.* (eds), *Language and Understanding*, Oxford: Oxford University Press.

Short, M. (1996), *Exploring the Language of Poems, Plays and Prose*, London: Longman.

Short, M. and W. Van Peer (1989), 'Accident! Stylisticians evaluate: Aims and methods of stylistic analysis', in M. Short (ed.), *Reading, Analysing and Teaching Literature*, London: Longman, 22–71.

Simpson, P. (1993), *Language, Ideology and Point of View*, London: Routledge.

Simpson, P. (1997), *Language through Literature*, London: Routledge.

Slimani, A. (1992), 'Evaluation of classroom interaction', in J. C. Alderson and A. Beretta (eds), *Evaluating Second Language Education*, Cambridge: Cambridge University Press, 197–220.

Somekh, B. (1993), 'Quality in action research: the contribution of classroom teachers', in J. Edge and K. Richards (eds), *Teachers Develop Teachers Research*, Oxford: Heinemann, 26–38.

Sperber, D. and D. Wilson (1986), *Relevance: Communication and Cognition*, Cambridge, MA: Harvard University Press.

Spiro, J. (1991), 'Assessing literature: four papers' in Brumfit, C. (ed.), *Assessment in Literature Teaching*, London: Macmillan.

Spittles, B. (1992), *Joseph Conrad: Text and Context*, Basingstoke: Macmillan.

Spolsky, B. (1994), 'Comprehension testing, or can understanding be measured?', in G. Brown *et al.* (eds), *Language and Understanding*, Oxford: Oxford University Press.

Styan, J. L. (1975), *Drama, Stage and Audience*, London: Cambridge University Press.

Talbot, M. M. (1995), *Fictions at Work: Language and Social Practice in Fiction*, London: Longman.

Toolan, M. (1988), *Narrative: A Critical Linguistic Introduction*, London: Routledge.

Toolan, M. (ed.) (1992), *Language, Text and Context: Essays in Stylistics*, London: Routledge.

Traugott, E. C. and M. L. Pratt (1980), *Linguistics for Students of Literature*, New York: Harcourt Brace Jovanovich.

Turner, G. (1973), *Stylistics*, Harmondsworth: Penguin.

Ur, P. (1981), *Discussions That Work*, Cambridge: Cambridge University Press.

Van Peer, W. (1986), *Stylistics and Psychology: Investigations of Foregrounding*, London: Croom Helm.

Van Peer, W. (1989), 'How to do things with texts: towards a pragmatic foundation for the teaching of texts', in M. Short (ed.), *Reading, Analysing and Teaching Literature*, London: Longman, 267–97.

Verdonk, P. (1988), 'The language of poetry: the application of literary stylistic theory in university teaching', in M. Short (ed.), *Reading, Analysing and Teaching Literature,* London: Longman, 241–66.

Verdonk, P. and J. J. Weber (1995), *Twentieth-Century Fiction. From Text to Context*, London: Routledge.

Vietor, K. (1882), *Der Sprachunterricht muß umkehren – ein Beitrag zur Überbürdungfrage*, Heilbronn: Henninger.

Vincent, M. and R. Carter (1986), 'Simple text and reading text', in C. J. Brumfit and R. A. Carter (eds), *Literature and Language Teaching*, Oxford: Oxford University Press, 208–222.

Wellek, R. and A. Warren (1949), *Theory of Literature*, New York: Harcourt.

Widdowson, H. G. (1975), *Stylistics and the Teaching of Literature*, London: Longman.

Widdowson, H. G. (1992), *Practical Stylistics: an Approach to Poetry*, Oxford: Oxford University Press.

Wilkins, D. A. (1976), *The Notional Syllabus: A Taxonomy and its Relevance to Foreign Language Curriculum Development*, Oxford: Oxford University Press.

Williams, R. (1958), *Culture and Society*, London: Chatto and Windus.

Williams, R. (1976), *Keywords: a Vocabulary of Culture and Society*, London: Fontana.

Yazigy, R. (1994), 'Perception of Arabic as native language and learning of English', *Language Learning Journal*, 1: 68–74.

Zwaan, R. A. (1993), *Aspects of Literary Comprehension. A Literary Approach*, Amsterdam/ Philadelphia: John Benjamins.

## SECTION B: LITERARY TEXTS

This section includes only those texts which are quoted and/or discussed at some length or for which context may clarify comment. In the case of short stories and poems, we give the title of a collection in which they appear. For all items, we have tried to choose an easily accessible edition or collection, not necessarily the earliest.

In many cases, but especially for the stories, novels and plays discussed in Chapters 5, 6 and 7, it would be helpful, though it is not absolutely necessary, to read the complete texts before and/or after reading what we say about using them in the classroom.

Burns, R. (1990), *Complete Illustrated Poems, Songs and Ballads of Robert Burns*, London: Lomond.

Conrad, J. (1973), *Heart of Darkness*, Harmondsworth: Penguin (first published 1902).

cummings, e. e. (1966), *Complete Poems 1913–1962*, New York: Harcourt Brace Jovanovich.

Dolley, C. (ed.) (1967), *The Penguin Book of English Short Stories*, Harmondsworth: Penguin.
    Cary, J. 'The Breakout'
    Hardy, T. 'The Withered Arm'
    Kipling, R. 'The End of the Passage'
    Lawrence, D.H. 'Fanny and Annie'
    Maugham, S. 'The Force of Circumstance'
    Waugh, E. 'Mr. Loveday's Little Outing'

Dolley, C. (ed.) (1972), *The Second Penguin Book of English Short Stories*, Harmondsworth: Penguin.
    Amis, K. 'Interesting Things'
    Greene, G. 'The Destructors'
    Lawrence, D. H. 'The Horse Dealer's Daughter'
    Mansfield, K. *'Feuille d'Album'*
    Powys, T. F. 'The Bucket and the Rope'
    Spark, M. 'You Should Have Seen the Mess'

Emecheta, B. (1994), *Second-Class Citizen*, London: Heinemann.

Gardner, B. (1966), *The Terrible Rain: the War Poets 1939–1945*, London: Methuen.

Gray, T. (1966), *Complete Poems of Thomas Gray*, Oxford: Clarendon.

Harrison, G. B. (ed.) (1937), *A Book of English Poetry*, Harmondsworth: Penguin.

Ishiguro, K. (1993), 'The Gourmet', in *Granta: Best of Young British Novelists 2* (Granta 43 Spring 1993).

Jones, P. M. (ed.) (1957), *The Oxford Book of French Verse*, second edition, Oxford: Clarendon.

Joyce, J. (1961), *Dubliners*, Harmondsworth: Penguin (first published 1916).

Kipling, R. (1939), *Sixty Poems*, London: Hodder and Stoughton.

Lawrence, D. H. (1977), *The Complete Poems of D. H. Lawrence*, Harmondsworth: Penguin.

Lochhead, L. (1989), *Mary Queen of Scots Got Her Head Chopped Off*, Harmondsworth: Penguin.

Lucie-Smith, E. (ed.) (1970), *British Poetry since 1945*, Harmondsworth: Penguin.

MacDiarmid, H. (1987), *The Complete Poems of Hugh MacDiarmid*, Harmondsworth: Penguin.

MacLaverty, B. (1984), *Cal*, Harmondsworth: Penguin.

Macleod, K. (1996), *The Stone Canal*, London: Legend Books.
Miller, A. (1961), *All My Sons*, Harmondsworth: Penguin (first published 1947).
Reber, F. (ed.), (1986), *Mitten in einen Vers*, Bern: Stattlicher Lehrmittelverlag.
Reed, H. (1946), *A Map of Verona*, London: Methuen.
Sandburg, C. (1950), *Complete Poems*, New York: Harcourt Brace Jovanovich.
Scott, T. (ed.) (1970), *The Penguin Book of Scottish Verse*, Harmondsworth: Penguin.
Shakespeare, W. (1958), *The Complete Works of William Shakespeare*, London: Spring Books.
Stallworthy, J. (1973), *The Penguin Book of Love Poetry*, Harmondsworth: Penguin.

# Index